ART OF THE FIFTIES, SIXTIES AND SEVENTIES

ART OF THE FIFTIES, SIXTIES AND SEVENTIES

THE PANZA COLLECTION

Interview
with Giuseppe Panza
by Christopher Knight

Preface by
Richard Koshalek
Sherri Geldin

Copyright © 1999
Editoriale Jaca Book S.p.a., Milan, Italy

ISBN 88-16-69001-1

On the front jacket:
Bruce Nauman, *Triangle Room*, 1978-1980

On the back jacket:
Robert Morris, *Untitled (Aluminium grating),* 1969

Printed and bound in Italy

Antique Collectors' Club:
5 Church Street, Woodbridge, Suffolk IP12 1DS, England
Tel. 01394 385501 Fax. 01394 384434
and
Market Street Industrial Park
Wappingers' Falls, NY 12590, USA
Tel. 914 297 0003 Fax. 914 297 0068

Editoriale Jaca Book:
Via Gioberti 7, 20123 Milano, Italy
Tel. 39 2 48561520/29 Fax. 39 2 48193361

Notes for Readers

Works belonging to the Panza Collection currently in the custody of museums and foundations are indicated in the captions to illustrated pages, in the photographic catalogue and in the revised list of works in the Collection as follows:

MOCA
indicates that the work was acquired by the Museum of Contemporary Art in Los Angeles in 1984.

The Solomon R. Guggenheim Foundation
indicates that the work was acquired by the Foundation in 1990.

The Solomon R. Guggenheim Foundation (Panza Gift)
indicates that the work was donated by Giuseppe Panza to the Foundation in 1992.

FAI (*Fondo per l'Ambiente Italiano*)
indicates that the work is one of the group donated by Giuseppe and Giovanna Panza to the FAI in 1996, together with Villa Menafoglio Litta Panza at Biumo Superiore, Varese.

The Solomon R. Guggenheim Foundation (Panza Gift) on permanent loan to FAI
indicates that the work is one of the 13 donated to the Foundation and permanently located at Villa Menafoglio Litta Panza, Biumo Superiore, Varese.

FAI (Fondo per l'Ambiente Italiano) on permanent loan to Guggenheim
indicates that the work is one of 13 donated to the FAI on permanent loan to the Foundation.

Where possible, the installation site and year in which the photograph was taken are indicated in the captions to illustrated plates.

Editor's note
The Story of the Panza Collection

Over time, the Panza Collection has put together for the art of the 50s, 60s and 70s one of the critical examinations most aware of the artistic phenomena known as *Minimalism*, *Conceptual Art* and *Environment Art*, which followed the *Informelle*, *Action Painting*, *Pop Art* and *New Dada* movements.

Giuseppe Panza's work must be considered the result of genuine historical and critical research, in stark contrast to much nineteenth and twentieth century collecting, and reveals an eye that has taken a highly personal yet wide-ranging look at the artistic world of the above decades. It is very personal since the route that can be traced in the Collection was born of the choices and judgements of its creator; and it is wide-ranging because the outcome of that critical scrutiny and personal involvement embraces many of the crucial moments in the artistic life of the years concerned.

It was a artistic period when the work was often conceived by its author in terms of specific installation codes. Correct positioning and display was therefore, in addition to the necessary occasion of contact with the public, a kind of formal completion of the work itself. From this point of view, Giuseppe Panza's labours have contributed to pose questions that may seem obvious in the case of environment art but which also regard other modes of artistic expression. The ambience in which a work of art is contemplated is far from being a neutral space. It has a continuous relationship with the work and participates decisively in exactly the same way as the work may play a crucial role in determining perceptions of the site where it is located.

Attention to the environment surrounding the work of art has always been a fixed point of Giuseppe Panza's work and indeed may be thought of as an integral part of his collecting activities. In a publication dedicated to the Panza Collection, it was therefore important to catch and reproduce works when museum exhibitions or installations enabled the artist's creation to find an appropriate collocation. Such opportunities, however, are relatively infrequent and isolated since, given the limits of what the artist can provisionally arrange and the areas the collector has available, there are very few spaces that will permit a complete formal presentation of art of this kind.

Giuseppe Panza's efforts have shown that this ongoing dialogue between work and environment is neither unvarying nor susceptible to once-and-for-all codification. The space in which a work is installed may be more or less suitable but this does not imply that there is only one set of appropriate environmental conditions nor that any such set of conditions should be constantly reproduced over time. There is, of course, in each work an internal logic which it is the fundamental duty of the collector, like any museum director, to appreciate and protect. But there are as many sets of conditions in which that logic may find expression as there are opportunities on which to exhibit the artist's work to the public. On each occasion, there comes into play a personal choice and a personal interpretation of the single work and of the corpus of works that is translated into a personal collocation of art objects in exhibition space. However once again that choice can and must focus on revealing the work's internal logic.

The ten years that have passed since the first edition of this book have also witnessed many changes in the Collection.

It has been a period of intense activity during which the Panza Collection has acquired about 1,500 new works, most by Americans but also from Italian, British, Belgian and German artists. Panza's searches and acquisitions have embraced the new developments in art during the 80s and 90s, involving for the most part artists not represented in his previous collecting activities. This latest phase has taken Giuseppe Panza's total to 2,500 works acquired over the 42 years he has been collecting.

It is the aim of this book, partly in the light of the Panza Collections new directions, to provide a retrospective of the earlier collecting period that embraced the 50s, 60s and 70s and which involved many of the greatest artists of the time.

A number of exhibitions, organized over the last ten years at some of the main museums of contemporary art in Europe and America, have helped to bring the Collection to the notice of a wider public and to give a greater "historic depth" to the artistic panorama it records. Of these, we would like to mention two exhibitions held in 1988, one at the Centro de Arte Reina Sofia with works by Carl Andre, Dan Flavin, Donald Judd, Robert Morris, Bruce Nauman and Richard Nonas, and the other at the Musée Rath d'Art e d'Histoire in Geneva with works by Robert Mangold as well as Andre, Flavin, Judd and Morris again. In 1989, works by Dan Flavin were exhibited at the Musée Saint Pierre d'Art Contemporaine in Lyons, and by Richard Long and Bruce Nauman at the Musée d'Art Moderne in St. Etienne. In 1990, the Musée de la Ville in Paris hosted an exhibition of minimal art with works by Sol LeWitt, James Turrell, Lawrence Weiner and other artists already mentioned. Many of the photographs that illustrate this book come from these exhibitions focusing on the artistic production of the 60s and 70s.

The Panza Collection's most recent phase of acquisitions has been on display at exhibitions of works from the last two decades at the Museo Cantonale d'Arte in Lugano (1992, 1995, 1997), at the Palazzo delle Albere in Trento (1996) and at the Llonja in Palma de Majorca (1997).

The last few years have also seen the Collection's co-operation with museums and foundations continue, providing further testimony of the role it has played in the artistic life of recent decades.

In 1990, the Solomon R. Guggenheim Foundation in New York acquired 202 works of 60s and 70s minimalist painting and sculpture on particularly favourable conditions; in 1992, the same foundation received a donation of 150 works and 330 works of minimalist, conceptual and environment art from the same period on a ten-year loan.

In 1993, the Getty Center for the History of Art and Humanities acquired the Panza Collection archives for the years 1956-1986, containing documentation of works acquired and correspondence between Giuseppe Panza and artists over the period.

In 1995, the MOCA in Los Angeles received a donation of 70 works by Californian artists in the 80s and 90s, which joined 80 others from the Collection already on display in the museum's permanent collection since 1984. The original 80 include works from the 40s, 50s and 60s.

In 1996, the FAI (Fondo per l'Ambiente Italiano, or Italian Foundation for the Environment) received a donation of the eighteenth century Villa Menafoglio Litta Panza at Biumo Superiore in the province of Varese, together with 133 works of contemporary art ranging from the 60s to the present day as well as furniture and furnishings from the sixteenth to nineteenth centuries and a collection of African and pre-Colombian sculpture. The Villa will be open to the public from autumn 1999.

Since December 1998, the Palazzo Ducale at Gubbio has been exhibiting 50 works from the Collection held in trust for five years.

Finally, the new museum at Rovereto, designed by Mario Botta, will receive a further 50 works from the Collection to be held in trust for five years.

The Collection's aims of exhibiting and making better known its works have imposed this distribution to a number of different art institutions. Allocation has always been on the basis of the Collection's own internal logic and links between the works and artists concerned.

But the Collection still possesses its original cohesion and a unity of its own. It is to that unity and fundamental nature that this book wishes to bear unadorned witness.

Preface

Giuseppe Panza di Biumo has emerged in his lifetime as one of the most significant collectors of the art of our era. His commitment to the art of his time calls to mind such celebrated predecessors as the Medicis in Renaissance Florence, Duke Vincenzo I Gonzaga in 17th-Century Mantua, Richard Boyle, Earl of Burlington, in 18th-Century England, and Gertrude Stein and her brother Leo, Dr. Albert C. Barnes, and Samuel Courtauld in 20th-Century Europe and America. Each of them created remarkable collections of art reflecting their respective periods in history, at the same time establishing vital links with the seminal artists who were then advancing the various disciplines of art.

Theirs was not simply a passion to amass the very best work being produced at a particular time, but to actively engage and support the leading artists of the period, thereby affecting the evolution of art history in a profound fashion. While the collected or commissioned works themselves survive in the world as permanent testimony to the superb aesthetic judgement shared by these collectors, equally essential to their ultimate achievements was a certain spirit of inquiry that inspired them to seek and confidently support the most compelling artists then at work. In addition to their responsiveness to and acceptance of new ideas, it is also a strong commitment to patronage that distinguishes these universally respected collectors and that assures Dr. Panza a place among them.

While the works Dr. Panza has assembled over two decades obviously carry tremendous inherent value, they do not in themselves confer upon the collector the unique status he has achieved. Rather it is the combination of a probing and prescient eye, an intellectual rigor, and a quest for beauty and understanding that toghether have propelled Dr. Panza to make a truly distinctive mark on the world of art. It would seem, in fact, that he did not set out to be a "collector" at all, but was almost predestined to assume that role by virtue of his highly inquisitive attitude, which has come to characterize his approach to contemporary life. It is his desire for an integrated understanding of the complexities and nuances of human existence that have drawn him to the art of his time.

In the mid, 1950s, Dr. Panza began building what was to eventually become an extensive collection by acquiring the work of Antoni Tapies, whose work he found to "reflect aspects of traditional Spanish spiritual life."[1] He then turned to the work of the French expressionist Jean Fautrier, in whose work he perceived a "refined sensitivity to color and shape, an almost post-impressionist sensibility for the beauty of color and elemental shapes of matter." In both cases, Dr. Panza's acquisitions were prefaced by a prolonged and serious study—a search for the elemental meaning behind the works of art.

Following a trip to the United States, Dr. Panza became intrigued by the pioneering work of American artists: the New York School paintings of Franz Kline and Mark Rothko; the transitional and historically important «combines» of Robert Rauschenberg; and the pop culture-inspired imagery of Claes Oldenburg, James Rosenquist, and Roy Lichtenstein—works that had not been extensively shown or collected in Europe. With each individual artist, Dr. Panza felt compelled to acquire a defined series of works that would more comprehensively reflect the scope and depth of that artist's expression. "My experience was not simply intellectual but also the opportunity to share life in some way with the artist."

Although Dr. Panza's early collecting primarily involved paintings, even then the appropriate installation of these individual works was of paramount importance. He strongly believed that the works of each artist should be presented together within their own controlled space, allowing for a reverberating energy among them and thus making possible a greater comprehension of the artist's ideas and concerns. This instinctive sensitivity on the part of the collector to the inseparability between works of art and their installation spaces logically evolved into the exploration of environmental works which he began to pursue in the mid-1960s. Focusing on such artists as Donald Judd, Dan Flavin, Sol LeWitt, Bruce Nauman, Richard Serra, Robert Morris, Robert Irwin, James Turrell, Douglas Wheeler and Maria Nordman, he devoted his energies to studying the perceptual, intellectual and emotional impact of this symbiotic interchange between the work of art and a specific space.

In particular, Dr. Panza's intensive involvement with artists of Southern California derived from what he perceived to be their forging of a "new kind of relationship between man and his perception of space." He considers the work of these artists to be "extremely important in art history, because something new has been discovered. This discovery is related to the development of space exploration, because it was necessary that scientist consider experience beyond the earth and acquire knowledge of an environment that is completely alien to human senses." Dr. Panza finds the works of Robert Irwin, James Turrell, Maria Nordman, or Doug Wheeler to have a resonance beyond their existence as art—to possess a fundamental connection to the broader questions of life itself.

By his own account, it was "a deep interest in being alone, a love of the desert, a need to live in a silent space, and a pessimistic attitude toward the reality of daily life" that initially drew Dr. Panza to an artist such as Antoni Tapies, but these same fundamental forces are equally manifest in this affinity for the minimal, conceptual, and enviromental works that form the later part of this collection. Just as Dr. Panza refuses to be constrained by the established art historical dogma that sepa-

---

[1]   All quotes from Dr. Panza are from an interview with Julia Brown Turrell included in *The First Show: Painting and Sculpture from Eight Collections, 1940-1980*, ed. Julia Brown and Bridget Johnson (Los Angeles: The Museum of Contemporary Art, in association with The Arts Publisher, New York, 1983), 69-90.

rates the artist of one idiom from another, so too does he discard the automatic assumption that what is contemporary is by definition distinct from what is past. While he acknowledges that the shapes, forms, and artistic approaches may be different, he maintains that the essential ideas, the foundation of each really important work, are basically the same. "We cannot believe in art if we do not believe in some kind of unchanging attitude toward, or a timeless standard of, what is beautiful, what is important, and what is essential in life."

Here is a collector whose primary impulse has been not to enrich his personal domain by acquiring the cultural symbols of his time, but rather to enhance his understanding of the evolution of mankind through the continuum of art. This is not a collection formed either in self-tribute or in tribute to the artists whose work is included, but an investigation into humanity itself and the enduring qualities that have set mankind apart in the universe. Dr. Panza sees art as "the visualization of men's minds," and he considers the artist in society to be a window of sorts through which we can gain a deeper understanding of life.

The activity of collecting therefore becomes one that requires a serious commitment of time and extended periods of concentration. To identify a "masterpiece" is to find a work that holds repeated surprises and new discoveries, even after multiple viewings over many years. And to collect such masterpieces cannot, according to Dr. Panza, be learned, but rather must be a genuine and intuitive expression of the collector's unique sensibility.

Richard Koshalek
Sherri Geldin

Archives of American Art - Smithsonian Institution

Interview with Giuseppe Panza

Conducting an interview is a bit like trying to drive through a snowstorm while looking only in the rearview mirror. You have a vague idea of where the destination lies (even if you can't see it in the blinding distance ahead), but the only way to inch resolutely forward is to keep your thoughts spiraling resolutely backward. In part, the aim is purely archival: to record, in the respondent's own voice, the people, places, and events that have been of primary significance in his past. Equally important, however, is the goal of articulating such decidedly less concrete but nonetheless tangible qualities as the sensibility, convictions, personality, and values that have given shape to a human life.

Fortunately, this approach is perfectly appropriate to a conversation with Milanese art collector and businessman Giuseppe Panza di Biumo. Ask him about a Robert Rauschenberg "combine", a James Turrell light-and-space installation, or a Robert Ryman painting of delicate, feathery-white brush strokes, and he quite naturally responds with an erudite reference to Leonardo's *Virgin of the Rocks*, an aspect of Renaissance philosophy, or a detail in a painting by Raphael. The union of past and present, cast as an intricate relationship between nature and mortality, is a leitmotif in his understanding of the very character of art; and these perceived qualities of art itself have informed the remarkable progress of his life as a collector, as well.

The interview on the following pages was conducted in three-hour sessions over a sequential three-day period in the spring of 1985. Six weeks earlier, the Los Angeles Museum of Contemporary Art had opened the inaugural exhibition of eighty paintings and sculptures, encompassing Abstract Expressionist and Pop art, that it had acquired the previous year from the Panza Collection. On the mornings of April 2, 3, and 4, we sat in a hotel room on Sunset Strip, high above the haze-filled basin of Los Angeles, and talked about Panza's life, his family, the development of his abiding interest in art, the philosophical crisis engendered by the human tragedy of World War II, the "mail order" purchase of a Franz Kline painting that sparked his affinity for postwar American art, his faith in nature as pre-eminent touchstone and, not least of all, the healthy blend of insight, luck and even errors that conspired to shape one of the most important private collections of contemporary art in the world today. This book constitutes a catalogue of the entire collection and a reflection on its formation.

The interview was conducted as part of the oral history program of the Archives of American Art, a department of the Smithsonian Institution, Washington, D.C., and was funded through a generous grant from the Edythe and Eli Broad Family Foundation.

Los Angeles 1986   Christopher Knight

CHRISTOPHER KNIGHT   *We should start at the beginning: When and where were you born, and what were your parents like?*

GIUSEPPE PANZA   I was born in Milan in March 1923. My father was from Monferrato, in Piedmont. He had come to Milan when he was very young, and he was in the wine business. It was a business of wine distribution from the south to the north, from the area of production to the area of consumption, buying when the market was low, selling when the market was high. The task of a good dealer. My mother was from Varese, and her family was also in the wine business. My parents had four sons; I am the third.

My father always lived the life of the good bourgeois in Milan. He was very successful in business and increased his wealth substantially, but he was also a man with great respect for people and for work. He worked hard all his life. Because he had a very strong will and a feeling for opportunities in life, he was able to make wise decisions at the right moment. In business, when he realized he had to lose money he was ready to lose money, because to lose some soon was better than to lose more later.

CK   *So he was very down-to-earth and practical?*

GP   Yes. He was devoted to reality, to making his life useful. He came from a family who lived in a small town in Piedmont, near Alessandria. My grandfather was not a wealthy man. He was a dealer, too, and had a small business in his town.

My mother was completely different. Her family was her main interest, but she also had a sensibility for fine things. Before she married, she liked to paint. There are still some of her paintings at home, and they're good, because we can feel how she liked to look to nature. When I was a boy she brought me to see museums and exhibitions, especially on Sundays.

My mother's sister had the same interest in art. Even when she was very old she liked to paint. My aunt was different in temperament from my mother, a very active woman. She married an industrialist. When my uncle died, she ran his business. She went through difficult times but ran the business well. When she retired, she spent weekends driving to see museums and old cities. She had a love for art.

CK *Did you travel much in Europe when you were young?*
GP No. We traveled to Rome, Florence, Turin – in Italy, mostly, but rarely outside the country. We did take a long boat trip to Spain and Portugal in 1932 and another to Istanbul in 1933. But we didn't travel much.

CK *When did your family acquire the Villa Litta in the town of Varese, north of Milan?*
GP The house was bought by my father in 1931. It was built in 1751 by the Marquis Menafoglio, who was a banker. During the time of Empress Maria Theresa, the Duke of Modena was also the governor of Milan, and the Marquis Menafoglio was his minister of finance. All important people in Italy needed to have a large house as a symbol of power. In 1780 the Marquis died, and his son sold the property.
   Early in the 19th century it was bought by the Litta family. They had political difficulties during the war against Austria for the unification of Italy. They were liberals and they were involved with Napoleon when the French came to Italy. When there was a revolution against the Austrians in 1848, the Litta family paid to equip a regiment of soldiers against them. General Radetski, the Austrian soldier in command of northern Italy, seized the family's property.

CK *How did your family title come about?*
GP It was given to my father in 1940 by the King of Italy, Vittorio Emanuele III. My father was active in business, a wealthy man, and was for many years mayor of the town where he was born. He was the head of several public associations related to wine production. For these reasons he was given his title.

CK *Would you describe your family as intellectually inclined?*
GP Well, my father was a man who didn't read much. He started his business very young. An uncle, the brother of my mother, was very interested in art. Before the last war he restored a castle, built in the Middle Ages near Varese, that he had bought in the '30s. He restored many frescos in this building, paintings from the 13th, 14th and 15th centuries that were all under a coat of paint. When I was a boy I liked to help him. There was a restorer doing the main job, but it was easy to remove the coat of paint with a small blade. I spent hours removing this coat of paint to see the frescos emerging.

CK *You grew up in a city that houses one of the most famous paintings in the world – Leonardo's* Last Supper *– as well as the extraordinary Brera Museum. What is your earliest recollection of art?*
GP In the '30s my father bought an old farm, and there were many paintings left in this old house. Some were good. So this was my earliest interest in art. But when I was fourteen years old, I got a common childhood disease, scarlet fever, which is contagious. So it was necessary to stay home from school, shut up in a room for forty days, to avoid spreading the disease. In my room I

kept an Italian encyclopedia – a very large one, about thirty-five volumes – with a lot of articles and pictures devoted to art history. I spent these forty days studying art. By the end, I was able to hide the label below each picture and remember the name of the painter, the school and the approximate date. I learned a lot. It was mostly Italian art, but not modern. The encyclopedia only went up to the 19th century, not the 20th. This was in 1937.

CK   *Had you studied art in school?*
GP   No. In the gymnasium, which is the middle school in Italy, there was no art teaching. Only in the last three years of high school, and then only one hour a week. When I started at high school, I was the best in the class!

I was interested in every kind of cultural activity. I liked to read poetry; I liked philosophy, history, literature. Between sixteen and eighteen I read Dostoesvky and Tolstoy. I was fascinated by Dostoevsky. I felt very close to his world, because the problems he explored in his novels were very close to my problems. When I was fourteen, I began to have psychological problems, as all young people have. I was very pessimistic. One way to be happy was to read, to improve my education, which was against the main trend of my family life. I was educated at a time in Italy when the authority of the father was important. My father had a kind of religious respect for work, and for people who worked. People who were just thinking, not making something, were beneath consideration. And I was a son who liked to think. He was really worried about this, and believed I was a "lost son" who would be unable to run the family business. Happily, I had an older brother.

CK   *Did you fight about this with your father?*
GP   No. It was impossible to fight my father. He was a man with a very strong will.

CK   *This was in the late 1930s. What effect did the political situation in Italy have on you?*
GP   Almost everybody in Italy was a Fascist. In the beginning the Fascist regime was popular, because Mussolini was successful in most everything he did. He brought Italy out of the economic recession of the '30s. He made that stupid war in Ethiopia because the Italians felt deprived of something after World War I. We had an inferiority complex in relation to France and England. These two countries had great power because of their colonies, but Italy and Germany had nothing. The ambition to be as powerful as France and England was strongly felt, and Fascism used this to win popularity. The unions had become stronger, and people of the middle class felt that a left-wing revolution was possible. There was fear of a communist uprising. Fascism was able to use this situation to gain power.

Few were against Fascism. Young people were educated in the Fascist way, but I had a chance. I wasn't interested in studying Latin and mathematics, so I couldn't go to public school. In Milan, there was a very good private school, called the Malagugini, staffed by teachers who had been fired from the public schools for political reasons: they refused to teach in the Fascist way. The Malagugini was excellent because it had the best teachers from the public schools. It was named after the head of the school; after the war he became a deputy in Milan, from a left-wing Socialist party. So the school had a liberal, socialist orientation.

CK   *Milan had been the center of the Futurist movement in the 'teens, and it's generally felt that Futurism played a significant role in shaping Fascism. Were you aware of Futurist art?*
GP   Yes, but in the '30s there was very little interest left in Futurism. Most people considered Futurism a strange idea; there wasn't much interest in it anymore. Good art was "well-painted art," not this strange alteration of shapes. We were moving into a conservative situation, and there wasn't much interest in contemporary art. I remember in 1931 there was the first exhibition of Modigliani in Milan, which caused a lot of talk. My mother and aunt took me to see it, but I don't remember much because I was too young. But they weren't much interested in Modigliani. They liked the Italian Renaissance masters like Titian or Michelangelo.

CK   *Tell me about your life during the war.*
GP   I was in Milan at the beginning of the war but wasn't drafted because I was still a student. When the armistice came on the eighth of September, 1943, and the north of Italy was under the control of the German army, I was on the list to be drafted by the Germans. In order to avoid this, I left Italy and went to Switzerland as a political refugee. My brother was in the Italian army but when the armistice came he refused to fight for Germany. I went with him to Switzerland and spent a year and a half there until the end of the war. The war had a devastating impact. I came back to Varese in May 1945. Varese is north of Milan, and only a few miles from the Swiss border.

CK   *When you returned from Switzerland, did you go back to school?*
GP   I studied law in Milan, and I graduated as a doctor of law in 1948.

CK   *I imagine your father was pleased with your law degree.*
GP   Oh yes, he was very pleased. He realized I was willing to work for the family business rather than become a philosopher! I took my degree in '48 and started to work but my father died in '49. For me, to work in business was a painful decision. After the war, our wine business closed and my father began a business making industrial alcohol. He also had interests in real estate, which I thought was better to develop. I felt my temperament was not adapted to working in trade because I did not have the ability to make decisions fast. When you work in trade, you have to make decisions fast – to sell when you realize the market is going down, to buy when you realize the market is going up. But I was a very slow thinker. So trade was something completely alien to me. I felt very uncomfortable.

CK   *Did you continue to pursue your interest in art?*
GP   Oh, yes. When I was in the refugee camp in Switzerland, I bought a lot of books on philosophy, art history, literature, poetry. This period in Switzerland was good for me because my vision of life changed. I felt very deeply the changes taking place after the war. The rationalist vision of life and the idealist philosophy of culture had been popular in Italy. But I came to feel it was not a good answer to real problems, because the war was such a tragic event. It was deeply shocking to the belief in man's rational capacities that had developed since the Renaissance. Science had become the religion of Europe, and we had believed reason and science

would make everything better. To see how reason failed totally during the war was a great crisis for European culture.

I had been interested in Renaissance art history, and in Titian, Michelangelo, Leonardo, Giorgione, Tintoretto, Botticelli. Piero della Francesca was perhaps the one I liked most. I believed Raphael was superficial-which was a mistake I understood only a lot later.

Rationalism and expressionism are the main aspects of art-death, life, suffering, why we have to suffer, why we have to die. These artists lived with these problems, which were important to me.

CK   *Piero's art, especially, is completely rational, ordered and clear, but it's taken to such lengths that it becomes almost abstract.*
GP   Yes, because he realized art is a vision of something ideal. It was the projection of a perfect world which the artist has seen but which is not real. It's an attempt to make it real. When we look at nature we find that this ideal beauty could exist, because nature has this quality. When I was young, I liked to be in the country, to be alone in the mountains, to walk alone in the garden at night when there was a full moon. I felt happy just being in nature.

CK   *You began to collect contemporary art in 1956, yet most of the artists you have mentioned so far are not contemporary. How did your interest in new art develop?*
GP   I wanted to make a collection of high quality, and to buy paintings of high quality from the past was financially impossible. I did not wish to have second rate paintings. This was the first requirement of the collection.

Also, I was always very curious about the new. In Switzerland I had read many books about science, biology, natural history, physics and astronomy. The attempt of physical theories to understand the mystery of matter is a struggle between the known and the unknown. I was interested in new art because it was something yet to be understood. Through art history I realized that many artists were not understood in their own time. I was interested to know why van Gogh, during his lifetime, never sold a painting. It was something strange to me. For this reason, I believed my task was to find the best new artists. And with the limited means available to me, it was the only way to make a collection of masterpieces, not medium quality paintings. When I realized that something was second-rate, I couldn't bear to look at it. I had to push it away.

A painting has to be very beautiful or it cannot stay with me, because I have a personal relationship with the work. A beautiful work speaks to me in an endless way, because each time it looks different. When I am sad and look at a beautiful painting it changes my mind. But I have to throw a bad one away.

CK   *How much time elapsed between your decision to start collecting and the first purchase you made?*
GP   A short time. I began after I got married in 1955. I had a house with empty walls. Because I had early 19th-century furniture, in the beginning I bought some paintings of the period, just to fill the house. But I also had some money to spend, and the first thing I wanted to do with it was find

good paintings. So I began a systematic investigation. I looked at Italian art in Milan. Afterward, I went to Paris to look at art made in France. I bought several paintings by young artists, some Italian but mostly French. I realized a year later that these paintings were no good.

This search began in January 1956. But the first important purchase was made in the spring of 1956 in Paris, when I bought several paintings by Antoni Tapies. In September, or perhaps October, I read an article in the magazine *Civiltà delle Macchine*, which means "The Civilization of Machinery." It was a good magazine, published by the state-owned steel industry. There were some illustrations of paintings which had some relationship to industry, such as Charles Sheeler's. There was also a Franz Kline because it looked like a steel structure, only broken. And I was impressed by this image. I read that the painting was from the Sidney Janis Gallery in New York. I wrote to him to ask for photographs of Franz Kline's work, and through them I selected the first painting, which is *Buttress*. The price was about $550. I asked Sidney Janis to reduce it to $500. He agreed.

CK   *A mail-order purchase! Were you at all surprised when the painting arrived at your door?*
GP   Oh no, I was very pleased. It was better than I was expecting. I loved Franz Kline because it reflected my state of mind. I always had this desire to reach something I could not reach. Man is born to be happy, but he cannot be happy. We want to reach perfection, but we cannot. We are deeply deprived of perfection, and deeply deprived of happiness. The world has limits. This opposition of reality and desire for something more beautiful was always strong in my mind. The images made by Kline gave me the same feeling. This man was looking for something which was impossible to have but which he desperately needed. This kind of tension was my condition, and I felt close to his art for this reason.

CK   *Had you imagined what sort of scale this picture would have? It's a very small painting by Kline's standards.*
GP   Yes, this one is small for Kline, but it was already bigger than the European standard. I came from a culture in which the paintings of Morandi were the usual size. Three feet was already big. Before the war there was the belief that a small painting was better than a large one. The paintings of Paul Klee, for example, were perfection because they were very small. To make something small was to produce something more perfect, more beautiful. Perhaps it came from the impact of Baroque paintings in the churches in Italy. They were big paintings but with little meaning.

CK   *When you bought the Kline painting, had you ever been in the United States?*
GP   I had made a long trip between 1953 and 1954. After my father's death, I was interested in doing something else. I was looking afetr to the real estate inherited from my father, but my eldest sister was also working in the administration of the real estate business because she was not married. My sister had some of my father's qualities, but not the best ones. She was very authoritarian. She had a kind of idolatry for my father, and believed what he said had to be followed without discussion. She had no consideration for my interests in art and philosophy, in things that did not provide income. So there was always a potential confrontation between us. For this reason I made the trip,

first to South America, then to North America, to learn about business. I spent several months in Brazil and Argentina, and then seven months in America. I didn't speak English. I spent three months in New York to learn English and then traveled through Canada, California, Texas, Louisiana, and so on.

CK *Did you look at art in America?*
GP Yes, but not much. I went to the Metropolitan and to the Museum of Modern Art, but I didn't go to galleries. I wasn't yet collecting. I was more involved in finding a solution for my life as a businessman. I visited many kinds of industries.

I was fascinated by life in America, by the landscape, by a way of living that was more free. In Italy there was a lot of social convention. In America the relationship among people was based more on individual capacity, not on social status. Crossing the continent, there was nature still untouched, still as it was before the arrival of the white man. The light was so different from the north of Italy, which is always gray and foggy because of the humidity. Here, especially in the midwest and the west, the light is pure. It gives the sense of a world which is more ideal.

When I went back to Italy, I believed America was starting a new kind of civilization. It was possible to develop a different culture because the social situation was so different from Europe. We have the weight of the past, of what was inherited from the centuries. Respect for rules made in the past was too strong. In America, perhaps it was possible.

CK *When the Kline painting arrived at your door a few years later, did you sense in it any of what you had felt in America?*
GP Oh, yes. I felt strongly the life of New York. I was very impressed the first time I went to

MOCA, Los Angeles, « The Temporary Contemporary», February-September 1985, Kline Hall

New York. For me it really was a new world. It looked to me like a romantic city – a city struggling for things impossible to possess but that it was trying to have anyway. The only goal was the infinite.

CK   *Your mother passed away shortly after you began collecting?*
GP   Yes. She died in November 1956.

CK   *In 1956 and 1957, you were buying Tapies and Kline; the following year you began acquiring work by Jean Fautrier and in 1959 Robert Rauschenberg and Mark Rothko. What led you, from the beginning, to concentrate only on specific periods of an artist's work, and to buy several pieces from those concentrated periods?*
GP   Because I was looking for the best period of each artist. Artists of the 20th century, more than artists of earlier times, have a shorter period of strong creativity. When this period is finished, the later work is not as good as the earlier work. There are exceptions to this rule, like Picasso, but not many. But even in Picasso there are periods that are better than others. Braque is an example, because the Cubist works are very much better than all the later ones.

CK   *Why do you think 20th-century artists have shorter periods of excellent work?*
GP   Information moves faster and the social context changes much faster than before. Each artist develops his work in a context, and if this situation changes, art changes. De Chirico is a clear example. He created masterpieces between 1912 and 1918, but afterward the quality of his work went down. For others, like Morandi, it was not the same, but most of the artists of the beginning of the century, the historical avant-garde, stopped doing important work around 1930. Miró did his best work earlier. Dalí also. And Magritte. Max Ernst, too.

CK   *So you have no interest in "late De Chirico" or "late Picasso"?*
GP   No. The market is buying the late period works of artists anyway because many people don't understand art but like to have it, so they buy the signature. They don't buy the painting. They pay for the reputation of the artist, not for the work itself.

Tapies made his best work between 1955 and 1959. Like other European artists, Tapies lived through the crisis of the last war. If you look at his paintings you always see the matter of the earth and forms that look like dead bodies. Near the edge you will see the horizon, but never the sky. The colors are all dark, and you have a pessimistic vision of life. But this was the attitude of Europeans after the tragedy of the last war. We needed to find new motivations, valid motivations, to begin again after the suffering of the crisis that all Europe was going through.

CK   *At this time did you make it a practice to meet the artist when you bought his work?*
GP   In some cases it was necessary, but it wasn't a goal for me. What was important was to see as many of his works as possible. And to have documentation, to have plenty of photographs. I spent a lot of time at home just looking through photographs, which is useful if you have already seen the original. You can have an intuition about what the artist wants to express but to be sure you have to live with the work. I spent all my evenings at home looking at paintings, or looking at

photographs and documentation. Only in this way do we know the artist. We rebuild his mind inside our head. This kind of partnership with the work is beautiful.

CK   *Shortly after you began collecting Rauschenbergs and Rothkos, in 1959, you stopped buying the work of Tapies. Subsequently, you've collected primarily work by Americans and very few by Europeans. Why?*

GP   A very simple reason: in America there were more important artists than in Europe. Soon after the war, the best artists in Europe were Fautrier, Jean Dubuffet, and Wols. In America, only Dubuffet is well known. Francis Bacon was important, but in some way he was very far from my vision of art. Even if I respected him very much, I was never too interested in his art. I was shocked by the Bacon world. It was too expressionist, a kind of expressionism with a wrong erotic attitude. I was more interested in American art. Rauschenberg and Jasper Johns had a different vision.

Also, their relationship to Duchamp was very interesting. I discovered Duchamp through Rauschenberg. Before, I didn't pay too much attention to Duchamp. His work looked too eccentric. But what looked too eccentric to me was not at all. I realized that his ready-mades are not objects picked up to illustrate a personal choice, but are made to give the viewer the opportunity to make an analogical connection to other facts related to his own life. This I discovered through Rauschenberg, and because of Duchamp I started to look at Italian Renaissance art in a different way.

I looked at Leonardo da Vinci more closely, and I discovered another Leonardo who was richer and more original than I had thought before. I discovered Italian Mannerist painting, which I had considered of not very good quality and I discovered how great these artists are. I understood why Raphael is great. What is important in Raphael is not the first look, but what you see slowly as you pay attention to the details. The detail becomes a painting in Raphael. If you look at a finger of the virgin, you see a landscape because this finger is part of nature.

This steady transition from the part to the whole is extremely interesting and I understood it through Duchamp.

Before, I always had a very emotional relationship to art and not enough of an intellectual relationship. Through Duchamp, I realize how this intellectual relationship opened up new emotional fields, which cannot be perceived if we stop at the image.

CK   *So Duchamp was the source of a more conceptual interest in art?*
GP   Yes.

CK   *Were you spending much time in New York then?*
GP   Well, I was going once or twice a year, and each time spending two weeks.

CK   *Coming from Italy only once or twice a year, how did you find artists whose work you wanted to see? Where there dealers or critics or curators you were listening to?*
GP   I was always asking people which young artists were interesting to see. I had a long list of names and went to galleries and studios all day. I always gathered documentation and when I was

back in Milan I looked at it. After long study, I decided what to buy. I was sure the work had to be purchased to the largest extent possible.

CK   *The eleven Rauschenbergs in your collection are astonishing. How did you first learn of his work?*

GP   I knew about Rauschenberg through John Cage. He came to Milan in 1958 to work at the Italian National Radio in the studio of electronic music-with Berio, I believe. He knew that I was buying American art, Kline and Rothko, and for this reason so he wanted to meet me. He came to lunch at my home and spoke to me about Rauschenberg and Jasper Johns.

I bought the first Rauschenberg not from Leo Castelli but from Larry Rubin, because he had a painting he was willing to sell called *Kick Back*. It was shown at Documenta in Kassel in 1959, where I saw it. In the catalog I saw it belonged to Rubin, and I bought it from him for $750.

At the same time I wrote to Leo to send me photographs, but he didn't send any. He told me sometime later he didn't believe an Italian really wanted to buy Rauschenbergs! Anyway, he finally sent the photographs and I began to buy Rauschenberg's work. In 1960 I was in New York and went with Leo to the warehouse-a room full of beautiful Rauschenbergs from the 50s. I bought several.

CK   *John Cage had also spoken to you of Jasper Johns. Why didn't you collect his work?*

GP   Because Johns was doing very few paintings, and a few collectors in New York were buying them. They could come to his studio and buy the painting as soon as it was finished. I wasn't interested in commissioning work, or in asking an artist to keep a work for me because I wanted to choose. I never bought without having seen the work, so I lost the opportunity to buy Johns.

CK   *You bought Rauschenberg's* Factum I, *but not* Factum II. *Why not?*

GP   Because I didn't understand the relationship between the two paintings. I chose Factum I because it looked more beautiful than Factum II. I didn't understand it would be better to keep the two paintings together. Rauschenberg did what Leonardo da Vinci did with the *Virgin of the Rocks*. Leonardo himself completed the first version, which is at the Louvre. And in collaboration with his best pupil, Ambrogio de Predis, he made the version that is in London. They are very similar. It's often difficult to find a difference; only some details are different. The quality of the two paintings is excellent. Both are beautiful. And this introduced the problem of duplication. Which is the original, and why can't the copy be like the original? How important is the hand of the artist? Does the artist have to do the work himself, or could it be done by somebody who followed the artist's mind very closely? Is the work of the hand more important, or that of the mind of the man that makes the hand work?

This is the problem, and this is why it would be very important to keep the two Rauschenbergs together. But at the time I hadn't yet understood Duchamp and Leonardo enough. I believe *Factum II* is now in the Neuman collection in Chicago.

CK   *Whether or not their reputations were widely established, most of the artists we've been discussing had been working in their mature styles for at least a few years when you began to collect their work. But in 1962 you began to acquire the work of Claes Oldenburg, Roy Lichtenstein, and James Rosenquist. They had only just begun their best work. After six years of collecting, were you feeling more confident in your own taste?*

GP   Oh, yes. I believed these artists were important.

CK   *Three of the Lichtensteins you acquired form a wonderful capsule response to Abstract Expressionism. There's the diary, which is "autobiography"; the slab of meat, which is "beefy"; and the hand-grip exerciser, which is "muscle". All three are painted as machine-made reproductions. It's a very neat critical commentary on the clichés of Abstract Expressionism.*

GP   The connection between Abstract Expressionism and Pop art was made through Rauschenberg. If you look at Rauschenberg, you see the sign of the painting. For this reason it was natural for me to arrive at Pop art.

When the Rauschenbergs first came into my house there were some people who were interested, but not many. Some were fascinated by the work of Rothko, Kline, Tapies, but to see Rauschenberg's art, so different, so vulgar, made with objects found by tipping over a trash can, was scandalous to these people. But I was greatly interested in Rauschenberg's work because of its relationship to the past. His work is an inducement to memory. All the ties are made to something real, which is fading away. The perishable materials – the paper, the wood, the objects – add distance to memory. It's a matter of fact, but we experience it as the distant past. Through memory, it's in some way changed, made more beautiful, because it loses reality and becomes more an ideal reality. This process is very strong in the work of Rauschenberg, especially from the '50s.

CK   *It would seem a very long way from Fautrier and Tapies to Lichtenstein and Oldenburg, but you just used the word "perishable" in relation to Rauschenberg. In my review of the portion of your collection now owned by the Museum of Contemporary Art in Los Angeles, I suggested that a notion of death and rebirth informed all the work that you acquired between 1956 and the early 1960s. Is there any legitimacy to that speculation?*

GP   Oh, yes. I believe this opposition of death and life, and the search for endless life, is a constant problem of every human being. If we didn't have the notion that life, in some way, will go on, it would be impossible to live. To have this hope is essential to living. When we realize that we will have to disappear, it is really shocking, a deep wound in our being. We are crushed by the fact that we cannot live forever.

CK   *In addition to questions of mortality, what other philosophical threads do you see running through the work in your collection?*

GP   The problem of truth. It is the basic problem of philosophy, whether knowledge is relative or absolute, is there something which is true, valid forever and in any situation? I was always interested in this problem because it's the basic problem of philosophy. If we don't solve this one, we cannot solve any other.

CK   *Is it a problem that can be solved?*

GP   No, but we have to try to solve it. We cannot rest if we don't try to solve it. We are human because we are trying to solve this problem that cannot be solved. But we can prove that wrong solutions are wrong, and this is very important.

CK *On a rather more mundane level... why did you acquire only four pictures by Lichtenstein?*
GP Because I made a big mistake. It was one of the biggest mistakes of my life as a collector. In 1962 I bought seven Lichtensteins for $600 each. My wife, Giovanna, didn't like Lichtenstein. She is always with me in my judgments of art, and is the main support for the collection. Without her it would be impossible to have the collection I have. She's smarter than I am. She understands immediately if an artist is good or not. She tells me, "Don't buy, it's no good", or "Buy, it's good." I don't trust her immediately because I want to study, to think, but I arrive at the same conclusion! She understands sooner. But on the Lichtensteins, we had different judgments. I liked them very much, but she didn't. So I decided to trade in three Lichtensteins for three Rosenquists – which was not really a mistake. But it was a mistake to lose the Lichtensteins, which were beautiful. It was 1963. I traded with Sperone, a dealer in Turin.

CK *What paintings were they?*
GP One was a ring on a cushion, called *The Engagement Ring*. Another was the hand of a woman with a sponge cleaning a glass window. The other was called *Engagement*, a very beautiful painting with a boy and a girl exchanging an engagement statement. Every time I think of this mistake I feel bad!

CK *Yesterday I was talking with Andy Warhol, who had just come from seeing your collection at the Museum of Contemporary Art. He was very complimentary and very sorry that he wasn't represented in it.*
GP Yes, that was another mistake. When I was in his studio it was full of beautiful paintings, about fifty of them, piled on top each other. This was in the fall of 1962. There were all the most famous paintings, many of which I saw in the Saatchi collection two weeks ago. Then, they were for sale for $600 and I didn't buy. I believed Lichtenstein was better, and in 1962 Warhol looked to me very close to Lichtenstein, but not as good. But it was a mistake, because it wasn't true. They're very different. Lichtenstein's goal is to make beautiful what is not beautiful, to make archetypal images of common images, images that don't have any aesthetic quality. He gives cultural dignity to images that don't have any. This way of making art is very close to the way of making paintings in the past, when the image was an opportunity to make something beautiful. It completely loses its usual capacity for communication because it's no longer just information.

Warhol is very different, because his art is a criticism of American society. His goal is to show how this society is wrong. He's very harsh, very aggressive in this attitude. It's direct and without compromise. Using photographs is the best way for him to realize this.

CK *In 1962 you also went to Claes Oldenburg's* Store *in downtown New York. What sort of experience was it?*
GP It was a beautiful experience. To reach the *Store* we had to go through the Jewish section in downtown New York, which was full of shops selling second-hand dresses. You had the strange

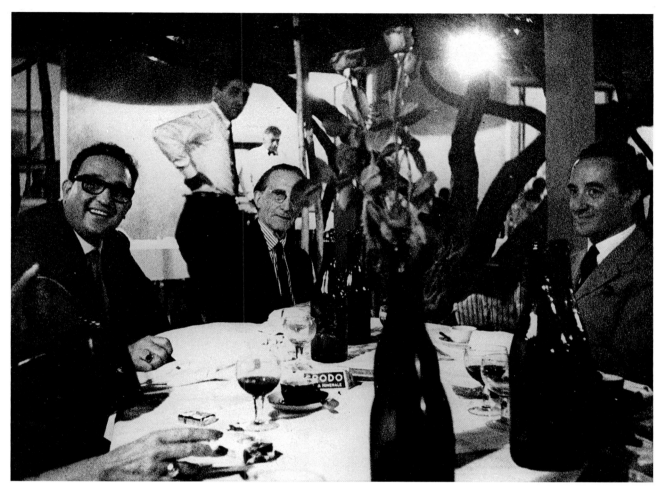

Arturo Schwarz, Marcel Duchamp and Giuseppe Panza, Milan 1963.

feeling of seeing used dresses as good and beautiful things, so different from what you saw in the shops on Fifth Avenue. The Oldenburg *Store* was on a small street, after the Jewish section. It was glowing with beautiful color. These poor objects, which had lived so long with somebody who didn't use them anymore, so closely linked to individual lives, were changed into something brilliant by Oldenburg's strong, pure colors. The contrast was strange, very moving. I went to the *Store* because, a few days before, I had seen his exhibition at the Green Gallery, which impressed me very much. At first I was shocked because it attempted to make beautiful what was ugly. I realized these ugly things had a strong attraction, that in reality they were beautiful. I asked Dick Bellamy to show me more, and he took me to the *Store*.

CK   *In an interview you did with Bruce Kurtz for* Arts Magazine *in 1972, you said that when you met Oldenburg and saw his work, you felt a relationship with German Expressionism.*
GP   Yes, because of the opposition of different colors. The German Expressionists used the same technique of putting very strong colors next to one another – not different tones, but pure colors

without any transitions. This was used to give violent force to the expression, and I found the same thing in Oldenburg.

CK   *Pop art is usually considered such an American sensibility, but in this case you connect it with a European tradition.*
GP   In some ways, yes. Perhaps I am wrong, but it was helpful in my understanding of Oldenburg.

CK   *Were there artists who were telling you about other artists that you should see?*
GP   Most of the Pop artists I met through Leo Castelli. In his gallery in 1960 I first saw a painting by Lichtenstein, which wasn't so good but was very interesting. In '61 I saw an exhibition of young artists at the Martha Jackson Gallery with some early work by Oldenburg – which was good, but which looked too much like Dubuffet in some ways. In June 1962 I met Ileana Sonnabend at the Venice Biennale. We had an appointment with Leo. They showed me some photographs of Lichtenstein and Rosenquist, and asked me to see them in New York. So I went in October and bought many works.

CK   *The installation you designed for your Abstract Expressionist and Pop works at the Museum of Contemporary Art is very precise: great attention was given to lighting; there are no labels; an attempt was made to remove all distractions. It's almost chapel-like and very much like the converted stables that serve as galleries at the Villa Litta.*
GP   I wanted a situation in which the viewer is inside, not seeing one work but a totality. This is possible only when there's a single artist represented in a room. In some way, you breathe the soul of the artist. This is a quality we can only achieve when there are several works by the same artist together in a private space, without any interference. You live with the artist, you are inside his mind. This is a different dimension, which is difficult to realize in museums.

CK   *The precision of the installation is very different from, say, Oldenburg's* Store.
GP   Well, in some way it's not. When I was in the *Store*, the whole space was filled with his work, only his objects, so brilliant in color. This accumulation was extremely strong. But when you are in a museum you cannot do the same thing, because to repeat the experience of the Store it would be necessary to have forty Oldenburgs, not just sixteen.

CK   *You'd also need the Jewish neighborhood to walk through!*
GP   Yes, the context was important, influential. You saw a reversed situation in the street outside. When you were inside the Store, you saw the same objects in a different dimension, like seeing a person who came back to life.

CK   *I'm curious about the reaction of your family when you began to collect art.*
GP   Well, the reaction of my family was negative, especially on the part of my elder sister. She was brought up with my father's concept: money spent for art was really risky. Investment in art is a volatile investment. If the market is not strong when we have to sell art, we lose money. This was

very counter to my father's way of thinking. Indeed, he never bought art. He used an example from the 1930s, when there was a crisis in Italy. There was a rich industrialist that built up a large collection of modern art in the '20s but it was a collection of the fashionable artists of the time. Not French Impressionists, but Italian followers. When the crisis came, he was forced to sell the paintings acquired at high prices ten years before, but they didn't sell because the market was down. This conviction was dominant in my family: don't spend money for art because it is a risky investment.

But my desire to own good art was so strong that I didn't pay attention to the advice. I started collecting. At the beginning I was not spending our family's capital, which I had inherited from my parents, but just the income. And I was spending all the income I could spend. I avoided leisure travel or a bigger car. With time, I realized my family's idea was wrong. If we buy art from successful artists the risk of losing money is strong, because later, when their success is over, the value goes down. The best artists aren't the successful ones. They are artists who have real quality related to art history, not to the fashion or the taste of the moment. This was my concept, and I believe it is correct because events have shown that it is right. But I always had to fight against my family, against the idea that money spent on art was wrong. Except with my wife, who always helped me.

With time, I was willing to spend more, even part of my capital. I had an inheritance from the family of my mother, and I sold off the estate in order to buy art. And this was judged a crime by my brother and my sister, who saw it as an attempt to destroy the family wealth, the wealth accumulated by a lifetime of work by our grandparents and by our father. I was destroying it. This was what they thought.

CK   *So you had no investment considerations whatsoever?*
GP   No, no. Indeed, it was impossible to have investment considerations when you were buying something everybody else refused to buy. For instance, when I bought Kline in 1956 everybody said that I was crazy, that a child was able to do these paintings, just throwing some black paint on canvas. Even the opinion of competent people - so-called competent people - was similar. A few said that Kline was very good, but the majority were against a positive judgment for Kline. In this situation, to buy as an investment was unthinkable.

CK   *Did your sister think the primary reason to buy art was for investment?*
GP   She was against any kind of investment in art because she followed my father's ideas. Investment in art had to be avoided. It was fine to buy something in order to have some good paintings in the house, to have a better house, but not as an investment.

CK   *To what degree do you think your having collected the work of certain artists has made them successful or has contributed to their success?*
GP   I never bought art with the idea that I would contribute to the success of the artist. I always bought because I was interested in a work's ideas, because I felt it was sympathetic to my way of life, because the vision of the artist was also my vision, because the work gave me new experiences and new possibilities to better understand situations of life about which I had a confused notion.

This experience of art enabled me to live better, to understand important things which I was not able to learn otherwise.

I never thought I was making a contribution to the success of the artist. I was giving moral and psychological help because I was somebody sympathetic to his work, who understood and loved it. But this was, in my opinion, my contribution to the artist. For a new artist, who usually sees his work refused, to find somebody who liked it could be psychologically helpful. And I also gave him some money, which could be useful for solving his practical problems. But no more than that. I never thought I had any influence on the market.

CK   *I understand you were once offered a Jackson Pollock painting for $4,000, and you turned it down.*
GP   Yes. It happened that in 1956, when I was buying Franz Kline, I was also interested in other painters. Sidney Janis offered me a painting by Pollock that was less expensive than other drip-paintings because it was made in an unusual way. It was not on canvas but on a large glass plate, about two meters wide and 1.5 meters high. But the price was too high for me. I was buying Franz Kline at $500, and to pay $4,000 for a single painting looked to me to be too much. I preferred to buy eight Klines with the same sum rather than a single Pollock, even if I realized that the Pollock was very beautiful. Indeed, I believe it is now in a university museum.

CK   *Do you regret not having the Pollock?*
GP   Oh surely. But unfortunately I missed many other opportunities. In 1960, I met Barnett Newman. I was in his studio and in his home, and he offered to sell me several works for $6,000 – very large works from the '50s, the best of Newman. When I was in his studio he was finishing *Vir Heroicus Sublimis*, which is now in the Museum of Modern Art. He was still working on the painting, yet there were others he was willing to sell. But it was too much for me in 1960. I missed a wonderful opportunity.

CK   *It has been said that you've never paid more than $10,000 for a single work of art. Is that true?*
GP   Yes, certainly.

CK   *Was that amount a conscious decision on your part?*
GP   No, it was just dictated by the fact that I didn't have too much money to spend. I had to organize my expenditures wisely in order to obtain the maximum results with the minimum of money. Otherwise it would have been impossible to make a large collection. For this reason I had to concentrate on artists who didn't already have an established reputation. The time to buy at a low price is very short. It lasts only one, two, three years. If you miss this short period for buying, the price goes up, becomes twice as costly, and you lose the opportunity.

CK   *Given your philosophically inflected attitude toward collecting, and the period and place in which you began, I've often wondered why Yves Klein was not part of your collection.*
GP   This was another mistake I made. I met with Klein several times. He was a very close friend of Pierre Restany, who was my friend and who often spoke to me about Klein. I saw the first exhi-

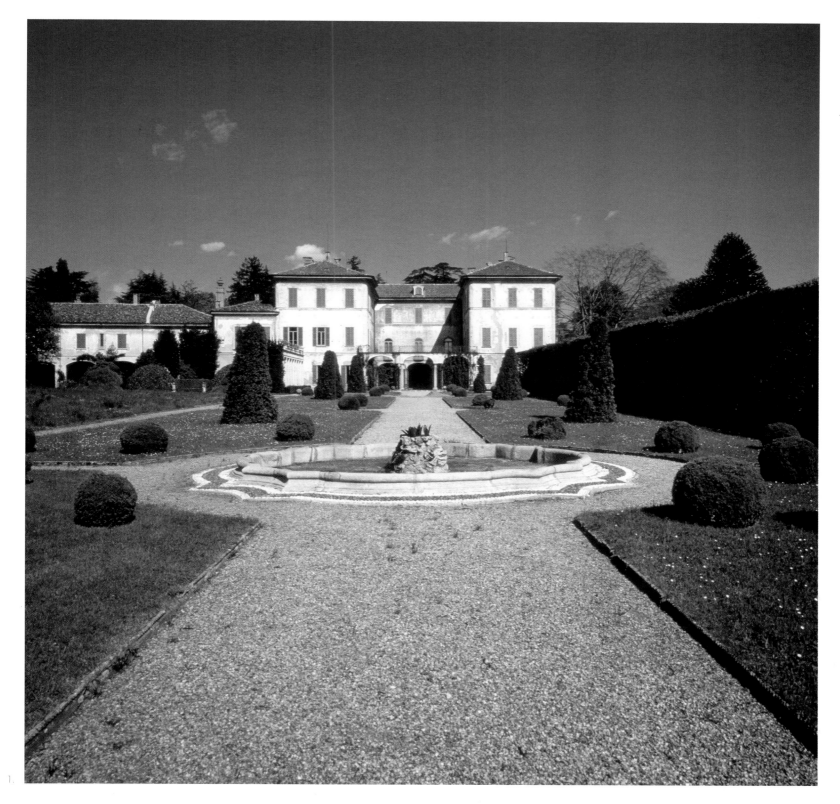

1. Villa Menafoglio Litta Panza,
   Biumo Superiore, Varese, Gift to
   FAI (Fondo per l'Ambiente
   Italiano).

2. Giuseppe, Giovanna Panza.

3.

3. Villa Menafoglio Litta Panza, staircase, 1966. Photograph by Ugo Mulas.
   Mark Rothko, *Black and Dark Sienna on Purple*, 1960, MR 7, MOCA;
   Black, Ochre, Red over Red, 1957, MR 4, MOCA;
   Brown, Blue, Brown on Blue, 1953, MR 1, MOCA.

4. Villa Menafoglio Litta Panza, dining room, 1966. Photograph by Ugo Mulas.
   Franz Kline, *Orleans*, 1959, FK 10, MOCA;
   Monitor, 1956, FK 4, MOCA.

5. Villa Menafoglio Litta Panza, main entrance, 1966. Photograph by Ugo Mulas.
   Robert Rauschenberg, *Gift for Apollo*, 1959, RR 8, MOCA.
   Claes Oldenburg, *Umbrella and Newspaper*, 1962, CO 11, MOCA.

▶

6. 7. Dan Flavin, *Varese Corridor*, 1976. DF 19, The Solomon R. Guggenheim Foundation (Panza Gift).
Installation: Villa Menafoglio Litta Panza (Varese) 1977.

4.

5.

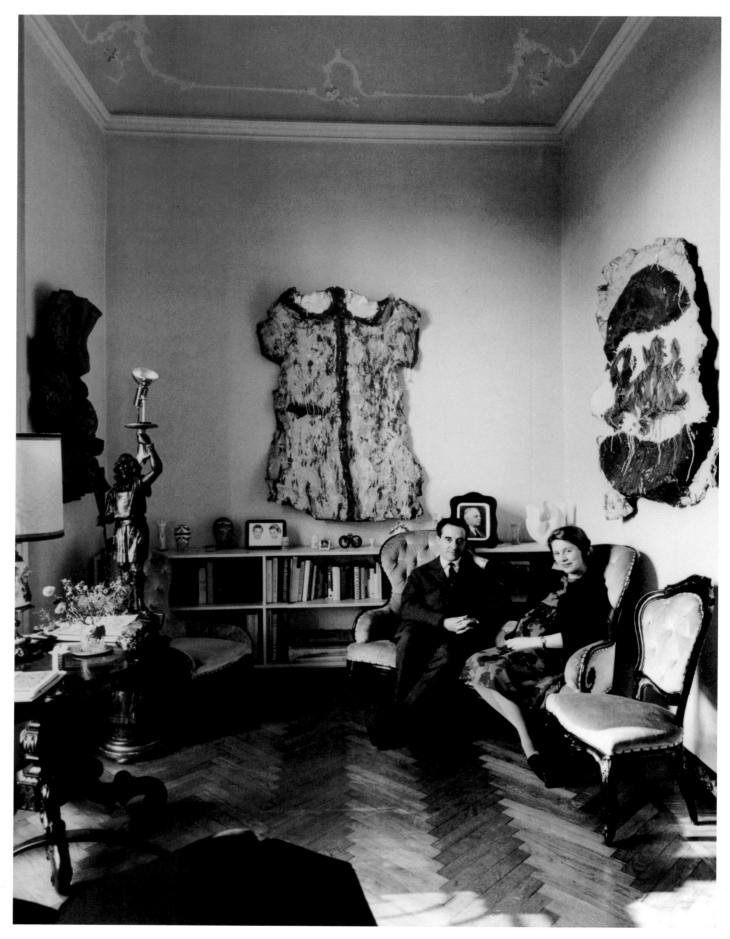

8. Villa Menafoglio Litta Panza, study, 1966. Photograph by Ugo Mulas.
Claes Oldenburg, *Fragment of Candies in a Box*, 1961, CO 3, MOCA;
Mu Mu, 1961, CO 1, MOCA;
Pepsi-Cola, 1961, CO 7, MOCA.

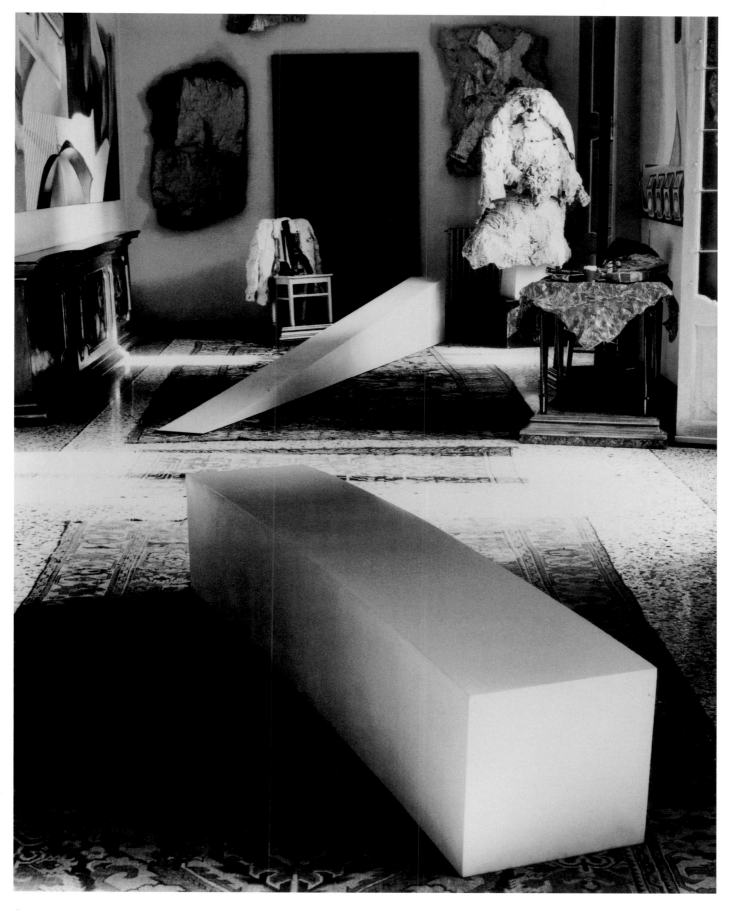

9. Villa Menafoglio Litta Panza, main entrance, 1966. Photograph by Ugo Mulas.
   Robert Morris, *Untitled (Wraped Bench)*, 1965, RM 3, The Solomon R. Guggenheim Foundation;
   Untitled (Door Stop), 1965, RM 4, The Solomon R. Guggenheim Foundation;
   in the background pieces by Claes Oldenburg and James Rosenquist.

bition he did in Italy, at the Galleria Apollinaire in Milan in 1958. Each painting cost 20,000 lire, which was about $150. But I didn't understand his work. In 1958 I hadn't yet learned the importance of Duchamp, and Yve Klein looked much too radical to me. The paintings didn't have enough visual qualities. It was too intellectual, too conceptual. Only later did I realize the importance of the conceptual in art. For this reason I lost entirely this opportunity.

CK *That was in 1958, and you came to understand Duchamp through Rauschenberg, whose work you began to collect in 1959. It's too bad the Klein show wasn't a year or two later.*
GP Yes, because in just two years the value of Klein changed rapidly. When he began to exhibit in the United States the work became expensive, and it was no longer so easy to buy it locally, in Paris or Milan.

CK *In addition to your friendship with Pierre Restany, you've had a long friendship with the critic Germano Celant. How did you meet?*
GP I believe it was in 1970, when he did the Arte Povera exhibition in Turin. I went to Turin often to see exhibitions at the Galleria Sperone, which was the first gallery to show American art in Italy. He began with Pop art in 1963. I might have met Germano Celant before – I don't remember exactly – but surely 1970 was a turning point. I saw a lot of work by the Arte Povera artists, who were interesting to me but less so than the Americans. They were the best Italian artists of the period, with an international value, not only an Italian phenomenon. But at this time I was buying the work of Richard Serra and Bruce Nauman – especially Serra – both of whom are close to the concepts of Arte Povera. But in my opinion, they were stronger. I decided to keep my attention concentrated on the Americans, not the Italians.

CK *Your friendships with Restany and Celant apparently have been important to you, but you obviously had an independent mind in choosing the work to collect.*
GP Oh, yes, surely. These people were friends, and they were very useful to me because we had an exchange of ideas. But I was very independent in my judgments. With them, I had a confrontation on how to judge art. I always did that with people who had other opinions, people who I respected. But at the same time I was judging from my feelings, from my opinions, from my ideas. I wanted to keep my independent judgment because I believe the only way to make fewer mistakes is to make our own mistakes, not to also make the mistakes of others.

CK *In 1966 you began to collect Minimal art.*
GP I began first with Robert Morris and Dan Flavin, and soon after Donald Judd, and in 1969 Carl Andre, Serra, and Nauman. At this time I was not traveling to New York, because my business had been depressed since 1963. I was going through a difficult time, and from 1963 to 1969 I had little cash available. But in 1966, through photographs I got from Leo Castelli, I became interested in the works of Robert Morris. I bought several, which were still very cheap at the time.

Also in 1966 there was a Flavin exhibition in Dusseldorf, and then at the Sperone gallery in

◄

10. Dan Flavin, *Monument for those who have been killed in Ambush (to P. K. who reminded me about death) 2/3,* 1966, The Solomon Guggenheim Foundation (Panza Gift), Installation: Villa Menafoglio Litta Panza (Varese) 1977, DF 11.

Milan. Sperone had a gallery in Milan for a short period of time. I bought several Flavins from this exhibition for 220,000 lire each, which was about $400.

CK   *What did you respond to in Morris's work and in Flavin's work?*
GP   The attempt to look for something essential in shapes was very interesting, to avoid what is not necessary and to look only for what is permanent. Rational forms are related to something permanent. Pure shapes are an image of the ability of man to think. At the same time this art finds a great variety of solutions, even using very simple shapes. Simplicity is not just one way. There is an endless array of possibilities because the ability of minds to think is endless.

These shapes looked cool to me, but at the same time warm because they were the result of a struggle for simplicity. It was the end of a long process of balancing all the elements necessary to make the shapes. These shapes, which are apparently so intellectual, really hide something extremely emotional. I believe that the greatest emotion of life is knowledge, the discovery of truth. The search for truth is the main goal of man. This art revealed the search for truth through simple forms.

CK   *In what way was it emotional?*
GP   It is emotional because it is the image of this process, the process of thinking, of learning, of understanding life, of understanding the law of nature – the real law, the deep, hidden law of nature.

CK   *Around this time I believe you also bought the two sculptures by George Segal.*
GP   Actually, I bought them some years later, I believe in 1971 or '72. I missed the opportunity to buy them in the '60s, but they were still reasonable in price. I went to Segal's chicken farm in New Jersey, and I found these two works there. It was a beautiful place. I took a bus on the freeway to New Jersey, about 100 miles south of New York. The freeway runs along the coast, which is heavily industrialized – a very interesting landscape of huge steel constructions. There are many chemical plants and docks and shipyards, and there are many beautiful, minimal structures. I very much like this kind of industrial landscape. Segal's "chicken factory" was a very large wooden building with several rooms. In each room there were sculptures. These white plaster people in this empty space were like ghosts, but at the same time alive in some way. The opposition of these real and unreal qualities was strong.

CK   *Given your interests at this time, it's surprising you didn't collect the work of Robert Smithson.*
GP   Well, I didn't understand the quality of Smithson's work. I met him several times, and I read his articles, which were beautiful. He was a good writer, an intelligent man. I had great respect for his personality, but I had less consideration for his work as an artist. It was a mistake because the work is very good. Also, perhaps, I never had the opportunity to see a good, full-scale exhibition of his work. I saw only a few works at the John Weber Gallery, or reproduced in photographs. They looked too intellectual, too much an attempt to make concepts visual, but without the right relationship between concept and shape – which is essential. But I was wrong.

Also, I didn't much like the Earthworks he made. The *Spiral Jetty* and the others didn't seem to me really connected to the environment. They fight against the natural situation around them. This looked wrong to me.

CK   *Do you still feel that way today?*
GP   Still, yes. But the sculptures are different, because they don't have this relationship to the environment. They're objects with their own qualities.

CK   *You began collecting Minimalist sculpture two years before the Primary Structures exhibition at the Jewish Museum in 1968. Did you see that show?*
GP   No, unfortunately not.

CK   *Was Flavin the first artist who worked with light whose work you acquired?*
GP   Yes. When I saw his exhibition in Milan in '66 I was impressed by the ability of light to fill the space in which the work was exhibited, to have this color which made the work. It wasn't only the shape of the fluorescent tubes. In Flavin there are two qualities. The composition of the fluorescent tubes is like the lines in a Mondrian painting. The way they are combined makes the work. But this quality is less important in Flavin. It's more important that the work is not confined to the shape of the material but expands into the volume of the room.

For the first time I realized how light could have a very strong emotional effect, as well as a very strong capacity to make a new relationship to something of which we have a common experience. Light is something physical and not physical, it's radiation made by photons. The photons don't have mass when they do not move, which in some way is not logical, but they are real, they have color, they make surfaces warm. They don't have mass but everything real has mass and weight. The photon doesn't have this quality, only radiation. For the first time I realized that light is extremely beautiful. The colors of this artificial light were very moving.

One of the first works in the gallery in Milan was a square made of blue fluorescent lamps. The blue color filled the empty room.

Blue is the color of the sky. Everything that is perfect, everything that is ideal, we believe comes from the sky, because instinctively we think that the sky is the perfection of nature.

CK   *Let's take what you've been saying about Flavin and double back to the very beginning of your collecting activities: Tapies, Fautrier. What connections do you or don't you see between where you started and where you were at this point with Flavin?*
GP   I believe there is always a link between different situations. Flavin is an artist who deals with some kind of metaphysical entity. He's a man looking for something that is not tangible and he feels very strongly the need for something absolute. In his work I believe this research becomes very clear, very strong.

And I felt the same kind of attitude in Tapies. The paintings by Tapies I bought were interesting to me because there was this struggle of a man, involved in a pessimistic view of life, for something great, something beautiful, which was not possible to achieve. He was involved with matter and the physical limits of everything but at the same time he was looking for this infinite freedom of mind. These two facts are present in both artists, who look so different. Tapies deals with an earthly material. His colors are without light. It is matter suffering the conditon of being matter. And in Flavin there is the ability to overcome the limits of matter using light.

CK   *So you could begin with Flavin and work all the way back to the Venetians and to Raphael.*
GP   Oh, yes.

CK   *Was Larry Bell the first artist from Southern California whose work you bought?*
GP   Yes. I bought one cube by Bell, and one disk by Robert Irwin, in 1968. I saw the 1968 exhibition by Bell at the Ileana Sonnabend Gallery in Paris, and at Documenta I saw two disks by Irwin. I was very attracted to these works, which dealt with light, with illusion, with perception. They were a step beyond the experience I had with Flavin. Flavin was using light, and Larry Bell was using light, because glass is a transparent material. This material is partly reflective and partly transparent. It creates an exchange between the two qualities. Sometimes you see reflections in these surfaces, sometimes you see what is behind – you go through the material.

In the work by Robert Irwin I found another field of research: the attempt to establish the limits of perception, to understand what perception is. To see how perceptions relate to memory, to our personality, to our participation in making judgments. We believe we see reality as it is but we see what we believe it is. All the work by Irwin reveals this fact, that our knowledge is mostly something related to our memory, to our preconceived judgment. We judge, we recognize and we experience what we already know. Seldom do we have new information from experience. We can only experience something new if our judgment is able to envision something new. Otherwise, our experience of reality is always a repetition of something we already know.

CK   *You first saw Bell's work and Irwin's work in Europe. Had you spent any time in Southern California, aside from your brief trip in the early 1950s?*
GP   No. I was in Los Angeles in 1954, but only for a few days, just passing through.

CK   *When did you first come to Los Angeles for any length of time?*
GP   It was in the fall of 1973.

CK   *What were the circumstances?*
GP   I wanted to buy more work by Irwin. I had news of Doug Wheeler, Jim Turrell, Eric Orr, and Larry Bell, and I wanted to know more about them. In New York, it was impossible to see art from Los Angeles because it wasn't shown much. I had seen a room installed by Irwin at the Museum of Modern Art. Before that I saw a beautiful show at the Stedelijk Museum in Amsterdam in 1970, with work by Wheeler and Irwin. There was the plastic square by Wheeler with the neon light on the edge and a large environment with light coming out of the edge of the wall, which was a beautiful work. And there was the disk by Irwin.

The room by Irwin I saw at MOMA, I believe in '69 or '70, was great. There was a scrim from the

Rothko, Red and Blue
over Red, *1959*
Villa Menafoglio Litta Panza,
living-room.
Photograph by Ugo Mulas, 1966.

ceiling taking up half the room, and there was a string of steel, very small, crossing near the end of the room. It was very impressive - so absolute, so simple, so strong, and involving only light and space.

I was, very involved, between 1969 and 1973, in Minimal sculpture and paintings. In 1970 I had acquired many paintings by Robert Ryman. I had seen Ryman, and also Brice Marden, in New York in 1967. But I didn't then realize the quality of their work. When Ryman showed at the Lambert Gallery in Milan in '69, suddenly I realized how beautiful this radical way of painting was, how strong this way of conceiving art was. I decided to buy all the Ryman paintings available in Europe and America. At this time Ryman had several shows in Europe, but he sold almost nothing. So it was possible to buy about twenty paintings in just a few months, which was all Ryman's production over several years.

CK   *You've described Ryman in the past as among the most important artists of this century. That's a fairly grand statement. Could you elaborate?*

GP   I believe Ryman has the same quality as Rothko. He's a man who has developed a strong exploration of his own mind. And the greatest thing in nature is surely the human mind. The wrong side of our mind prevails, because we are always acting, always willing to do something but we are less able to think, to look inside ourselves. The world inside us is a universe. Life becomes life the moment men have self-awareness. Matter does not. The highest achievement of life is self-consciousness, the capacity to understand that we are alive. Animals have some kind of consciousness, but in man this ability is most complete.

Our lives would be different if we were to use this capacity inside our minds but it is difficult. It's much easier to act rather than make this exploration, which demands a great deal of energy more energy - than lifting up heavy weight. We are lazy in using our brains, and we have the habit of repeating what we usually do. But self-exploration is the discovery of the flux of life inside us, and is the most creative act. Life every instant is the possibility of a creative act.

Ryman revealed this capacity. He was able to establish a direct relationship between what is inside our mind and what could become visible. The great achievement of Ryman is this connection between the hand, the finger, the nervous system – the objects for making paintings – and our mind. I realized how different art is if seen in this way. Because of this, I realized how great Raphael is. If you look at Raphael, with a magnifying lens, you see the quality of a Raphael painting in the details. You see a whole world in a small part of his painting. How the pigment is laid on the canvas shows the personality of the artist. This simple act is beautiful, just the moment when the pigment is laid down on the canvas. When the artist is able to achieve full control between his nervous system and his mind, it's great. The total relationship is complete. At this moment he's able to create masterpieces.

CK   *So obviously you would see a direct relationship between Ryman and the work of Robert Irwin or Doug Wheeler.*
GP   Oh, yes, sure.

CK   *Why do you suppose that it was easier for you to see Irwin's and Wheeler's work in Europe, rather than New York, and that you had to come to Southern California to see more?*
GP   Because this attitude is against the attitude of New York. New York is a city where people work. People work making art. People are competing for something to be made. Some people have a different attitude - like Rothko, Ryman, Flavin. But the dominant taste of dealers and collectors is against the attitude of artists from Los Angeles. They were making things that were hard to sell. We can sell painted canvases, white canvases by Ryman, if a person is able to understand the quality of his work. But it's more difficult to sell a room by Irwin or by Wheeler because space is difficult to get. Such a room is difficult to install as well. Galleries in New York weren't willing to engage money and time in something that is difficult to sell. I believe these were the two reasons why it was not possible to see this art from Los Angeles in New York.

CK   *Was it primarily a market reason?*
GP   A market reason and also a different cultural attitude. New York as a city is closer to the will to act than the will to think.

CK   *In addition to the artists you've mentioned, whom did you meet when you came to Los Angeles in 1973?*
GP   We met Jim Turrell at his studio in Los Angeles – in Santa Monica. We went to his house in

the late afternoon. The house was white, with empty white walls and almost nothing else around. There was a doorway, but no door. There was an empty room in his house with light coming in near the floor, and at the top of the front wall, facing west toward the ocean, there was an opening to the sky. It was a small opening, about three feet wide, and the room was perhaps 10 feet by 20 feet. We sat in this room and watched the sunset through the hole.

At first, the sunset was dark blue and the space inside looked empty. The dark blue appeared to be on the surface of the wall, because there was a sharp edge around the opening and you couldn't see the thickness of the wall. The wall and the opening appeared to belong to the same plane, to the same surface. The opening looked like a surface, not a void. When the light of the sunset began to change, this feeling shifted from an empty space to a surface to a solid colored material. It was very strange to see something that didn't exist but, at the same time, was real. The colors were always changing, but in a way we don't realize when we see the sunset outdoors. The sunset started with dark blue, became pale blue, and then red, light red, dark red, gold, green, violet – a steady variation of color.

Turrell is a man, like Irwin, with a broad knowledge of science and philosophy – a cultivated man with a strong cultural background. What is different about Turrell from many other artists is his ability to do everything related to technique himself. He's a pilot and restores old planes to resell to collectors. He makes a living in this way because his is not an income-generating kind of art. He's a fascinating man, because he's devoted to making an art that is difficult to sell but he does it because it's beautiful.

His vision of the universe is great, his interest in nature and its importance to our lives. Life came from inside the universe, but we don't know how the universe was made. These theories about the "big bang" are very interesting but how did the "big bang" happen? What was the beginning of the "big bang"? There was an infinite density of energy, which is something no scientific theories can explain. The beginning was an undifferentiated situation, but the world became so different. There is a wonderful, logical architecture to nature, where every phenomenon is connected to every other phenomenon. How beautiful this construction is!

Western civilization has lost interest in this because we work for other goals. We spend our energy, our time, to have a better life. We use resources from nature, but we don't pay attention to the fact we are alive because the universe was born one day, that everything we have is a gift we received. We are intelligent not because we made man intelligent, but because nature made man intelligent. Our culture has lost this essential relationship. Turrell was making this relationship evident again. For this reason I believe his work is so important.

In Turrell's house in Santa Monica there was another room that was completely dark. The room was near a street corner with a stoplight. One side of the room overlooked a small road with a little track. The other side faced the main street with many cars passing by. In the end wall of this room, Turrell had made several holes, windows that could be opened and closed, in different positions on the wall. If you opened the hole facing the stop light, the room filled for some minutes with a beautiful red light. And after that, a yellow one. And after that, a green one.

Closing this window and opening another one, it was possible to see only the lights projected by the cars passing in the main street. This light flashed inside the room like lightning, filling the room with very strong light but only for a short time. Afterward, the light disappeared and the room became dark again.

Opening another hole, it was possible to see only a light coming from the small road. For some minutes the room was dark, but then a small, dim light came into the room and got stronger and stronger. This light had a shape, and the shape went around the room as the car outside turned into the main street.

Opening another one, it was possible to have only the light coming from faraway street lights. This light was very dim, but it filled the room in a very peaceful way. It looked like moonlight. It gave the same kind of emotion because only the shadows of objects were visible inside the room. There was a confused notion of the volume of the space. The room looked much larger, almost endless because there were only very faint shadows. Everything inside the room looked like it had lost its material quality and gained some kind of ideal entity – which wasn't earthly but heavenly. It was very strange, very metaphysical. This series of beautiful experiences was made in a very simple way and showed the qualities of many kinds of light. Only the hole in the wall was the work of the artist.

After our visit to Turrell's house, my wife and I decided to have him make some rooms at our house in Varese.

CK   *How long did you stay in Los Angeles on this first visit?*
GP   In the first trip we spent about ten days. We saw the galleries and we met Betty Asher. She was working at the County Museum of Art and had a beautiful collection – especially Pop art. We also met her son, the artist Michael Asher, and we met with Bell, Wheeler and Bruce Nauman. Nauman's work I had seen many times before, in New York. I had started to buy Nauman's work from Leo Castelli in 1969 – early works.

CK   *Did visiting Los Angeles and seeing Turrell and other artists change the way you thought about Nauman's work?*
GP   No, because Nauman was involved in a different area. He was more concerned with the relationship of the space to the perception of the viewer and his physical presence. The relationship between space and our body is the main research of Nauman. The work he made with televisions is a way to duplicate ourselves, to explore the perception we have of ourselves through our own senses. This was very interesting, but different from the work of other Los Angeles artists. It was more physical. It dealt with the constraints to which our life is submitted every day. Man was made by nature to live inside nature, not in an urban landscape. But we live in an urban landscape and, because of this, we lose the connections to nature and to our own bodies. We believe we are the center of everything but in fact we are not. We are a temporary living object in a fast-changing environment. When we split our senses from our perception, we realize this opposition in a powerful way. This is the main lesson I learnt from looking at Nauman's work.

CK   *Would you say, then, that the primary aspect of Nauman's work is to manipulate artificial, constructed elements in such a way that one "rediscovers" his own body and perceptions?*
GP   Yes.

CK *Who else did you see on your first trip to the West Coast?*

GP After our meeting with Turrell, we paid our first visit to the desert, which is a beautiful space. We planned to stop in Nevada to see the Earthworks of Michael Heizer and Walter De Maria. I met De Maria some years before in New York and was very interested in his work. Few works were available, and they already cost more than $10,000, but I was interested in seeing the work he made in Nevada. I came with Helen Winkler and Heiner Friedrich. He had galleries in Cologne and New York, where I had bought several works by Flavin and Ryman. He was also the dealer of De Maria. Helen Winkler had come to the West several times with De Maria to look for a site for the *Lightning Field*. He made a test site near Flagstaff and made a work in Nevada, not far from Las Vegas. There was also Heizer's *Double Negative* to see on the Mormon Mesa, near Overton and Lake Mead. Because Turrell had to go to Nevada, too, we used his airplane.

CK *You have a reputation as a "collector of uncollectable art". What that were the works the first installation or environmental work that you purchased?*

GP The first was the disk by Robert Irwin. After that were the works by Turrell and Wheeler, in 1973. But these didn't exist yet. They were just projects. I knew Wheeler's work from the show in Amsterdam, but when I went to his studio there was nothing completed. He was thinking about making a room with rounded corners in order to obtain an illusion of disappearing, limitless space.

CK *So you bought the plans for that work?*

GP Yes.

Villa Menafoglio Litta Panza, entrance, 1966

CK *Had you already converted the stables at the Villa Litta into galleries?*

GP I was beginning to make them. In 1973, I commissioned Irwin to come to Varese to realize three works in three different rooms. At the same time, my wife and I asked Turrell to do the same with five other rooms which were available in Varese. We had also met Maria Nordman, because we went to the University of California at Irvine to see a room she had made there. We were very impressed by it. We asked her to do one in Varese, which she made in 1975-76.

I bought many other projects in 1975 - for instance, fourteen by Wheeler. But I soon ran out of money and it was not possible to complete the installations. Indeed, all the space in Varese was occupied. There was no way to instal even one room by Wheeler, whose work I like very much.

CK *Are the plans you've acquired works that could be executed by someone other than the artist - say, fifty years from now?*

GP I believe all the works by Wheeler could be executed by someone else because they don't have a specific relationship to the environment. If there is the right space, they could be made anywhere. The work by Irwin is different because Irwin is very concerned about the relationship to the environment. For Turrell, the participation of the artist is necessary because the relationship to the outside is important. There are other works by Turrell made with light-projectors where this is less important, but there are adjustments to the projectors that are better made by the artist. The works by Irwin, Turrell and Nordman in Varese were commissioned for the existing space. They could be remade elsewhere, but only with the participation of the artist.

CK *So you were not using the stables as galleries before 1973?*

GP I started to use the stables in 1968 and '69 for the large works by Robert Morris. In this period I bought about thirty works by Morris, twenty-eight by Donald Judd, forty by Nauman. I had many works by Flavin, Andre, Serra, Marden, Ryman. There were a lot of things to put inside! It was only possible to show part of this work. I was using all the space available, even for storage.

CK *The paperwork alone for a collection of that size is staggering. Museum have staffs. Did you have help?*

GP I did everything myself. I never had a secretary helping me. My wife was busy with the family, with her own charitable activities, and she didn't have the time to help. I had people working in my office, but this work I liked to do myself. However, it was very time-consuming. I used all my free time for the collection. In the evening, I would usually go to bed around one o'clock. From nine o'clock, after dinner, to one o'clock, I would work on the collection. On Sundays I didn't go for drives, I went to Varese to work on the collection, to write, or to look at photographs. On holiday, I would often work on the collection. Sometimes I would walk in the mountains, but almost every available hour I worked on the collection.

I never watched television, and very seldom would I go to the movies or the theatre. I like music very much, and I would listen to records to relax for an hour after dinner. I liked to listen to operas by Wagner or Bach. I also liked to read articles in science magazines. Science is something that fascinates me. And I read magazines or books on art.

CK   *Not much time to go to La Scala.*
GP   No, I hardly ever go to La Scala. I go once every three years!

CK   *What unique problems do you face as a collector of environmental and installation works?*
GP   The problem is to find the right space. Not only is the space itself important, but also its relationship to the space around it. With the window by Irwin at Varese, it's important that it faces a garden with many dark green trees in the background and large branches in the fore-ground. From the empty room, which is all white and neutral, you see nature full of life. The opposition of the empty space inside, to the outside seen through the opening, looks like a painting. The window becomes like the frame of a painting – a very strange painting which is real and not an illusion. This shifting image is very interesting. It's beautiful to see this wall of green, living trees. If there weren't any trees, if there was a street behind this wall of the house, everything would be lost.

CK   *Different picture?*
GP   Yes.

Kline, Tower, *1953. Milan,*
Panza's House, 1962.

CK   *Do you own any of Irwin's stripe-paintings?*

GP   No, but I have a beautiful dot-painting done, I believe, in 1964. Unfortunately, it is in storage, like the two disks and the plastic column. I have several projects which were made by Irwin at the Pace Gallery in New York and the Ace Gallery in Los Angeles, but they exist only as projects. My problem is to find the space to install these works permanently. It's my greatest concern, because I believe these works are an important achievement of our culture. But they don't exist. It's important to find a way to give the public access to these works. For this reason, I am actively trying to find space in museums interested in keeping this work in a permanent way.

CK   *In the late 1960s and early 1970s you began collecting the work of Joseph Kosuth, Lawrence Weiner, and other Conceptual artists. At the same time you were collecting the work of Richard Serra. His sculptures are so physical, so much about gravity and weight and tensions. How do you reconcile the purely Conceptual work of Kosuth or Weiner with your simultaneous interest in Serra?*

GP   Conceptual art deals with ideas, with philosophical problems but it can also have a strong visual impact if it's shown in the right way. Because these artists are artists, not philosophers, they are able to make concise definitions of our thinking, and these concise definitions become art.

If we make an analysis of intuition, we realize it is not a simple thing but a very complex one. We can go on and on analyzing intuition and find out how many aspects it contains. It looks very simple, but it's not. There is understanding in the first second, but at the same time it has all the qualities of a complex intellectual development of ideas.

This is very new in the history of art, and it is new because it was never possible before. Leonardo da Vinci or Piero della Francesca were artists with strong philosophical backgrounds and the work they made was related to these philosophical ideas. When we look at their work we can understand this background, but the relationship is very indirect. We can see the relationship if we know the philosophy behind it, if we know other sources and the prevailing ideas of the Renaissance. But looking at a work by Kosuth or Weiner or Robert Barry or Sol Lewitt, you have a more direct reference to philosophical research about knowledge, language, the relationship between meaning and expression, and about how something could be valid as a tool for translating thought into images.

Linguistic philosophy is a very interesting field. For instance, the work by Lawrence Weiner, which is made of words, is something absolutely new in art history. In the early Renaissance and, especially, Medieval times, we see words used in relation to paintings. There are many examples. But these words belong to speech. They explain the image. In the work by Lawrence Weiner, the word becomes something completely independent of speech. It becomes art because it is independent of the development of logical reference to a situation. Both words and images have an essential quality: to be able to express different contents; to be symbols used for saying different things, to have different meanings. Usually we don't pay attention to this fact. When we open the dictionary and look at a word, we realize how many different meanings it could have. If its position in speech changes, its meaning changes.

CK   *And from language to language, as in Kosuth's* Definition of Nothing *in six different languages.*

GP   Words can be art because of this ambiguity. Images and words are useful because of this capacity for having different meanings. The fact that the meaning is not exact, but can shift, gives the viewer the possibility of stimulation to think about different things. Art is art because of this. A work of art is beautiful when it gives different ideas and different suggestions to the viewer.

CK   *And how does this mesh with your simultaneous interest in Richard Serra?*
GP   As with every great artist, the meaning of his work can be read in different ways. It's physical because the weight of the mass deals with gravity, which is a force that acts on everything, but at the same time it's something we don't see because it's a force. We feel it but we don't see it. The more mass an object has, the more we feel its heaviness. If an object is large but light, these perceptions of mass change.

The force acting in Serra's work is energy. Intelligence is also energy. We cannot see the process of intelligence – how it moves, how it works, yes. There are two aspects of intelligence: logic, which is a process of dealing with quantities and definitions of facts; and intuition, which is completely different.

CK   *You said earlier that Robert Ryman's paintings gave evidence of the moment of consciousness of the self. This is very much the kind of experience offered by Maria Nordman's piece in Varese, which is one of the most remarkable light-and-space installations I've ever seen. So whether it's a painter or an installation artist, the work you were acquiring is an extension of a central concern that goes back to the work you were collecting in the 1950s. In this regard, I wanted to ask you about your collection of death masks.*
GP   I was interested in these skulls because I believe the problem of death is the main problem of life. We cannot understand life if we cannot have a clear awareness of death. Life and death are two aspects which cannot be split. It's wrong to think of life as endless. We don't have much time and must use well the time available to us. If we see life in this perspective, it becomes different. Many things which look important are in reality less so. Life is good if we leave behind us something useful to others. I believe this is the main goal of life. For this reason, I was interested in keeping these objects, which give evidence of this idea.

Most of them are skulls carved in ivory. They're Japanese, Italian and German from the 15th, 16th and 17th centuries. Some are African. It's a small group, and not very important as a collection. But it's important to me because it reminds me of this fact that life and death are two things which always go together.

They were *memento mori*. The attitude of people in the 16th and 17th centuries was different than today. Now we try to avoid the image of death in any way we can. People like to think death doesn't exist and they take care to avoid anything which recalls this fact.

CK   *How did you acquire these masks?*
GP   Mostly, I found them in antique stores in Milan. The *memento mori* was a common object in the past.

CK   *Was it in 1975 that you stopped collecting?*

GP   Yes, I stopped in '75. There are a few works that came into the collection in 1976, but they were works which had been engaged in '75.

CK   *How many pieces were there in the collection then?*
GP   There were 600 of museum quality and a hundred more which were good but, being small, would not be interesting in a museum installation. Some small paintings by Robert Mangold and Ryman, for instance. It wouldn't be right to put them in a museum next to larger works.

CK   *After collecting for almost exactly twenty years, why did you stop?*
GP   I stopped for economic reasons. I ran out of cash! There was no more money available. I always spent all the money it was possible to spend. Unfortunately, after 1975 my business wasn't as good as before. I had already taken a risk, from a financial point of view, having spent so much money between 1969 and 1975.

CK   *Your sister warned you!*
GP   Yes, I was just undermining the financial situation of the family. For this reason, I had to stop. It was a very difficult decision, but it was dictated by the situation. Indeed, I was very busy looking for a way to show the collection, which was almost completely hidden in storage. This became a full-time job, just trying to find a way to show the collection.

CK   *If you had about 600 major works that you had collected over a twenty-year period, that works out to about one new acquisition every twelve days. Was it difficult to stop?*
GP   Oh, yes, it was a terrible decision. When I see an artist who I realize is good, I feel a tremendous need to buy. And I cannot. It isn't easy for me. But although it is something I cannot do now, I hope to resume buying if the situation improves and I am able to sell my business in Italy. I don't know if it will be possible.

CK   *Are there other collectors you admire?*
GP   Yes. I believe the best collection assembled recently was in Zurich, Switzerland. It's shown now in an old factory made available by the city of Schaffhausen. It was assembled by Raus Muller, an artist who for several years ran the Ink Institution, a space in Zurich for showing art. He made a beautiful collection of American artists of the '60s. There are also European artists of the period, but mostly American. He didn't have any money but he had a group of friends who gave him the means to buy the collection. The collection is called Crex. It really is the most beautiful collection of American art of the '60s in the world.

The Ludwig collection in Germany is very large but that was made with a different goal. It's very broad, having documentation of every event in art, and is not as selective as the Crex collection. That one was made like mine, a careful selection of the best work of the best artists.

The Saatchi collection in London is very good but it has a different orientation. The Minimal art is excellent. There are also many works by the German Neo-Expressionists and the Italian Trans Avant Garde, which interest me less. I believe the good artists of the '80s are not the Trans

Avant Garde and the German Neo-Expressionists. I believe that the best artists of these years are in Los Angeles, and some in New York. Not in Europe.

CK   *Why aren't you interested in the German and Italian painters?*
GP   Because these artists are expressing instincts coming from a lower part of the body. I like artists who express instincts from a higher part of the body!

This kind of art is very far from my vision of life. It's not concerned with the problems that are essential to me. For me, art is something which improves the quality of life, the quality of thought, the quality of our inner intellectual activity. This art gives no improvement. It's an art which looks to the past, not to the future. It doesn't take the risk of making something new that tries to expand the experience of existence.

If you look at this art, you find elements coming from German Expressionism of the early years of the 20th century. You find forms from Surrealism, Metaphysical art, Abstract Expressionism and all these brought together. But these were important because they were new experiences and all of them were motivated by an idealistic view of their situation. It was a test to explore the human mind, a new answer to a changing social situation. It was a projection, or a forecast, of how life in the modern world was changing. But the relationship of Neo-Expressionism to the art of the past is completely stripped of this motivation. It only uses the formal body, the shell of this earlier art, not its meaning, not its content. In this way it's useless. Art is art when shapes have a direct relationship to a given experience. When this relationship doesn't exist, it's just an intellectual exercise about shapes. Shapes without anything behind them are nothing, just a void.

CK   *So you're an idealist?*
GP   Oh, yes, of course.

CK   *German Expressionism attempted to reconnect contemporary culture to its source in nature. Neo-Expressionism, with its interest in history, seems to me a reflection that nature is no longer the source from which culture derives. Today, culture is itself the source from which culture derives, and culture has a life, a "nature" of its own. So the Neo-Expressionist interest in the "nature of history" and the "nature of images" suggests that nature has become indistinguishable from culture.*
GP   I believe that the lack of reference to nature is a negative quality of this art. It's an exercise about past cultural experience. There is no engagement with anything, and this lack of engagement is the main reason the art is made. It is its main feature, and one with which I disagree very deeply. Art is not a pleasure, not a relaxing activity, an amusement or entertainment. Art is an engagement with life and reflects this engagement with life.

This lack of a relationship to nature is the lack of a relationship to a real motivation to be alive. If we don't feel this relationship to nature, we are cut off from reality. We are real because we are born from nature. And this art is useless to me because it's an intellectual experiment and nothing else.

The main reason this art is the way it is, I believe, is because it came out of a generation of people who lived through the revolution of 1968 in France. This revolution gave the hope of total freedom, the possibility of doing anything we wanted to do. But this kind of freedom is really not freedom. Real freedom is the obligation to make what is best for the evolution of man. This is the goal that nature gives to man, to continue evolving. We are thinking animals because we came from animals who do not think, who lived by instinct. Man has this privilege. The history of nature is evolution. From the "big bang" – from undifferentiated energy to physical differentiation – man is the very last event in the long history of evolution. He's the last, and perhaps he is the beginning of something else. We don't know where nature will lead us. But it's clear that we are the instrument of something else, and this "something else" is evolution.

Inside our mind we always feel this desire for things beyond what we have reached. This is the voice of nature speaking inside our mind, this endless desire for the best.

CK   *If in your view, the student riots in Paris in 1968 had a great deal to do with these developments, it's curious that the artists who have subsequently come to the forefront are German, Italian and American, and not French.*
GP   Well, Figuration Libre is a version of this in France.

CK   *But it has much less... notoriety, shall we say.*
GP   Yes, it came after but it belongs to the same psychological situation. These people who lived with the hope - the wrong hope - of 1968 were disillusioned very fast. It's clear that total freedom leads to self-destruction because it leads to nothing. They were disillusioned by what came after because not one of their great hopes for total freedom was realized.

The generation coming out of 1968 had no strong moral readiness to face disillusionment. And for this reason they make this kind of art which shows great disillusionment with life. They lack engagement because they don't have hope. If we do not have goals, we cannot be alive. If we have a goal, we have hope to reach something better than we have today.

CK   *So you believe that this desire for total freedom meant that there was no touchstone and that nature must be the primary standard?*
GP   Yes.

CK   *I believe you have two works by Joseph Beuys in your collection. How does Beuys – who many would regard as the father of certain of these recent developments – fit into your collection, and why did you stop collecting his work?*
GP   In 1968 there was an exhibition of Beuys and Robert Morris at the Eindhoven Museum. I went because I was collecting Morris's work, and it was a beautiful exhibition of his early work. In this way, I also saw the Beuys exhibition. It was the first time I saw Beuys's work, the first time I had even heard his name and I was extremely impressed by him. But his work has nothing to do with the post-Expressionist art of Germany. It's related to the experience of a real German Expressionism, to the whole culture of Central Europe. And it's very much related to Surrealism. He's the parallel of Rauschenberg in a certain way.

The art of Beuys is extremely important. It's related to the Medieval life of Europe - not to the Renaissance tradition but to the hidden world which is deeply inside our mind. It's the exploration of instincts which lay down every act we make, things of which we have no notion but which are basic in our lives. This exploration is carried out in a powerful way, through analogy, through opposing objects which have some relationship to memory, as in Rauschenberg. But Rauschenberg is romantic in his own way. Beuys goes to the roots of Central European culture, which comes out of the Middle Ages. The Renaissance in Germany didn't have roots as strong as in Italy. The Italian Renaissance was closely related to Greek and Roman culture and rediscovered classical harmony. But German culture is more closely related to the Middle Ages, to the gods, to this world we don't see. It relates to the Medieval belief that hell and the devil are true. This is very strong in the Beuys experience, as is the mystical experience. Both of these are together, a strong erotic and mystical experience and the opposition of good and evil. To look at Beuys's work is like reading the *Divine Comedy* of Dante.

His best work was done in the 1950s and early '60s. I tried hard to buy his work, but a German collector was buying all Beuys's work at this time. There were no good ones available, and soon his work became expensive. I only have two small objects. Stroher, the collector, had acquired a collection of Pop art from New York but his main commitment was to Beuys, whom he started to collect very early. There are four rooms devoted to his early work at the Darmstadt Museum – the core works are really powerful. The work Beuys made in the '70s and '80s is fine, but not as strong.

CK   *So the pressure of the marketplace kept you from being able to acquire Beuys's work. The market has changed dramatically since you first began to buy art in New York in the 1950s. What other effects do you think market pressure has on art?*

GP   Today the market pressure is very negative. It's costly to live in New York. Artists have to make things which can be sold. The prevailing taste is for this kind of art, Neo-Expressionist art, which is an art that can be sold easily. It's figurative art. There are strong colors, large canvasses, we recognize images and we understand what the painter is saying. For this reason, people are happy to buy it. They believe they are buying avant-garde art. Collectors with a modest cultural background in modern art buy it because they've found some avant-garde art they can understand. This is why prices are so high. It's successful art and I never liked successful art because, usually, it's easy art. After a few years this art will disappear. Many times I have seen so-called famous artists be forgotten.

CK   *When you began collecting Robert Ryman's paintings, they were very inexpensive. Shortly after you began acquiring them, their prices increased significantly. Although investment has never been a consideration for you, your stature as a collector would seem to have an effect on the market. Would you agree?*

GP   Perhaps. I don't know. There are some artists whom I bought early who went on to become famous. There are others whom I believe are very important artists who didn't become famous at all. I can give some examples. One of the few Italian artists whose work I have is Maurizio Mochetti. He makes kinetic art. I believe he's the best at this kind of work. Kinetic art is related to time, and I believe nobody expresses the value and meaning of time as well as Mochetti. But nobody knows him. Have you ever heard his name?

CK   *No.*

GP   Yes, but in my opinion he's a very important artist. I also collected paintings by Bob Law and Peter Joseph, who are very good artists but not famous at all.

CK   *So you're saying you are only one factor among many.*
GP   Yes. There are situations in which an artist is not able to find a good dealer, or is not able to have a relationship with dealers. Or he makes something which other people don't react to the way I do. This work is left out of the market. However, if I do collect some good art, people around are not stupid and they collect it, too.

CK   *You've never collected figurative art, except for art that derives from photographic sources, such as Pop. Nor have you ever collected photography* per se. *Although Douglas Heubler and Jan Dibbets use photographs, they aren't really photographers. Why do you favor abstraction?*
GP   It is a distinctive quality of 20th-century art to explore new dimensions and visions of reality. I don't believe that abstract art is better than figurative art because there is no difference. For instance, some artists of the Italian Renaissance, the so-called Mannerist painters, were in reality abstract painters. For them, the quality of the image was more important than its meaning. What was important was the relationships of color and the harmony of shapes, not the fact that the image was related to something real. The image was only a way to build forms that were intellectual creations.

But I believe that modern science, revealed to our knowledge a world which is far above what is possible for our eyes to see. Our eyes have limits in perceiving reality. But knowledge goes far above this limit. For this reason we no longer need the images which our eyes can see. The world we can know through our intellect is wider than the image that arrives through our eyes. If you look in the microscope, you see an abstract image. If you look at photographs of the stars, they are abstract images. Abstraction is a closer image of the reality around us. It's a more efficient tool to inform us about reality.

CK   *How do you reconcile being an idealist and a realist?*
GP   Well, we cannot really be an idealist if the idealism is only an intention. Life is not made of good intentions. If the intentions are not related to the facts, they're just words. Words are no good if they're not related to something real. Idealism and realism have to exist together. The quality of our idealism is in relation to our attempts to make it real. We can fail, but what is important is the commitment we have to make it real. It's not important if we fail, but it's important that we try. Commitment is the only important thing in life. It's not so important that the ideal becomes real but it's extremely important that our energy be devoted to the goal we have in mind.

CK   *Would you describe that as a political dimension for art?*
GP   It's a political dimension for art because I believe it's an obligation which everyone has.

CK   *In 1980, a comprehensive exhibition of your collection had been planned in Dusseldorf.*
GP   Yes, in the Kunsthalle and in the City Museum. But the City Museum was closed for restora-

tion so we used a large room at the fair nearby. There was also a plan to make a long-term loan to the Dusseldorf Museum of Nordrhein Westfalen of the works which are now owned by the Museum of Contemporary Art in Los Angeles. The director was Mr. Schmalenbach, who had assembled a beautiful collection of modern art. But this program could not be carried out because of the Italian law forbidding long-term loans abroad of works of art.

CK   *So the exhibition was never completely realized?*
GP   No. In the early '70s, I had already bought many works of art and the need to find space for them was pressing. Only a small number of them could be shown at my house in Varese. So I began to investigate museums in order to find one that would be interested in having the first part of my collection. I believed this was the more interesting part for a museum to have because it was made up of well-established artists. I asked many museums but the first answer came from Germany, from the Moenchengladbach Museum and, afterward, from Mr. Schmalenbach at the Dusseldorf Museum.

Johannes Cladders, the director at the Moenchengladbach Museum, was an excellent man. He made beautiful, early exhibitions of several American and European artists, and I went to see them many times. They were of the same artists I was beginning to collect. The museum was in a small old house but there was a plan with the city to build a new museum. The task was given to Hans Hollein, whom I read this morning was given a very important prize for architecture, which was awarded last year to Richard Meier.

CK   *The Pritzker Prize.*
GP   Yes I'm very happy because I like his work very much. But the museum was yet to be built, and I was very interested in making a long-term loan. The city didn't have the money to buy the collection but was very interested in having it for a fifteen year loan. Negotiation started in 1973. In '74, we reached an agreement and I crated all the works. I sent them to storage in Switzerland, expecting construction to begin the following year and to be finished no later than 1978. But unfortunately, there was an economic depression in Germany in 1974 and the start of construction was postponed. So the museum wasn't ready until 1982. Because the possibility of building the museum appeared to have vanished, I was approached by Mr. Schmalenbach to loan the works to Dusseldorf.

Schmalenbach had built up a beautiful collection of modern art, starting with Cubism, Metaphysical art, Surrealism, abstract art, and Pop art. There are just a few paintings by each artist, but all are masterpieces. I believe it's the most beautiful collection made in postwar Europe, really top quality. There are no mistakes in this collection. It was made with funds provided by the state - about three million marks a year. The amount of money Schmalenbach had each year was not very much less than all the money I spent on art in my whole life!

CK   *What is the equivalent of three million marks in dollars?*
GP   Well, I'm not strong in money conversion. But when the dollar was very low in value, two marks bought one dollar, so it was about $1.5 million a year.

CK   *So you've spent a little more than that on your entire collection?*
GP   Yes.

CK *I keep thinking of your sister having told you to be careful. You have proven her wrong!*
GP Oh, yes.

Schmalenbach also had a plan to build a new museum. There was an international contest for the project. But for economic reasons, it was delayed, too. Indeed, this museum wouldn't be ready until 1986. I had stored my collection in Switzerland as a permanent export from Italy, in order to avoid complex regulations in force in Italy. When you have to export something, you cannot make it a long-term loan, only a loan of one or two years. It's very complex. So I set up a Lichtenstein Trust, which became the permanent owner of the collection, and this Trust was the property of my wife and he. In this way, I was free of all the complex formal obligations with the Italian administration.

CK *This Trust included only the eighty works which are now in the collection of L.A.'s Museum of Contemporary Art?*
GP Yes. This operation was possible in Italy at that time. It was not allowed by law, but if you did it there were no consequences. We had to pay a fine, but it was a small fine.

CK *It's a good thing you were a lawyer.*
GP But in 1976, the Italian government passed a new law which required that every Italian resident with property in a foreign country bring it back to Italy, or else sell it and send back the money. I asked the government not to impose this obligation because mine was not an investment abroad, not capital kept abroad. It was a cultural activity.

This law required me to dissolve the Trust I had made, which I did, and the works became mine. But the Italian administration rejected my request. We were obliged to bring back the work or the money in a very short period of time. We asked for an extension, but that was also rejected. Because the new law was very severe on anyone keeping money or property abroad, there was a risk of going to jail. We were reported to the criminal court in Rome because we were guilty! We ran the risk, my wife and I, of going to jail because we kept works of art abroad to be shown in museums!

CK *What reason did they give for refusing your request for a waiver for cultural reasons?*
GP Just because it was the law. There were no distinctions, even if there was some valid reason for keeping something abroad. This law was very simple: Everything had to come back - either the estate or the money - if it was sold.

CK *That was in 1976, and you sold the collection in 1984. So for eight years you were avoiding the police?*
GP Almost, because we had to await trial by the criminal court in Rome, which would establish whether we were guilty or not. And we had to wait six years because Italian law is very slow! The courts were in no hurry because they realized that our crime was not a risk for Italy. But my wife and I had to go on trial, to sit where the accused sit and argue with the three judges – in a very large, bare room in Rome.

CK *They didn't handcuff you?*

GP   No, we had a derate. I showed them catalogs, I explained why I was keeping these works abroad, because there was this cultural interest that was real, not just something I had made up. After having seen the material and having a short discussion with my lawyer, the court retired. They spent half an hour in the room where they had to decide our sentence. And we had to spend one of the worst half hours of our lives, waiting to see if we were guilty or not!

At last, they came out. They read the decision and we were declared not guilty. The interpretation that the court gave was this. When something was kept abroad for cultural reasons, it was within the intent of the law. The law was made only for people who had assets abroad for investment. So we were completely free, and we believed we had solved every problem and could make the long-term loan to Dusseldorf.

CK   *When the court looked at the catalogue, what did they think of the work of Hannah Darboven and Jan Dibbets?*
GP   Well, we also gave them many articles about the collection from Italian newspapers. They realized that, even if they didn't understand it, it was judged to be something good by competent people.

But the problem was not really solved. The Italian administration in charge of foreign exchange still interpreted the law differently from the court. And we still ran the risk of being caught again and going to another criminal trial, which was not an experience we wanted to repeat. So I decided to look for another solution, which was to sell the collection and bring back the money. I tried to sell the works to Schmalenbach, but unfortunately his funds had been cut by the state of Westphalia because of the economic depression in 1982. So in June of 1983, I wrote to Richard Koshalek, the director of the Museum of Contemporary Art in Los Angeles, to ask if the museum was interested. He said yes.

CK   *When you sold the collection, you had to return the money to Italy?*
GP   Yes. The dollars go to the Bank of Italy and the Bank of Italy gives me lire at the rate of exchange of the day.

CK   *That's very clever of them.*
GP   Yes. If I brought back the paintings, which was the other possibility, I would have to pay a value-added tax of 20% – that's millions of dollars – which was impossible. I would have to sell one-third of the collection just to pay the tax. I would have to break up the collection, which I didn't want to do. When I saw the only solution was to sell, I asked for an estimate from Christie's and Sotheby's. They raced to Milan the next day to make an estimate. The estimates were between $11 million and $15 million, if sold at auction in 1983, but they were prudent estimates. Christie's was the higher. They told me it would be the greatest sale of contemporary art in history, that it would draw museum directors and collectors from the world who wanted to have the paintings.

But money was not my goal. My goal was just to keep the collection intact, to have it housed in a beautiful museum. MOCA was the ideal solution.

CK   *But it was clear that the estimates were very conservative.*
GP   Oh yes. Leo Castelli told me recently that he had several offers when people realized that I

was willing to sell. There were institutions and collectors willing to give me $12 million in cash, immediately.

CK *Well, they could turn around the next day and practically double their money.*
GP Oh yes. Castelli told me if I wanted to sell these paintings I would easily get $20 million.

CK *So the $11 million that MOCA paid for the collection was the lower estimate that Sotheby's had given?*
GP Yes.

CK *You had benefited from an inheritance from your family. Do you feel a similar obligation, since you have five children?*
GP Yes. If I didn't have children, I would give my collection as a gift. I don't feel a need to be rich. I feel the need to achieve my goal, which is to have the collection installed in the best way possible in good museums. I am not a great businessman, but as an art connoisseur I think I am good. If I have inherited this talent from nature, I have to use it in the best way. It is my duty.

CK *You once wrote that art was essentially a vehicle for social integration. In reference to Renaissance frescos, you wrote that those artists "interpreted the feelings that were shared by a community, since they were works executed in buildings destined for public use. The individualistic conception of art which Romanticism introduced into our culture shattered this relationship."*

You seem to be saying that, in the intellectual and moral crisis of the 18th century, which gave birth to modern culture, we somehow made a wrong turn. Could you elaborate?
GP A Renaissance, Baroque, or Medieval artist was not working for a private collector. He was working for the church, for the king, for the duke, for the prince, but always for a building with a social and political function, whether church or palace. The palace, where policy was made, had to be decorated with works dealing with the social achievements of the man in power or, through symbols, to show the goal the prince wanted to reach for the good of the people for whom he was responsible. Only with the development of the bourgeoisie did this function diminish. Art was needed for private houses. This began in Holland in the 17th century, when the bourgeoisie became rich through trade with foreign countries. In Italy, paintings made for private use mostly had a religious function, to have religious images in the home. In the early 16th century it became common to make portraits to preserve the memory of the family in the house. It was related to the Medici commissions for paintings of mythological stories, which were analogies for what was happening in their family.

An artist's work was mostly carried out in connection with social or political events. He was the man who interpreted the moral and ethical life of the community. This was the goal of art. And it was used in this way by people who wanted to have art made.

CK *It was for a particular social class, though.*
GP Yes, that was one important consideration. The people who commissioned artists were the dominant social class. The most important families had sons who became cardinals or bishops of

the church, or sons who became soldiers and had political power – and sometimes even economic power. Leadership was concentrated in a few hands, in the class that had the highest level of instruction. There was no public education, with one teacher and twenty five pupils. Each son had his own teacher, who was a man with a high cultural reputation. The best writer, the best poet, the best painter lived in the palace to teach the son.

CK   *Wasn't the rise of individualism essential to changing that?*
GP   This happened because of the French Revolution. The system ended when the great monarchies collapsed at the end of the 18th century because the bourgeoisie was becoming more important economically. The system didn't work anymore. Power shifted into the hands of the people who had economic power. Social life was also changing. The quality of education of the new rich people was lower because they didn't have the best humanists teaching texts in Latin and Greek. The close relationship between the intellectual world and power was lost.

In Rimini, there is a beautiful church by Alberti, the great architect of the 15th century, which was built for a Malatesta prince. Outside the church are the graves of the prince and his court. The first is the grave of the prince. The second is the grave of the poet, who was the poet of the prince. The third is the grave of the painter, who was the painter of the prince. The fourth is the grave of the man of law. The fifth is the grave of the general. And so on.

But the poet is first. Today, it would be the minister of finance! The man who pays for the election is most important.

We can see how power and culture were together and couldn't be split. The prince, the man of power, realized that his power didn't have any justification if there was no cultural motivation. The identity of good government and the cultural appreciation of the value of life was the same. This was extremely important. It's not the same now.

CK   *Do you believe that the artists whose work you've collected are, in some way, attempting to do something similar?*
GP   Oh, yes, surely. The artist, being a man like other men, is also an interpreter of our social situation. And the artist is the best interpreter of social conditions because he's a man of higher sensibility who lives more intensely life shared with other men. Every one of us lives in the same way – in America, in Europe, in Japan.

CK   *Essentially, then, you have built a collection for private use, and the dilemma you're facing now is how to transform it into a collection for public use.*
GP   Yes.

CK   *While you were trying to place the portion of your collection that's now at MOCA – the Abstract Expressionist and Pop works – you also had begun negotiations to place the Minimal, Conceptual, and installation works in two palaces in Turin. How did that project begin, evolve, and finally fall apart?*
GP   In the mid-'70s, when the Italian newspapers found out that the first part of the collection would leave the country, they complained that it was not being kept in Italy. Some people

asked, Why not keep the rest in Italy? Why not make long-term, fifteen-year loans of my collection, or even a donation, to fill empty, historical buildings then under restoration but with no planned use?

The first suggestion came from a friend, Giuliano Gori, a collector who lives in Prato, to use the stables of a famous building near Florence: the Medici villa in Poggio a Caiano, which was built by Giuliano da Sangallo for Lorenzo Il Magnifico. It's a beautiful masterpiece of the Italian Renaissance, built between 1490 and 1498. Construction was begun while Lorenzo was alive, but it wasn't completed until after his death in 1494. Near the villa was a large stable, a beautiful space. On the ground floor were three naves with columns separating them, about 300 feet long and 80 feet wide. It looked like a big church. Above it was a similar space with a huge corridor in the middle and rooms on the sides. There had been a fire – part of the roof fell in – and the Department of Fine Art was starting restoration of the building. The Medici Villa is state-owned.

My friend asked me to make a proposal, and I suggested using the ground floor for a huge work by Dan Flavin – a series of fluorescent lamps, filling the left wall – and on the right a fluorescent work by Bruce Nauman. The space would be lighted by these two works but the view of the space would not be altered in any way. The second floor would have works by Los Angeles artists who use light: Wheeler, Irwin, Turrell, Nordman, Nauman.

If it was built, this museum would be maintained by the state administration of Tuscany, which was communist and socialist. I had several meetings with the politicians in charge, and they were in favor of my idea. I also met with the Minister of Culture, and everybody always said yes, yes, yes. But it was never done. It was a great pity not to be able to associate these beautiful works with a villa built for a great collector, intellectual, and politician like Lorenzo Il Magnifico, and built by a great architect like Giuliano da Sangallo. It was the ideal thing to do: to unite history and the art of the past with the best art made today. Nothing similar would be possible anywhere but in Italy.

Two years later, in the summer of 1978, I was in Turin. Previously, I had made two long trips through southern Germany to see the Baroque architecture, which is one of the great achievements of European culture. I was also interested in the Baroque architecture of Italy, and Turin was one of the centers of Baroque art because of the Savoy dynasty. Until 1563, the Savoy dynasty was French because they had power on the French-speaking side of the Alps and in Switzerland. The French kings needed to regain control of the natural border, along the Alps and the Rhine, in order to protect themselves from the pressure of the German empire. The French king was allied with the Canton of Bern, which also wanted to control this part of Switzerland. The Savoy Duke was allied with the Duke of Bourgogne, who lost the war, so the Savoy dynasty lost control of the whole French-speaking side of Switzerland and of the land on the French side of the Alps. They tried to expand their power in Italy, in Piedmont. In 1562, Duke Emanuele Filiberto moved the capital from Chambery, in France, to Turin.

Until then Turin had been a small town. With the help of the best Baroque architects, the duke planned a beautiful city and a large number of palaces were built. Two were falling into ruin: Rivoli Castle in the northen suburbs, which overlook the city; and Venaria Castle, the hunting lodge of the most powerful king of the dynasty, Vittorio Amedeo II, which was built between the end of the

17th century and the middle of the 18th century. It was a huge building with huge stables, designed by one of the best Baroque architects in Italy, Filippo Juvarra. The building had become an army barracks and was in ruins. Rivoli Castle has about 50,000 square feet, the Venaria Castle about 300,000 square feet.

CK *The Venaria Castle alone could accommodate the entire collection.*
GP Oh, yes. It was one of the biggest royal palaces built in Europe. It was smaller than Versailles, and smaller than Caserta, the royal Baroque palace near Naples, but it was bigger than all the other palaces of Europe.

I got in touch with friends, who in turn put me in touch with the administration in Piedmont responsible for the restoration of the Rivoli Castle. We signed an agreement for a long-term loan, lasting fifteen years, for the Minimal art by Morris, Andre, Flavin, Nauman, and Serra.

CK *So the Italian government would provide restoration of the building, and you would provide the collection?*
GP Yes, that's right.

CK *What was the cost of the restoration?*
GP For the Italian government, the cost was about $4 million. The value of the eighty large works to be housed in the Rivoli Castle was about $8 million.

I also made a proposal to house the whole collection in both castles. The money needed to restore Venaria Castle was about five times more than for Rivoli because the building was about five times bigger. We waited for the allocation of funds in order to sign an agreement.

While this was happening, another possibility came up. Near Milan is the castle of Vigevano, built by the Sforzas in the 14th and 15th centuries. Part of the building was designed by Bramante, and Leonardo had lived and worked there while he was designing hydraulic works for land irrigation around the castle, which belonged to the duke, Ludovico il Moro. Leonardo spent much of his life in Milan, from 1483 until Ludovico was overthrown by the King of France in 1499. He returned to Milan in 1506 and remained until 1516, when François the First, who liked Leonardo's work very much, was king of France. The building is very large, at the top of a small hill in the old town, with wonderful spaces for art. And this connection to Leonardo and Bramante made it a very exciting opportunity.

The castle, which has a hundred rooms, was under restoration, albeit slowly. It was going to be used by the Brera Museum for paintings that couldn't be shown in Milan owing to lack of space. But Mr. Bertelli, who was director of the Brera, realized that there were too many large doorways and windows to accommodate the paintings and that many of the walls were not vertical because the building was originally designed as a fortress. He asked me to make a proposal for housing my collection there. I planned to show the Conceptual art, the Minimal art that wouldn't be shown at Rivoli Castle, several installations by Los Angeles artists, and so on.

It was necessary to obtain final approval for this plan from local authorities and the Minister of Culture. From Rome, he appointed a committee to decide. Because the castle is in Lombardy, the committee was led by the head of the Lombardy cultural administration. Instead of a long-term loan, Mr. Bertelli had asked me to donate one hundred works for this space. I agreed, but the committee refused the donation.

CK *Why?*
GP I don't know. They decided instead to use the building as a center for the art of Lombardy, which didn't mean anything because they didn't have any Lombardy art to put inside. The building is still empty.

In the meantime, there were many other negotiations. I went to Venice because people there asked me to use the Arsenale to house the collection. It is a huge building, designed as the shipyard of the Venetian Republic and built in the 13th, 14th, and 15th centuries. It was used by the Italian navy until a few years ago, but now it is empty.

There was also a possibility of using the Villa Doria Pamphili, in the middle of a huge park overlooking Rome. There was also a suggestion to use a villa in the suburbs of Milan but it was too small – only 10,000 square feet, too small for the collection. There was also a plan to use an abbey near Parma because the University of Parma was setting up an art collection. I contacted the director but when I told him I was willing to make the gift if the work would be shown permanently, he refused the donation.

In Varese I had started negotiating with the city in 1978 to turn my house into a museum. I was willing to give the collection in the house as a gift along with one-third of the property because the other two-thirds belong to my brother and two sisters. They were willing to sell their portion at a very reasonable price. But the negotiation never went through. Like all Italian politicians, they always say yes but never do anything.

CK *So you have been through a lot of negotiations all over Italy.*
GP Oh, yes. Just last year, before the sale of my collection from the '50s to MOCA, I asked the museum if they would give the option to Turin to buy the collection at a greatly reduced price – $7 million instead of $11 million – so that the entire collection could be kept in Italy. But the regional administration in Piedmont couldn't find the money. So I signed the agreement with MOCA.

CK *I understand there were protests against the proposal in Turin by Italian artists. Is that true?*
GP Yes. In March of 1984, a few months after I signed the agreement with MOCA, I offered to make the long-term loan of the Minimal sculptures for Rivoli into a gift. The restoration was almost finished, and the museum would open in December. But on April 26, the head of cultural affairs for the regional administration called and told me they were no longer willing to have my collection in the museum. They had appointed Rudi Fuchs, the director of the Eindhoven Museum, to prepare a program of international exhibitions. The main reason was to give space to the Arte Povera artists from Turin, who complained that they were not represented in my collection. If the museum had been made as planned, it would have become the first museum in Europe devoted to American art. This would be done by a leftist administration, communists and socialists, without any Italian art. So the program was changed. The gift was refused. The $8 million worth of art was lost.

CK *In a nutshell, the project got started because of complaints that the collection was going to leave the country, and it all fell apart because of complaints that it was going to stay in the country?*
GP Yes. It is a contradiction.

But the interests of politicians are stronger than anything else. They risked losing a few hundred votes from Italian artists. Because they feared losing the help of these people, they lost the $8 million gift. Rudi Fuchs made an exhibition that was a reduced version of the last Documenta. Some are good. Others are not good at all. And it is a temporary installation. All the work is on loan. The regional administration says it will spend a half million dollars a year on acquisitions. But I don't believe it's true because that's all the money they have for all cultural activities. They've asked for help from the big corporations in Turin but I am very doubtful that this help will be given them.

CK *I'm sure you were extremely disappointed when this plan didn't work out. Do you feel any bitterness about the difficulties you encountered?*
GP Oh, yes. For me this experience in Turin was a wound, a deep wound, because I trusted this administration. They were really knowledgeable about the quality of the collection and the importance of art. But the political interest was stronger than the interest for art. For me it was a very bitter fact to realize that the interest of parties and politicians were so far ahead of the public interest.

To lose this possibility really broke me because I always had the idea of putting together the culture of the past with the culture of our time. For me, it is the continuation of the same search. There is no difference between artists of the Italian Renaissance and artists of America. They share the same cultural roots and development, they're branches of the same tree. The opportunity to show this unity of past and present was unique, and it could be realized only in Italy. I looked in France, but there are no buildings large enough or with large rooms. I looked in Germany, but there are no large old buildings available. I looked in England and in Scotland but the situation is the same.

Another experience that wasn't positive happened in Basel, in 1976. I went to Basel often to see exhibitions. I was friendly with Franz Meyer, the director of the Kunstmuseum, and with all the directors of the Kunsthalle. I had spoken with them about my intention to find space for my collection. I met Mrs. Maia Sacher, the former wife of one of the owners of Hofman-La Roche Corporation, which makes chemical products.

CK *Valium, I think.*
GP Yes. She was willing to make a gift to the museum to build an extension to house the collection of contemporary art. The Hofman Foundation was buying beautiful contemporary art for the Kunstmuseum. Mrs. Sacher had come to Varese to see my collection because she knew I wanted to make a long-term loan. She was very intelligent and one of the best collectors in Europe. She had beautiful works by Max Ernst, Picasso, and Klee. Mrs. Sacher was seventy-six years old but she was still interested in contemporary art and was buying work by Barry, Weiner, Ryman, Morris, Andre, Serra and others. But the foundation didn't have more work to put in the new extension, so if another collector was willing to make a loan, that would be welcome.

She was very impressed by my collection in Varese. The stables were finished and there were works by Los Angeles artists and Minimalists. She said she was sure to find a way to do something similar in Basel and would look for a space. An old factory was found not far from the Kunstmuseum, in the old part of the city near the Rhine. It was owned by another foundation whose director, Hans Meier, was interested in art and willing to construct a museum. I advised the architect on how to make the interior spaces and how to use natural and artificial light. The top floor would have natural light reflected from the sky, supplemented with electrical light at dusk. We agreed to select work from my collection, from the Hofman Foundation and from the Kunstmuseum – all Minimal and Conceptual art of the '60s.

But then Mrs. Sacher's family and others who were not competent in art began to complain that she was spending five million Swiss francs to make a museum for the Panza collection, rather than for the Hofman Foundation which was paying for it. So they changed the program. They did give me one beautiful thing: a chance to exhibit my collection for eleven months. The top floor, with the natural light, was used for my Ryman paintings, and it was magical to see.

CK   *Was this the first time you had seen so much of your collection together in one place?*
GP   Yes. There were about seventy-six works – Bell, Andre, Judd, Lewitt, Kosuth, Weiner, Mangold, Serra, Nauman. The rooms of this museum were perfect, and I was very happy to have the opportunity. Unfortunately, it only lasted 11 months.

When she was eighty, Mrs. Sacher retired as president of the foundation because she wasn't in good health. The foundation started to buy successful artists: Julian Schnabel, Anselm Kiefer, Francesco Clemente, Enzo Cucchi, Mimmo Paladino, and so on.

CK   *That must have driven you crazy.*
GP   It wasn't the best work of these artists, unfortunately.

This was a bitter experience for me. With Mrs. Sacher we had started a beautiful program but afterward, everything fell apart. The original project would have been the first museum devoted to Minimal and Conceptual art of the '60s. Now it's a museum without an identity. Today, the Crex Collection in Schaffhausen is the only one devoted to Minimal and Conceptual art and we can see how much better it is than work bought by the Hofman Foundation.

CK   *Now that these various plans have fallen through, I imagine other museums have been knocking on your door. What are your primary criteria for selecting a home, or multiple homes, for your collection?*
GP   The primary criterion is to keep a coherent group of works together, as I have done at Varese and as I did with the first part of the collection at MOCA in Los Angeles. I would like to follow the same idea and have each museum specialized in a given period of a given group of artists, without mixing up different artists. I like specialized museums.

However, it's not possible to have forty Naumans together or thirty Rymans in a single place. It would be too much. It would be better to split them into two or three places - the early work of Ryman in one, the period of the '70s in another. Or the steel work of Robert Morris in one place, the fiberglass in another.

I still hope to keep intact the work I have in Varese.

CK *How do you assess the quality of a potential museum as a caretaker for your collection?*

GP It depends on the size, quality, and location of the space. Factories are often very beautiful because Minimal art goes well with very simple engineering structures. This art, which deals with man's intellectual capacity as a thinker, finds its natural home in these simple spaces. Lighting is extremely important in museums, not just for seeing details better but for creating an environment. Light is a key function in giving the feeling of a totality.

I have basically one idea: a museum is not an accumulation of more or less good works of art. It's not an elegant warehouse. It's a place where we live in a different condition when we are inside. We have to feel something ideal is present in the space. This is the goal a museum has to reach, or else it fails as museum. Very often museums are just accumulations of art.

I had a bitter experience at the Tate Gallery in London when I went to see the Saatchi Collection. The Saatchi Collection is installed in a beautiful old factory that was cleaned and restored. The spaces are very simple, with few works inside but beautiful ones: Judd, Marden, Warhol, Cy Twombly, Serra. The perfect space increased the quality. Afterward, I went to the Tate Gallery and saw fine works mixed with bad ones, just hung on the wall like stamps in a stamp collection. It was terrible, really very depressing. To see the Rothkos cramped in a small room with bad light was just sad.

CK *So your task is to find museums with the same conception as your own?*

GP Yes.

CK *I read that Johannes Cladders has said that your approach to installing the collection is admirable but impractical.*

GP Well, I believe that's not true because the experience I had in Basel was positive. It didn't last because the people in power had other interests, but the experience I've had with MOCA proves that it's possible.

The main problem for every museum is the space available. To find space is always difficult because museums are in large cities. In the center of the city, space is very valuable. To find a city willing to give up in order to have art is not easy. New buildings are very costly. But often, cities own buildings in depressed areas, old disused factories or dockside warehouses. The way of shipping materials in containers is different today, so we don't need warehouses in ports. Large buildings are available, for instance in Long Beach, San Francisco, San Diego.

CK *Those cities are in California, and one of the things that pleased you most with the project in Turin was the unique possibility to link past and present. What is unique about Southern California as an appropriate place for your collection?*

GP Well, a large number of artists represented in the collection live in California or worked there. They have a relationship to Californian culture. Los Angeles is midway between Europe and Asia. It is a city by the ocean at the end of the desert. There are few cities in the world with such beautiful light.

The investment that the State of California made in education in the past was very important. Now this country is shaping the future of the world in science and high technology. Science is the religion of the 19th and 20th centuries, but it is also a religion which could destroy humanity. Because of its great concentration of scientific research, California has a major role in the future. Science will be essential for improving life – if it's married with research in the humanities. The improvement of man's inner world is made through art – not only through art, but mostly. If science doesn't have this joint goal with human values, it will be dangerous rather than useful. For this reason, it is important to develop art and cultural activities in California.

CK   *You said earlier that the possibilities for art in New York have been limited by the marketplace. The art market in Los Angeles is not yet strong, but it is headed in that direction.*
GP   I believe that the fact that the market is not strong in Los Angeles is a positive thing for art. Positive for art, but not for artists! Many artists in Los Angeles must have a part-time job in order to live. In this way they are free to make what they want. They don't have all the restraints of the market. Freedom is essential for good art. Without it, we cannot have good art.

CK   *Having been involved in the art world for thirty years, who among the artists, curators, critics, and collectors has most informed your thinking?*
GP   Well, many people. Cladders was influential, and Pontus Hulten. We met in 1963 because he wanted to make an exhibition of Pop art in Stockholm and he came to Varese to see the work I had. Edy de Wilde was a close friend, and we had many similar interests. In New York, I was very often buying art just before de Wilde arrived. Or sometimes the reverse happened. A work was not available because it had been bought two days before by de Wilde.

CK   *Who do you believe to be the most interesting new artists working now?*
GP   I believe the most interesting young artists are in Los Angeles now. Perhaps I am not well informed about what is happening in Europe or New York. But here in Los Angeles there are many new artists who I like: Bob Therrien, Mark Lere, Michael Davis, Susan Kaiser-Vogel, Peter Shelton, Joann Callis. I have a lot of faith in the work they are making and believe they will become important in the future.

CK   *Could you talk about the work of say, Bob Therrien in relation to the art you've collected over the years?*
GP   Yes. Therrien interests me because he has a very simple way of making shapes, and he blends painting with sculpture. His shapes are not geometrical, like Minimal art, they're organic, close to the shape of a living body. What is most interesting is the sensibility behind his work. It deals in a way with life and death.

CK   *We were talking earlier about the "wrong turn" modern culture made toward individualism and away from social integration. Your collection was privately assembled, and I think it could reasonably be described as highly individualistic. How does one then make the transition from private collection to a public museum whose goal is social integration?*
GP   My collection is certainly individual because it is my personal choice. But I am a man. I am a man like others. I believe my goal is the goal of a very large portion of the population, no different

from that of others. Because of this, my choices are the potential choices of millions of people. Indeed, I was very pleased at MOCA to see how many people loved this art. This is my greatest pleasure. Nothing lovlier exists than the possibility of sharing this passion with other people. The greatest gift that art gives to me is this pleasure: seeing how many people love what I love. This is the most beautiful thing.

11. *Dépouille*, 1946, F 5, MOCA.

12. *Nu*, 1943, F 2, MOCA.   13. *Tête d'otage no. 14*, 1944, F 3, MOCA.

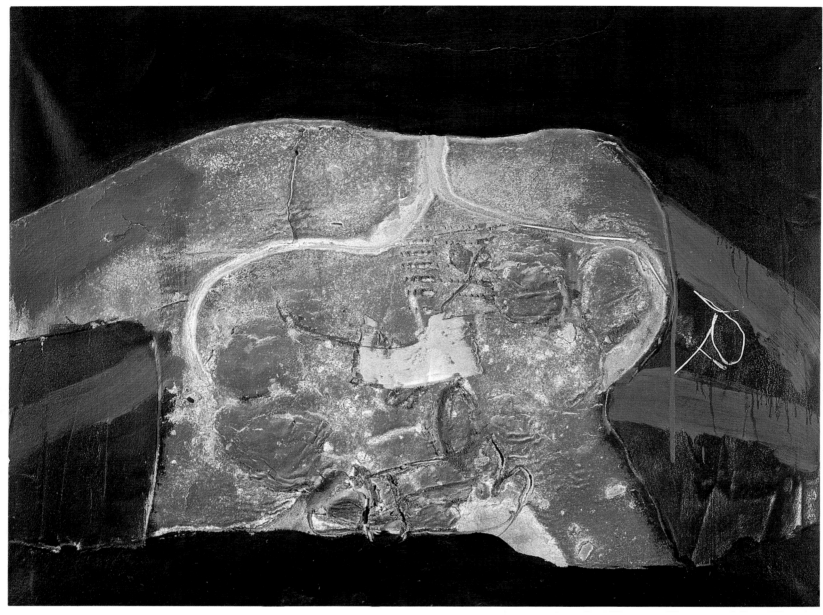

14.

14. *Red-Brown*, 1958,
AT 11, MOCA.

15. *Brown-Ochre with Black
Crevice*, 1957, AT 7, MOCA.

16. *Hammered Grey*, 1959,
AT 13, MOCA.

15.

16.

17. *Ilza*, 1955, FK 3, MOCA.

18. *Violet and Yellow in Rose*, 1954, MR 2, MOCA.

19.

20.

21.

22.

19. *Interview*, 1955, RR 2, MOCA.

20. *Untitled Combine*, 1955, RR 1, MOCA.

21. *Painting With Grey Wing*, 1959, RR 6, MOCA.

22. *Coca-Cola Plan*, 1958, RR 5, MOCA.

23.

23. *Vestigial Appendage*, 1962, JR 6, MOCA.

24. *Waves*, 1962, JR 4, MOCA.

24.

25.

26.

25. *Mu Mu*, 1961, CO 1, MOCA.
26. *Pepsi-Cola*, 1961, CO 7, MOCA.
27. *Breakfast table*, 1962, CO 16, MOCA.

27.

28.

28. *Meat*, 1962, RL 3, MOCA.

29. *Desk Calendar*, 1962, RL 2, MOCA.

29.

31.

◀ 30. *Untitled (Five Timbers)*,1969,
RM 18, The Solomon
R. Guggenheim Foundation,
Installation: Centro de Arte Reina
Sofia (Madrid) 1988.

31. *Untitled (16 Steel Boxes)*, 1967, RM
7, The Solomon R. Guggenheim
Foundation, Installation: Musée
d'Art de la Ville (Paris) 1990.

32. *Untitled (Piece with Battered
Sides)*, 1966, RM 32, The Solomon
R. Guggenheim Foundation,
Installation: Centro de Arte
Reina Sofia (Madrid) 1988.

32.

33.

34.

33. *Untitled (Aluminium grating)*, 1969, RM 9, The Solomon R. Guggenheim Foundation, Installation: Centro de Arte Reina Sofia (Madrid) 1988.

34. *Untitled (½ Round Piece)*, 1967, RM 19, The Solomon R. Guggenheim Foundation, Installation: Centro de Arte Reina Sofia (Madrid) 1988.

35.

35. *Untitled (Piece with Battered Sides)*, 1966, RM 32;
Untitled (Four Round Wedges), 1967, RM 5A;
Untitled (Four Wedges), 1967, RM 5;
The Solomon R. Guggenheim Foundation,
Installation: Gegenwartskunst Museum (Basel) 1981.

36. *Philadelphia Labyrinth*, 1974, RM 28, The Solomon R. Guggenheim
Foundation, Installation: Institute of Contemporary Art
(University of Pennsylvania), 1974.

37. *Untitled (5 Steel Plate Piece)*, 1969, RM 26;
Untitled (3 Steel Plate Piece), 1969, RM 24;
The Solomon R. Guggenheim Foundation,
Installation: Whitney Museum of American Art (New York) 1970.

38. *Untitled (Alluminium I-Beams)*, 1967, RM 27, The Solomon R.
Guggenheim Foundation, Installation: Albright-Knox Art Gallery
(Buffalo)1968.

36.

39. *Untitled (5 Steel Plate Piece)*, 1969, RM 26;
Untitled (4 Steel Plate Piece), 1969, RM 23;
The Solomon R. Guggenheim Foundation, Installation: Centro de Arte Reina Sofia (Madrid) 1988.

40. *Untitled (Square Donut)*, 1968, RM 33, The Solomon R. Guggenheim Foundation,
Installation: Centro de Arte Reina Sofía (Madrid) 1988.

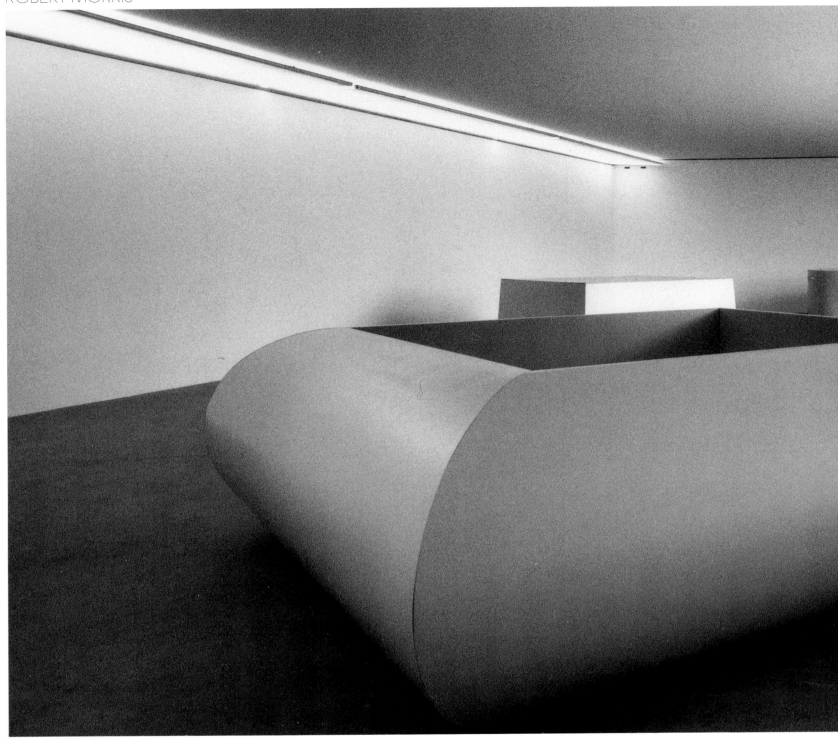

41.

41. *Untitled (1/2 Round Piece)*, 1967, RM 19,
    The Solomon R. Guggenheim Foundation,
    Installation: Gegenwartskunst Museum (Basel) 1981.

42. *Untitled (Aluminium I-Beams)*, 1967, RM 6,
    The Solomon R. Guggenheim Foundation,
    Installation: Villa Menafoglio Litta Panza
    (Varese) 1975-1976.

42.

43.

43. *Untitled (Aluminium I-Beams)*, 1967, RM 27,
The Solomon R. Guggenheim Foundation,
Installation: Musée d'Art de la Ville (Paris) 1990.

44. *Untitled (4 Steel Plate Piece)*, 1969, RM 23,
The Solomon R. Guggenheim Foundation,
Installation: Centro de Arte Reina Sofia (Madrid) 1988.

45. *Untitled*, 1968, RM 10;
Untitled (Aluminium grating), 1969, RM 9;
The Solomon R. Guggenheim Foundation,
Installation: Centro de Arte Reina Sofia (Madrid) 1988.

44.

45.

46.

46. *Portland Regulus*, 1973-1974, CA 12, The Solomon R. Guggenheim Foundation, Installation: John Weber Gallery (New York) 1974.

47. *2 x 18 Aluminium Lock*, 1968, CA 3, The Solomon R. Guggenheim Foundation, Installation: Galleria Nazionale d'Arte Moderna e Contemporanea (Roma) 1980.

48. *Hague Steel Piece*, 1968, CA 4, The Solomon R. Guggenheim Foundation, Installation: Villa Menafoglio Litta Panza (Varese) 1973.

49. *Fall*, 1968, CA 5, The Solomon R. Guggenheim Foundation, Installation: Villa Menafoglio Litta Panza (Varese) 1975-1976.

47.

50.

50. *2 x 18 Aluminium Lock*, 1968, CA 3, The Solomon R. Guggenheim Foundation, Installation: Centro de Arte Reina Sofia (Madrid) 1988.

51. *Fall*, 1968, CA 5, The Solomon R. Guggenheim Foundation, Installation: Musée d'Art de la Ville (Paris) 1990.

51.

52.

52. *Copper Square*, 1973, CA 10, The
    Solomon R. Guggenheim
    Foundation, Installation:
    Centro de Arte Reina Sofía
    (Madrid) 1988.

53. *Reef*, 1966, CA 1, The Solomon R.
    Guggenheim Foundation,
    Installation: Musée d'Art de la Ville
    (Paris) 1990.

53.

54. *Seventeenth Copper Triode*, 1975, CA 13, The Solomon R. Guggenheim Foundation,
Installation: Guggenheim Museum SoHo (New York) June - September 1992.

55.

56.

55. *Untitled*, 1967, RS 2;
    Tearing Lead from 1:00 to 1:47, 1968, RS 4;
    Belts, 1966-1967, RS 1;
    Angle Slabs, 1967, RS 3;
    The Solomon R. Guggenheim Foundation,
    Installation: Gegenwartskunst Museum (Basel) 1981.

56. *Belts*, 1966-1967, RS 1, The Solomon R. Guggenheim Foundation,
    Installation: Richard Serra Studio (New York) 1967.

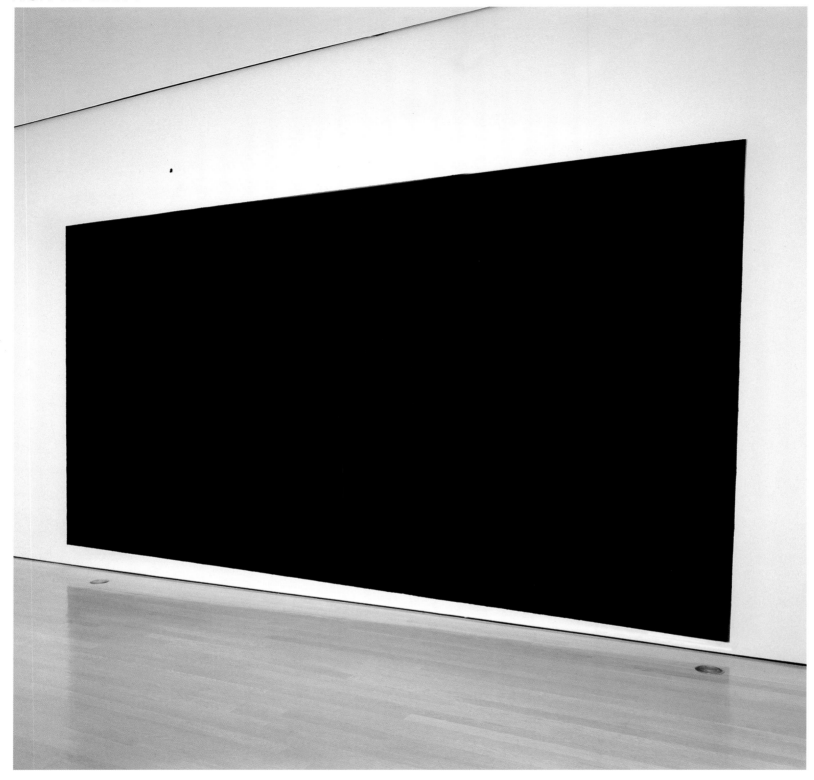

57. *Shafrazi*, 1974, RS 11, The Solomon R. Guggenheim Foundation,
    Installation: Guggenheim Museum SoHo (New York) May 1993 - January 1994.

58. *Different and Different Again Unequal Elevations*, 1973, RS 13. The Solomon R. Guggenheim Foundation.

59. *Clothes Pin Prop*, 1969, RS 8, The Solomon R. Guggenheim Foundation, Installation: Villa Menafoglio Litta Panza (Varese) 1973.

60. *Strike (to Roberta and Rudy)*, 1969-1971, RS 9, The Solomon R. Guggenheim Foundation.

61. *Shovel Plate Prop*, 1969, RS 5, The Solomon R. Guggenheim Foundation, Installation: Villa Menafoglio Litta Panza (Varese) 1973.

DAN FLAVIN

62. *Ultra Violet Fluorescent Light Room*,
1968, DF 17, The Solomon Guggenheim
Foundation (Panza Gift), Installation:
Villa Menafoglio Litta Panza
(Varese) 1981.

63. *An Artificial Barrier of Blue, Red and Blue Fluorescent (to Flavin Starbuck Judd)*, 1968, DF 20,
The Solomon R. Guggenheim Foundation, Installation: Centro de Arte Reina Sofia (Madrid) 1988.

64. *Untitled 1/3 (Green Light)*, 1963, DF 1, The Solomon R. Guggenheim Foundation (Panza Gift),
Installation: Centro de Arte Reina Sofia (Madrid) 1988.

65.

65. *Kunsthalle, Köln, Installation with circular lights,* 1972, DF 22, The Solomon R. Guggenheim Foundation, Installation: Centro de Arte Reina Sofia (Madrid) 1988.

66. *Untitled,* 1975, DF 52, FAI (Fondo per l'Ambiente Italiano) on permanent loan to the Solomon R. Guggenheim Foundation, Installation: Guggenheim Museum, SoHo (New York) September 1995 - January 1996.

67.

67. *Green Crossing Green (to Piet Mondrian who lacked green)*, 1966, DF 16, The Solomon R. Guggenheim Foundation, Installation: Guggenheim Museum, SoHo (New York) September 1995 - January 1996.

68. *Untitled (to Jan and Ron Greenberg)* , 1972-1973, DF 21, The Solomon R. Guggenheim Foundation, Installation: Guggenheim Museum, SoHo (New York) September 1995 - January 1996.

69.

69. *Green Light Corridor*, 1970, BN 24,
The Solomon R. Guggenheim Foundation (Panza Gift),
Installation: Villa Menafoglio Litta Panza (Varese) 1981.

70. *Yellow Room (Triangular)*, 1973, BN 38,
The Solomon R. Guggenheim Foundation,
Installation: Gegenwartskunst Museum (Basel) 1981.

►

71. 72. *Pink and Yellow Light Corridor (Variable Lights)*, 1972, BN 31,
The Solomon R. Guggenheim Foundation,
Installation: Villa Menafoglio Litta Panza (Varese) 1981.

73. *My Last Name Exaggerated Fourteen Times Vertically*, 1967, BN 6.

70

74.

75.

74. *Triangle Room*, 1978-1980, BN 29, The Solomon R. Guggenheim Foundation,
    Installation: Centro de Arte Reina Sofia (Madrid) 1988.

75. *Triangle Room*, 1978-1980, BN 29;
    Robert Morris, *Untitled (Aluminium I-Beams)*, 1967, RM 27;
    The Solomon R. Guggenheim Foundation, Installation: Musée d'Art de la Ville (Paris) 1990.

76. *Forced Perspectives: Open Mind, Closed Mind, Parallel Mind, Equal Mind (Allegory and Symbolism)*, 1975, BN 42, The Solomon R. Guggenheim Foundation, Installation: Musée d'Art Moderne (St. Etienne) 1989.

77. *Double Doors - Projection and Displacement*, 1973, BN 39, The Solomon R. Guggenheim Foundation,
Installation: Musée d'Art de la Ville (Paris) 1990.

78

78. *Sound Wedge (Double Wedge)*, 1969-1970, BN 16, The Solomon R. Guggenheim Foundation,
    Installation: Musée d'Art Moderne (St. Etienne), 1989.

79. *Double Wedge Corridor (With Mirror)*, 1970-1974, BN 32, The Solomon R. Guggenheim Foundation,
    Installation: Musée d'Art Moderne (St. Etienne) 1989.

79

80.

80. *Straight Single Tube*, 1974, DJ 24, The Solomon R. Guggenheim Foundation,
    Installation: Centro de Arte Reina Sofia (Madrid) 1988.

81. *Untitled*, 1972, DJ 9, The Solomon R. Guggenheim Foundation,
    Installation: Centro de Arte Reina Sofia (Madrid) 1988.

82. Untitled, 1971, DJ 8, The Solomon R. Guggenheim Foundation,
    Installation: Centro de Arte Reina Sofia (Madrid) 1988.

81.

82.

84. *Galvanized Iron Wall*, 1974, DJ 27, The Solomon R. Guggenheim Foundation (Panza Gift),
    Installation: Villa Menafoglio Litta Panza (Varese) 1977.

◄

83. *Untitled*, 1969, DJ 3, The Solomon R. Guggenheim Foundation,
    Installation: Centro de Arte Reina Sofia (Madrid) 1988.

85.

85. *Untitled*, 1973, DJ 11;
Untitled, 1966-1972, DJ 7;
The Solomon R. Guggenheim
Foundation,
Installation: Gegenwartskunst
Museum (Basel) 1981.

86. *Eight Hot Rolled Steel Boxes*, 1974,
DJ 26, The Solomon R. Guggenheim
Foundation,
Installation: Galleria Nazionale d'Arte
Moderna e Contemporanea (Roma)
1980.

86.

87.

88.

87. *Untitled*, 1970, DJ 4, The Solomon R. Guggenheim Foundation, Installation: Gegenwartskunst Museum (Basel) 1981.

88. *Untitled*, 1972-1973, DJ 12, The Solomon R. Guggenheim Foundation, Installation: Kunstmuseum (Dusseldorf) 1980.

ROBERT MANGOLD

89.

90.

91.

89. *Circle Painting 6 (Dark-Red),*
   1973, RMA 8;
   Distorted Square Within a Circle
   (Dark-Red), 1973, RMA 9.

90. *Neutral Pink Area, 1966, RMA1,*
   One-Third Grey Curved Area, 1966,
   RMA 33.

91. *Circle Painting 3 (Green-Grey),*
   1973, RMA 7;
   Circle Painting 1 (Yellow),
   1972, RMA 5.

92. *Distorted Square Within a Circle*
   (Violet), 1973, RM7;
   Distorted Square Within a Circle
   (Yellow), 1973, RMA 10
   Circle Painting 6 (Dark-Red), 1973,
   Model, RMA 32;

89, 90, 91:
The Solomon R. Guggenheim Foundation,
Installation: Gegenwartskunst Museum (Basel) 1981

93.

93. *Standard no. 5*, 1967, RRY 2, The Solomon R. Guggenheim Foundation.

94. *Four Units*, 1969, RRY 11, The Solomon R. Guggenheim Foundation.

95. *Empire*, 1973, RRY 30, The Solomon R. Guggenheim Foundation.

96. *Classico IV*, 1968, RRY 7, The Solomon R. Guggenheim Foundation.

97. *Three Units (nos. 1. 2. 3.)*, 1969, RRY 12;
Five Units (nos 1. 2. 3. 4. 5.), 1969, RRY 13;
The Solomon R. Guggenheim Foundation, Installation: Gegenwartskunst Museum (Basel) 1981.

98. *J. Green I*, 1968, RRY 9, The Solomon R. Guggenheim Foundation; ▶
Murillo, 1968, RRY 8;
Installation: Villa Menafoglio Litta Panza (Varese) 1977.

94.

95.

96.

97.

99.

100.

99. *D'après la Marquise de la Solana,* 1969, BM 3.

100. *Adriatic,* 1972-1973, BM 7.

►

101. Alan Charlton, *90 x 180 in., slit 156 in.,* August-November 1971, AC 8;
112 x 56 in., slit 100 in., March 1971, AC 7;
Outer piece 84 x 144 in., inner piece 68½ x 128½ in., channel 1³/₄ in.,
May-August 1972, AC 17.
The Solomon R. Guggenheim Foundation (Panza Gift).

EARTH TO EARTH ASHES TO ASHES DUST TO DUST

101.

102. *90 x 56 in., slit 44 in., September 1971, AC 11.*

103. *90 x 78 in., each slit 78 in., January 1972, AC 14.*

104. *82 in. Square, 1970-1972, AC 3.*

105. *Outer piece 60 in. square, inner piece 38½ in. square, channel 1³/₄ in., December 1973, AC 30.*

106. *Outer piece 58 in. square, inner piece 18 in. square, channel 1⁵/₈ in., September 1973, AC 26.*

107. *Outer piece 63½ in. square, inner piece 12 in. square, channel 1³/₄ in., September 1973, AC 28.*

102.

103.

104.

105.   106/107

108.

108. *Untitled (Cream Color with Black Border)*, May 1975, PJ 5;
Untitled (Cream Color with Dark Blue Border), 1976, PJ 8;
The Solomon R. Guggenheim Foundation (Panza Gift),
Installation: Gegenwartskunst Museum (Basel) 1981.

109. *Untitled (Cream Color with Brown Border)*, March 1974, PJ 1;
Untitled (Grey-Blue Color with Black Border), November 1974, PJ 4;
The Solomon R. Guggenheim Foundation (Panza Gift),
Installation: Villa Menafoglio Litta Panza (Varese) 1977.

110. *Untitled (Grey with Blue Border)*, 1975, PJ 7,
The Solomon R. Guggenheim Foundation (Panza Gift),
Installation: Villa Menafoglio Litta Panza (Varese) 1981.

109.

There was a Museum January 1972

111. *Discussion: January 1972*, IW 1.

112. *No. 83 (Crimson, Blue, Violet, Black)*, 1971, BL 7, The Solomon R. Guggenheim Foundation.

▶

113. *No. 64 (Purple, Plum, Black, Violet)*, 1967, BL 1,
The Solomon R. Guggenheim Foundation (Panza Gift),
Installation: Villa Menafoglio Litta Panza (Varese) 1977.

IT IS WHOLLY INDETERMINATE
IT HAS NO SPECIFIC TRAITS
IT IS ENTIRELY INEFFABLE
IT IS NEVER SEEN
IT IS NOT ACCESSIBLE

114. *It is wholly indeterminate. It has no specific traits. It is entirely ineffable.*
It is never seen, It is not accessible, 1970, RB 6, Installation: MOCA T.C. (Los Angeles) 1985.

▶

115. *Try. All in now. Here...*, 1972, RB 12,
The Solomon R. Guggenheim Foundation (Panza Gift),
Installation: Villa Menafoglio Litta Panza (Varese) 1977.

ANOTHER TIME

1000 GERMAN MARKS WORTH MEDIUM
BULK MATERIAL TRANSFERED FROM
ONE COUNTRY TO ANOTHER

117.

EARTH TO EARTH ASHES TO ASHES DUST TO DUST

118.

116. *Reduced*, 1970, LW 20, Installation:
Gegenwartskunst Museum (Basel) 1981.

117. *1000 german marks worth medium bulk material transfered
from one country to another*, 1969, LW 3.

118. *Earth to earth, ashes to ashes, dust to dust*, 1970, LW 12,
The Solomon R. Guggenheim Foundation (Panza Gift),
Installation: Villa Menafoglio Litta Panza (Varese) 1981.

▶

119. *The joining of France Germany
and Switzerland by rope*, 1969, LW 6,
Installation: Gegenwartskunst Museum (Basel) 1981.

THE JOINING OF FRANCE GERM

Y AND SWITZERLAND BY ROPE

120. *Wall Drawing no. 146*, 1972, SL 15, The Solomon R. Guggenheim Foundation (Panza Gift),
Installation: Villa Menafoglio Litta Panza (Varese) 1981.

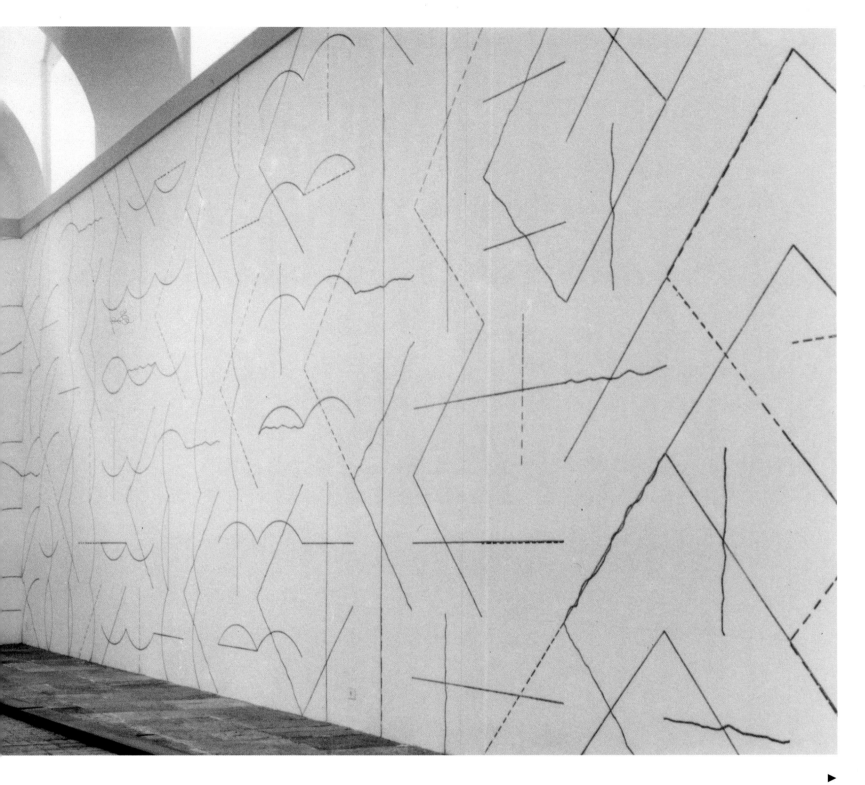

121. *Wall Drawing no. 266*, 1975, SL 12,
The Solomon R. Guggenheim Foundation (Panza Gift),
Installation: Villa Menafoglio Litta Panza (Varese) 1981.

122. *Wall Drawing no. 3*, 1969, SL 1,
Installation: Gegenwartskunst Museum (Basel) 1981.

123. *Wall Drawing no . 265*, 1975, SL 11;
Walter De Maria, *Balldrop*, 1961, WM 1;
The Solomon R. Guggenheim Foundation (Panza Gift),
Installation: Villa Menafoglio Litta Panza (Varese) 1981.

122.

123.

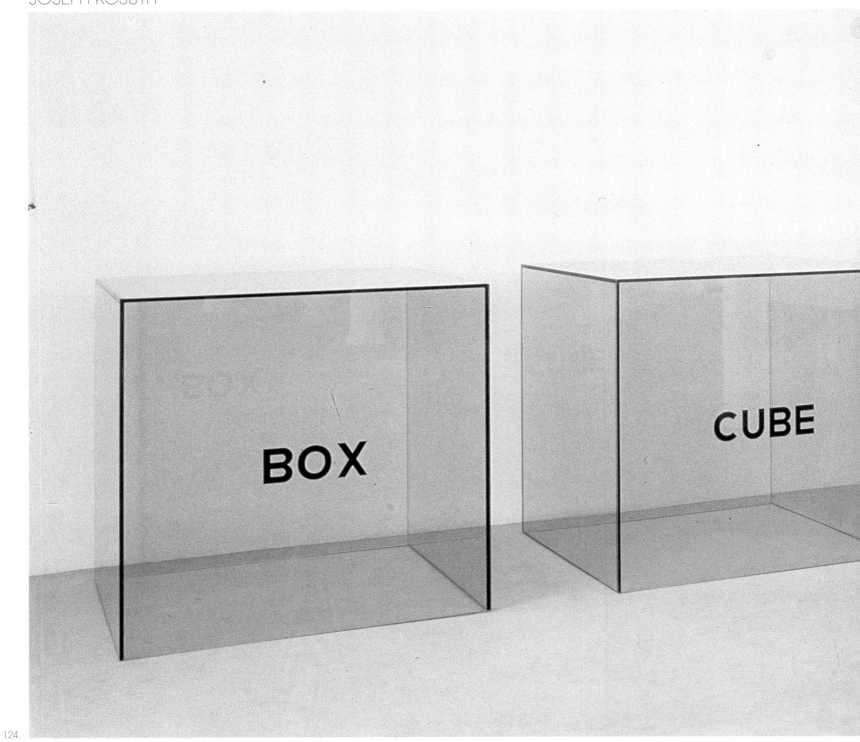

124.

124. *Box, Cube, Empty, Clear, Glass - a Description*, 1965, JK 7, Installation: Gegenwartskunst Museum (Basel) 1981.

125. *Titled (Art as Idea as Idea)*, 1966, JK 11, Installation: Gegenwartskunst Museum (Basel) 1981.

125.

148

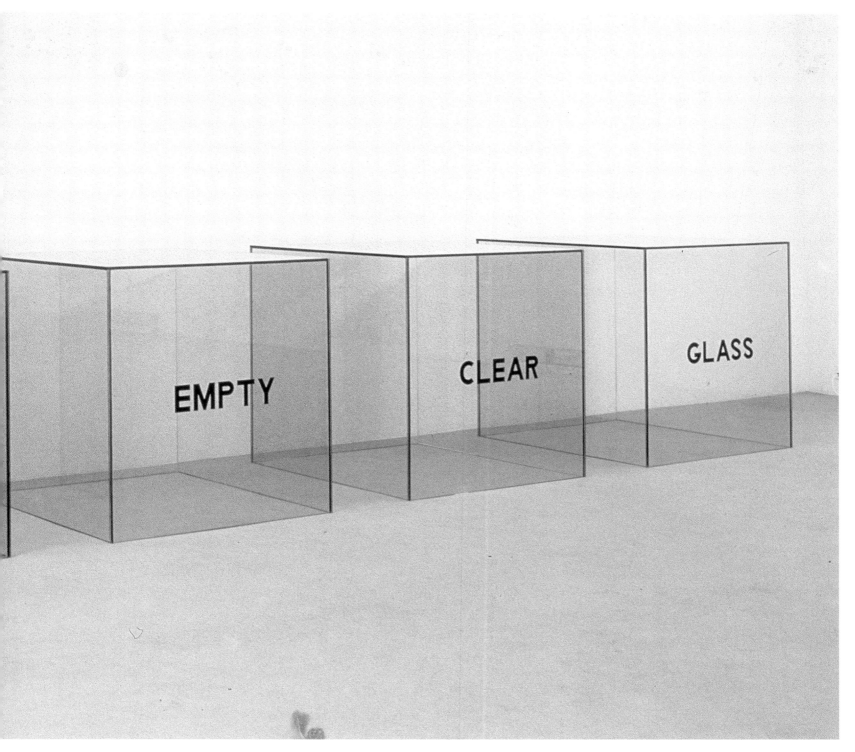

126. *Titled (Art as Idea as Idea)*, 1966, JK 14.

1. *Idea*, adopted from L, itself borrowed from Gr *idea* (*ἰδέᾱ*), a concept, derives from Gr *idein* (s *id-*), to see, for **widein*. L *idea* has derivative LL adj *ideālis*, archetypal, ideal, whence EF-F *idéal* and E *ideal*, whence resp F *idéalisme* and E *idealism*, also resp *idéaliste* and *idealist*, and, further, *idéaliser* and *idealize*. L *idea* becomes MF-F *idée*, with cpd *idée fixe*, a fixed idea, adopted by E Francophiles; it also has ML derivative **ideāre*, pp **ideātus*, whence the Phil n *ideātum*, a thing that, in the fact, answers to the idea of it, whence 'to *ideate*', to form in, or as an, idea.

126.

149

127.

127. *Self-Defined*, 1965, JK 2.

128. *The Eighth Investigation,*
Proposition 3, 1971, JK 24,
Installation: Leo Castelli Gallery
(New York) 1971.

128.

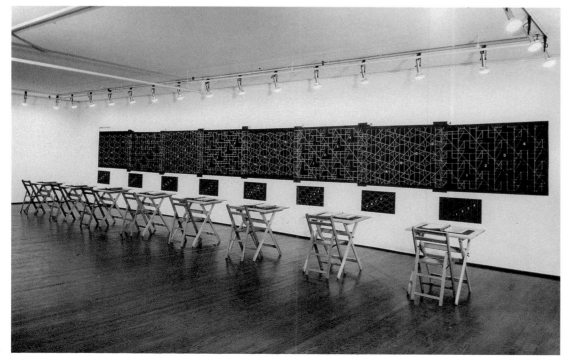

129. *The Tenth Investigation,*
Proposition 4, 1974, JK 26,
Installation: Leo Castelli Gallery
(New York) 1974.

129.

130. *Location Piece no. 1*, New York - Los Angeles, February 1969, DH 4;
Duration Piece no. 4, Paris, January 1970, DH 14, The Solomon R. Guggenheim Foundation (Panza Gift);
Installation: Villa Menafoglio Litta Panza (Varese) 1977.

131. *Disc Coloured Pale Grey, Green, Pink, Violet*, 1966-1967, RI 2,
      Installation: Villa Menafoglio Litta Panza (Varese) 1977

132.

132. *Varese Window Room*, 1973, RI 8, The Solomon R. Guggenheim Foundation (Panza Gift),
Installation: Villa Menafoglio Litta Panza (Varese).

133. *Varese Portal Room*, 1974, RI 10, The Solomon R. Guggenheim Foundation (Panza Gift),
Installation: Villa Menafoglio Litta Panza (Varese).

133

JAMES TURRELL

134. 135. *Sky Window I*, 1976, JT 5,
The Solomon R. Guggenheim
Foundation (Panza Gift),
Installation: Villa Menafoglio
Litta Panza (Varese).

134

136. 137. 138. *Sky Space I*, 1976, JT 4,
The Solomon R. Guggenheim
Foundation (Panza Gift),
Installation: Villa Menafoglio
Litta Panza (Varese).

139. 140. *Virga*, Varese 1976, JT 3,
The Solomon Guggenheim
Foundation (Panza Gift),
installation: Villa Menafoglio
Litta Panza (Varese).

135.

139.

140.

142.

142. *Light Brown Box*, 1968, LB 1, Installation: Villa Menafoglio Litta Panza (Varese) 1977.

143. *Two Glass Walls - Diagonal Top*, 1973, LB 2,
Installation: Galleria d'Arte Moderna (Bologna) 1976.

144. *Two Glass Walls*, 1971-1972, LB 3, Installation: Gegenwartskunst Museum (Basel) 1981.

◀

141. James Turrel, *Night Passage*, 1987, JT 20, The Solomon R. Guggenheim Foundation
(Panza Gift), Installation: Musée d'Art de la Ville (Paris) 1990.

143.

145.

145. 146. *SA MI DW SM 2 75 Continum Atmospheric Environment,*
1975, DW 11, The Solomon R. Guggenheim Foundation
(Panza Gift), Installation: Galleria Salvatore Ala (Milano) 1975.

146.

147.

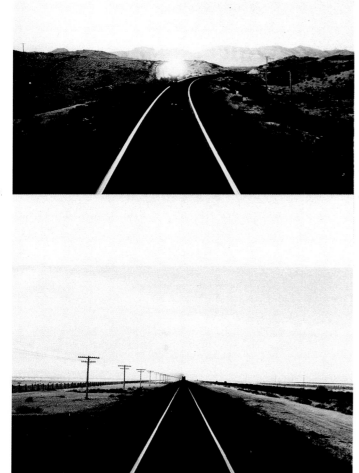

148.

149.

147. *Untitled (4 photographs with land of stone)*, 1970, HF 11.
148. 149. *Goat Fell Mountain*, Isle of Arran, Scotland, Spring 1970, HF 7.

150. *Varese Room*, 1976, MN 12 ,Solomon R. Guggenheim Foundation (Panza Gift),
Installation: Villa Menafoglio Litta Panza (Varese).

151.

152.

151, 152. *Untitled*, 1974, JH 1, Solomon R. Guggenheim Foundation
(Panza Gift), Installation: Villa Menafoglio Litta Panza (Varese) 1977.

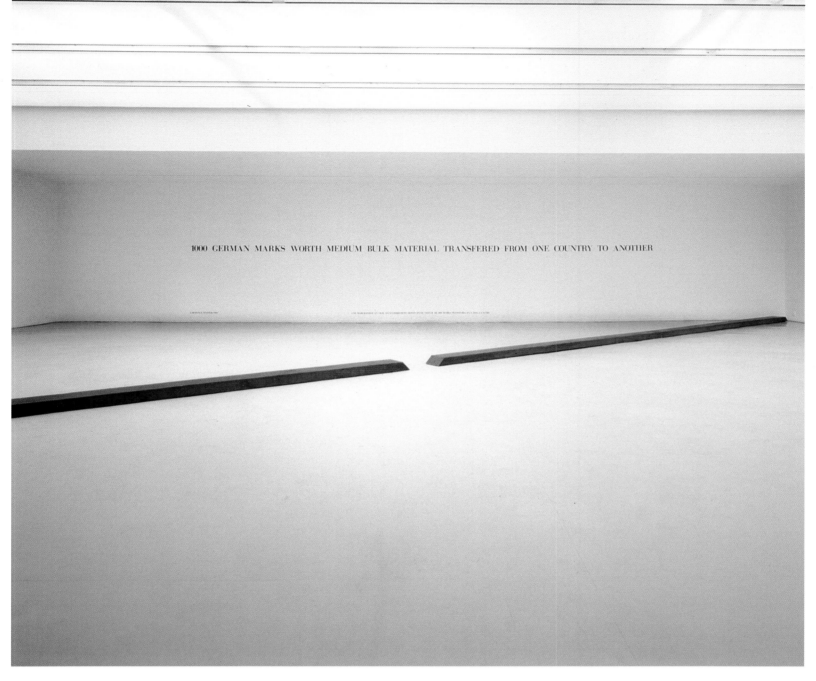

153. *Drive (Shortline Series)*, 1976, RN 36
Lawrence Weiner, *1000 german marks worth medium bulk material
transfered from one country to another*, 1969, LW3
Installation: Musée d'Art de la Ville (Paris) 1990.

154. *Fresno Shortline*, 1974, RN 9, Installation: Centro de Arte Reina Sofía (Madrid) 1988.

155. *Stone Circle*, Roma 1976, RLO 10, The Solomon R. Guggenheim Foundation,
    Installation: Gegenwartskunst Museum (Basel) 1981.

156. *Stone Circle*, Roma 1976, RLO 9, The Solomon R. Guggenheim Foundation,
Installation: Gegenwartskunst Museum (Basel) 1981.

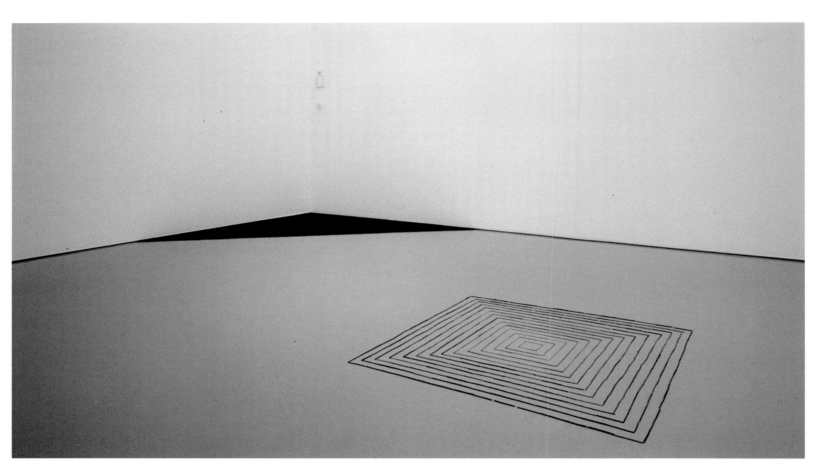

157. *Square Wood Sculpture*, 1967, RLO 1;
Sculpture at Galerie Lambert, 1969, RLO 4;
The Solomon R. Guggenheim Foundation, Installation: Musée d'Art Moderne (St. Etienne) 1989.

158. *Cross of Sticks*, 1983, RLO 15;
Arizona Circle, 1987, RLO 14;
Madrid Circle, 1986, RLO 18;
Installation: Musée d'Art Moderne (St. Etienne) 1989.

159. *00 → 99 = No. 1→ 2k → 20 k*, 1969-70, HD 10,
Installation: Museo Cantonale d'Arte (Lugano) 1992.

▶

160. Hanne Darboven, *49 Drawings*, 1971-1972, HD 18 (detail).
161. Hanne Darboven, *101 Drawings*, 1971-1972, HD 16 (detail).
162. Hanne Darboven, *51 Drawings*, 1971-1972, HD 4 (detail).

1. Buch I↓ Zusammenfassung 42. Buch I↓
1. index

	à 32	à 33	à 34	à 35	à 36	
1	2 -1657	2 -1556	2 -1455	2 -1354	2 -1253	1
2	3 -1758	3 -1657	3 -1556	3 -1455	3 -1354	2
3	4 -1859	4 -1758	4 -1657	4 -1556	4 -1455	3
4	5 -1960	5 -1859	5 -1758	5 -1657	5 -1556	4
5	6 -2061	6 -1960	6 -1859	6 -1758	6 -1657	5
6	7 -2143	7 -2061	7 -1960	7 -1859	7 -1758	6
7	8 -3344	8 -2143	8 -2061	8 -1960	8 -1859	7
8	9 -4445	9 -3344	9 -2143	9 -2061	9 -1960	8
9	10 -5546	10 -4445	10 -3344	10 -2143	10 -2061	9
10	11 -6647	11 -5546	11 -4445	11 -3344	11 -2143	10
11	8 -748	3 -647	3 -546	3 -445	3 -344	11
12	4 -849	4 -748	4 -647	4 -546	4 -445	12
13	5 -950	5 -849	5 -748	5 -647	5 -546	13
14	6 -1051	6 -950	6 -849	6 -748	6 -647	14
15	7 -1152	7 -1051	7 -950	7 -849	7 -748	15
16	12 -748	8 -1152	8 -1051	8 -950	8 -849	16
17	8 -1253	12 -647	9 -1152	9 -1051	9 -950	17
18	13 -849	9 -1253	12 -546	10 -1152	10 -1051	18
19	9 -1354	13 -748	10 -1253	12 -445	11 -1152	19
20	14 -950	10 -1354	13 -647	11 -1253	12 -344	20
21	10 -1455	14 -849	11 -1354	13 -546	12 -1253	21
22	15 -1051	11 -1455	14 -748	12 -1354	13 -445	22
23	11 -1556	15 -950	12 -1455	14 -647	13 -1354	23
24	16 -1152	12 -1556	15 -849	13 -1455	14 -546	24
25	12 -1657	16 -1051	13 -1556	15 -748	14 -1455	25
26	17 -1253	13 -1657	16 -950	14 -1556	15 -647	26
27	13 -1758	17 -1152	14 -1657	16 -849	15 -1556	27
28	18 -1354	14 -1758	17 -1051	15 -1657	16 -748	28
29	14 -1859	18 -1253	15 -1758	17 -950	16 -1657	29
30	19 -1455	15 -1859	18 -1152	16 -1758	17 -849	30
31	15 -1960	19 -1354	16 -1859	18 -1051	17 -1758	31
32	20 -1556	16 -1960	19 -1253	17 -1859	18 -950	32
33		20 -1455	17 -1960	19 -1152	18 -1859	33
34			20 -1354	18 -1960	19 -1051	34
35				20 -1253	19 -1960	35
36					20 -1152	36
Q	à 32	à 33	à 34	à 35	à 36	2)

$\frac{43}{61}$

6. Kapitel   7. Kapitel   8. Kapitel   9. Kapitel   10. Kapitel

II		index I ↓ 42.buch (—)	1.Teil 1×19	2.Teil 1×19	3.Teil 1×19	4.Teil 1×19	5.Teil 1×19	6.Teil 1×19	7.Teil 1×19	8.Teil 1×19	9.Teil 1×19	10.Teil 1×19	19.Teil II
II	1	10	1,	2,	3,	4,	5,	6,	7,	8,	9,	10,	12
1.	2/	43/ 2, 43	20,	19, 60	18, 59	17, 58	16, 57	15, 56	14,	13, 54	12, 53	1,
2.	3/	44/ 3, 44	2, 43	20, 61	19, 60	18, 59	17, 58	16, 57	15, 56	14, 55	13, 54	2,
3.	4/	45/ 4, 45	3, 44	2, 43	20, 61	19, 60	18, 59	17, 58	16, 57	15, 56	14, 55	3,
4.	5/	46/ 5, 46	4, 45	3, 44	2, 43	20, 61	19, 60	18, 59	17, 58	16, 57	15, 56	4,
5.	6/	47/ 6, 47	5, 46	4, 45	3, 44	2, 43	20, 61	19, 60	18, 59	17, 58	16, 57	5,
6.	7	48/ 7, 48	6, 47	5, 46	4, 45	3, 44	2, 43	20, 61	19, 60	18, 59	17, 58	6,
7.	8/	49/ 8, 49	7, 48	6, 47	5, 46	4, 45	3, 44	2, 43	20, 61	19, 60	18, 59	7,
8.	9/	50/ 9, 50	8, 49	7, 48	6, 47	5, 46	4, 45	3, 44	2, 43	20, 61	19, 60	8,
9.	10/	51/ 10, 51	9, 50	8, 49	7, 48	6, 47	5, 46	4, 45	3, 44	2, 43	20, 61	9,
10.	11/	52/ 11, 52	10, 51	9, 50	8, 49	7, 48	6, 47	5, 46	4, 45	3, 44	2, 43	10,
20.	12/	53/ 12, 53	11, 52	10, 51	9, 50	8, 49	7, 48	6, 47	5, 46	4, 45	3, 44	11,
30.	13/	54/ 13, 54	12, 53	11, 52	10, 51	9, 50	8, 49	7, 48	6, 47	5, 46	4, 45	12,
40.	14/	55/ 14, 55	13, 54	12, 53	11, 52	10, 51	9, 50	8, 49	7, 48	6, 47	5, 46	13,
50.	15/	56/ 15, 56	14, 55	13, 54	12, 53	11, 52	10, 51	9, 50	8, 49	7, 48	6, 47	14,
60.	16/	57/ 16, 57	15, 56	14, 55	13, 54	12, 53	11, 52	10, 51	9, 50	8, 49	7, 48	15,
70.	17/	58/ 17, 58	16, 57	15, 56	14, 55	13, 54	12, 53	11, 52	10, 51	9, 50	8, 49	16,
80.	18/	59/ 18, 59	17, 58	16, 57	15, 56	14, 55	13, 54	12, 53	11, 52	10, 51	9, 50	17,
90.	19/	60/ 19, 60	18, 59	17, 58	16, 57	15, 56	14, 55	13, 54	12, 53	11, 52	10, 51	18,
100.	20/	61/ 20, 61	19, 60	18, 59	17, 58	16, 57	15, 56	14, 55	13, 54	12, 53	11, 52	19,
Q	Q	Q	1.) 2.) → 3. Kürzung / 19 × 19 × 42									index II

$$100 \, \tilde{a} \, / \, 19$$

I↓ 2/20 /43/ /61

II ⇐ 2–20 /43/ /61

1. buch (+)

I↓ 43/61/ 2/20

II ⇐ 43–61 / 2/20

42. buch (—)

	↓ 19	↓ 19	↓ 19	↓ 19	↓ 19	↓ 19	↓ 19	↓ 19	↓ 19	↓ 19
Teil:	1,	2,	3,	4,	5,	6,	7,	8,	9,	10,

DIAGRAM

This is a diagram for the Sol LeWitt wall drawing number *152*. It should accompany the certificate if the wall drawing is sold or otherwise transferred but is not a certificate or a drawing.

163.

163, 164. *Wall Drawing no. 8*, January 1973, SL 18.

CERTIFICATE

This is to certify that the Sol LeWitt wall drawing

number ___152___ evidenced by this certificate is authentic.

```
Three-part Drawing:  1st Wall:  Straight
horizontal lines.  2nd Wall:  Not straight
horizontal lines.  3rd Wall:  Broken
horizontal lines.  The lines are about two-
inches (5 cm) apart.

Black pencil
First Drawn by:  Kazuko Miyamoto
First Installation:  Rosa Esman Gallery,
                     New York, NY.

January, 1973
```

This certification is the signature for the wall drawing and must

accompany the wall drawing if it is sold or otherwise transferred.

Certified by _Sol LeWitt_____

Sol LeWitt

© Copyright Sol LeWitt

Date

164

181

Location Piece # 8
Bradford, Massachusetts

    In April, 1969 a memorandum (facsimile below) was sent to the approximately 400 girls who form the student body of Bradford Junior College.

    On May 23, 1969 the ashes of 63 secrets were all mixed together and that mixture scattered in a random manner throughout the campus.

    This statement and the facsimile of the original memorandum constitute the form of this piece.

May, 1969   Douglas Huebler

Memorandum
Bradford Junior College
Bradford, Massachusetts

To: All students
From: Mr. Huebler
Re: A secret

    I need to use an important secret of yours in order to complete a project on which I am working.

    Simply write it down and then burn the paper on which it is written in an ashtray, seal the ashes in an envelope addressed to me and have it put into my faculty mail box.

    I will complete the project by combining all ashes so returned into one mixture and then scattering it randomly throughout the campus.

165.

Memorandum

Bradford Junior College
Bradford, Massachusetts

TO: All students

From: Mr. Huebler

Re: A secret

I need to use an important secret of yours in order to complete a project on which I am working.

Simply write it down and then burn the paper on which it is written in an ashtray, seal the ashes in an envelope addressed to me and have it put into my faculty mail box.

I will complete the project by combining all ashes so returned into one mixture and then scattering it randomly throughout the campus.

166.

165. 166. *Location Piece no. 8*, Bradford, Massachusetts, May 1969, DH 8.

Catalogue

by
Francesca Guicciardi

1.

2.

3.

JEAN FAUTRIER

1. *Profil*, 1945. F 4, MOCA
2. *Untitled*, 1936. F 7
3. *Untitled*, 1950. F 8
4. *Tête d'otage no. 1*, 1943. F 1, MOCA
5. *Le pot*, 1947. F 6, MOCA

4.

5.

1.

2.

3.

4.

5.

6.

7.

CLAES OLDENBURG

1. *White Shirt on Chair*, 1962. CO 10, MOCA
2. *Blue Pants on Chair*, 1962. CO 14, MOCA
3. *Bride*, 1961. CO 4, MOCA
4. *Umbrella and Newspaper*, 1962. CO 11, MOCA
5. *Hamburger*, 1962. CO 12, MOCA
6. *Piè à la Mode*, 1962. CO 13, MOCA
7. *Tennis Shoes*, 1962. CO 15, MOCA
8. *Pentecostal Cross*, 1961 CO 2, MOCA
9. *Cigarette Fragment*, 1961. CO 6, MOCA
10. *A Brown Shoe*, 1961. CO 8, MOCA
11. *Green Stocking*, 1961. CO 9, MOCA
12. *Fragment of Candies in a Box*, 1961. CO 3, MOCA
13. *Blue and Pink Panties*, 1961. CO 5, MOCA

8.

9.

10.

11.

12.

13.

ANTONI TAPIES

1. *Grey with Red Sign*, 1958. AT 12, MOCA
2. *Collage on a Black Group*, 1956. AT 5, MOCA
3. *Black-Ochre with Perforation*, 1957. AT 9, MOCA
4. *Grey and Black Cross*, 1955. AT 3, MOCA
5. *Sable-Ochre*, 1957. AT 10, MOCA
6. *Grey Relief Perforated by a Black Sign*, 1955. AT 2, MOCA
7. *All White*, 1955. AT 1, MOCA
8. *Grey on White*, 1956. AT 4, MOCA
9. *Grey With Six Marks*, 1959. AT 14, MOCA
10. *Ochre and Brown (New York)*, 1957. AT 8, MOCA
11. *Grey-Brown Composition*, 1957. AT 6, MOCA

8.

10.

9.

11.

191

1.

2.

3.

4.

5.

6.

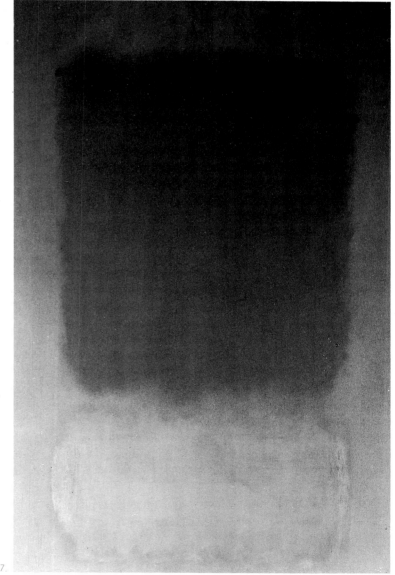

7.

JAMES ROSENQUIST

1. *Push Button*, 1960 - 1961. JR 2, MOCA
2. *A Lot to Like*, 1962. JR 5, MOCA
3. *Capillary Action*, 1962. JR 3, MOCA
4. *Shave*, 1964. JR 8, MOCA
5. *White Cigarette*, 1961. JR 1, MOCA
6. *Noon*, 1962. JR 7, MOCA

4.

1.

5.

2.

3.

6.

MARIO RADICE

Untitled, 1956. MRA 1

CY TWONBLY

Untitled, 1957. CT 1

GEORGE SEGAL

Man in the Armchair (Helmut von Erffa), 1969. GS 1, MOCA

Sunbathers on the Roof Top, 1963-1967. GS 2, MOCA

VITTORIO TAVERNARI

1. *Figura sdraiata*, 1971. VT 2

2. *Grande torso (il fiume)*, 1954. VT 1, The Solomon R. Guggenheim
   Foundation (Panza Gift)

FRANZ KLINE

1. *Monitor*, 1956. FK 4, MOCA

2. *Thorpe*, 1954. FK 2, MOCA

3. Drawing, 1957. FK 13

4. *Hazelton*, 1957. FK 6, MOCA

5. *Buttress*, 1956. FK 5, MOCA

6. *Black Iris*, 1961. FK 12, MOCA

7. *Black and White*, 1957. FK 7, MOCA

8. *Tower*, 1953. FK 1, MOCA

4.

8.

5.

9.

6.

7.

10.

JOSEPH BEUYS

1. *Untitled*, 1961. JB 2
2. *Fontana Dose*, 1963. JB 1

RAYMOND HAINS

Untitled, 1960. H 1

GILBERT AND GEORGE

We Are Only Human Sculptors, London 1970. GG 1

ROBERT RAUSCHENBERG

1. *South Carolina Fall*, 1961. RR 10, MOCA
2. *Small Rebus*, 1956. RR 3, MOCA
3. *Factum I*, 1957. RR 4, MOCA
4. *Trophy III*, 1961. RR 11, MOCA
5. *Gift for Apollo*, 1959. RR 8, MOCA
6. *Inlet*, 1959. RR 9, MOCA
7. *Kickback*, 1959. RR 7, MOCA

5.   6.   7.

ROY LICHTENSTEIN

1. *Cézanne*, 1962. RL 1, MOCA
2. *The Grip*, 1962. RL 4, MOCA

1.   2.

1.

2.

5.

3.

6.

4.

7.

DONALD JUDD

1. *Untitled*, 1972. DJ 9,
2. *Bern Piece no. 1*, Bern 1976. DJ 28
3. *Bern Piece no. 2*, Bern 1976. DJ 23
4. *Untitled*, 1972-1973. DJ 12
5. *Untitled*, 1970. DJ 5
6. *Bern Piece no. 3*, Bern 1976. DJ 30
7. *Untitled*, May 1972. DJ 13
8. *Untitled*, 1971. DJ 8
9. *Straight Single Tube*, 1974. DJ 24
10. *Untitled*, 1965. DJ 2
11. *Raised Top Plywood Piece (Lisson 1)*, 1974. DJ 29
12. *Untitled*, 1973. DJ 10
13. *Untitled*, 1965. DJ 1, The Solomon R. Guggenheim Foundation (Panza Gift)

1 → 12:
The Solomon R. Guggenheim Foundation

8.

9.

11.

12.

10.

13.

1½" ALUMINUM
8'×16' ABOUT 15° PARALLELOGRAM
INNER SHEETS PARALLEL

14/A.

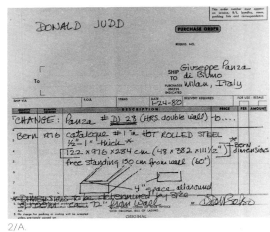

DONALD JUDD — PURCHASE ORDER

SHIP TO Giuseppe Panza di Biumo Milan, Italy
DATE 1-24-80

CHANGE: Panza # DJ 23 (HRS. double wall) to....

Bern 1976 catalogue #1 in HOT ROLLED STEEL ½"-1" thick *
122 × 976 × 284 cm (48 × 382 × 111½") } * Bern dimensions
free standing 150 cm from wall (60")
4" space all around

* Dimensions to be determined by size...
72" from wall

2/A.

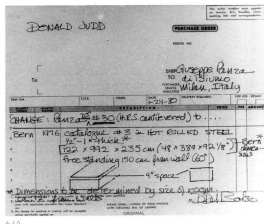

DONALD JUDD — PURCHASE ORDER

SHIP TO Giuseppe Panza di Biumo Milan, Italy
DATE 1-24-80

CHANGE: Panza # DJ 23 (Plywood, recess) to....

Bern 1976 catal #2 in HOT ROLLED STEEL ½"-1" thick *
122 × 966 × 704 cm (48 × 378¾ × 276") } * Bern dimensions
free standing 150 cm from walls (60")
9"

* Dimensions to be determined by size of room.
72" from walls

3/A.

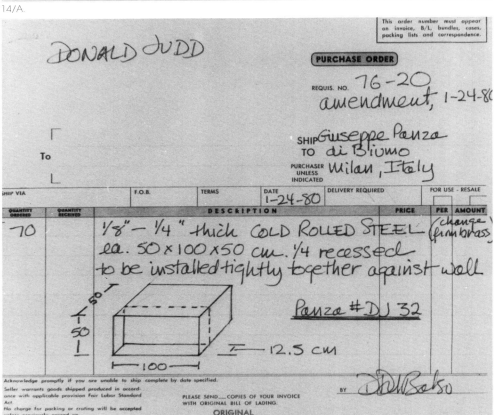

DONALD JUDD — PURCHASE ORDER

REQUIS. NO. 76-20
amendment, 1-24-80

SHIP TO Giuseppe Panza di Biumo Milan, Italy
DATE 1-24-80

QUANTITY ORDERED: 70

DESCRIPTION:
⅛" – ¼" thick COLD ROLLED STEEL (change from brass)
ea. 50 × 100 × 50 cm. ¼ recessed
to be installed tightly together against wall

Panza # DJ 32

50, 50, 100, 12.5 cm

Acknowledge promptly if you are unable to ship complete by date specified.
Seller warrants goods shipped produced in accordance with applicable provision Fair Labor Standard Act.
No charge for packing or crating will be accepted unless previously agreed on.

PLEASE SEND___ COPIES OF YOUR INVOICE WITH ORIGINAL BILL OF LADING.
ORIGINAL

BY [signature]

15.

Another purchase order (6/A):

DONALD JUDD — PURCHASE ORDER

SHIP TO Giuseppe Panza di Biumo Milan, Italy
DATE 1-24-80

CHANGE: Panza # DJ 30 (H.R.S. cantilevered) to....

Bern 1976 catalogue #3 in HOT ROLLED STEEL ½"-1" thick *
122 × 992 × 235 cm (48 × 389 × 92⅛") } * Bern dimensions
free standing 150 cm from wall (60")
4" space

* Dimensions to be determined by size of room.
72" from walls

6/A.

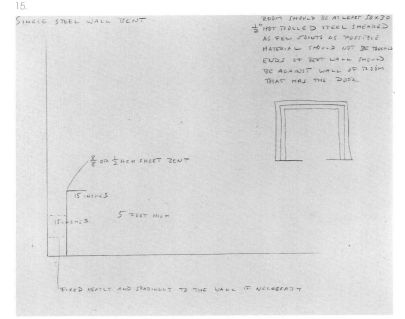

SINGLE STEEL WALL BENT

ROOM SHOULD BE AT LEAST 50×30
½" HOT ROLLED STEEL SHEARED
AS FEW JOINTS AS POSSIBLE
MATERIAL SHOULD NOT BE TOUCHED
ENDS OF BENT WALL SHOULD
BE AGAINST WALL OF ROOM
THAT HAS THE DOOR

⅜ OR ½ INCH SHEET BENT
15 INCHES
15 INCHES
5 FEET HIGH

FIXED NEATLY AND SPARINGLY TO THE WALL IF NECESSARY

16.

DONALD JUDD — PURCHASE ORDER — INVOICE

made by: Opizzi
SHIPPED TO Giuseppe Panza di Biumo, Milan

INVOICE DATE 1979

Panza # DJ 31 (change from alum. to HRS)
HOT ROLLED STEEL - 3 cm thick (1 5/16")
5 × 15 × 8'
with parallelogram inside
(see archit. drawing)

Thank You!

14/A.

CERTIFICATE

I, _Donald Judd_, hereby declare and confirm that on _____, I sold and/or transferred sole ownership of the work of art described below, ("the work") to Dr. Giuseppe Panza di Biumo, his successors and assigns, for good and valuable consideration and that he is now its sole and exclusive owner:
Title, description and medium of the work: _LC 286_

Eight plywood boxes: open back   _4' x 4'_

This work has not yet been constructed or realized and its existence is presently evidenced solely by the following, which is hereinafter referred to as "the Document":

Peter Ballantine has const. information.

If the Document listed above consists of more than one item, all of the items taken together shall constitute the Document.

I hereby grant Dr. Panza, his successors and assigns the right to have the work constructed or realized, provided that this is done by reference to and in strict and exact compliance with the Document and all of the details and instructions set forth therein and provided further that I, or my personal representatives or my Estate, am notified in writing of the realization.

CERTIFICATE

I, _Donald Judd_, hereby declare and confirm that on _____, I sold and/or transferred sole ownership of the work of art described below, ("the work") to Dr. Giuseppe Panza di Biumo, his successors and assigns, for good and valuable consideration and that he is now its sole and exclusive owner:
Title, description and medium of the work: _LC 303_

Eight plywood boxes: closed back
_6' x 6'_

This work has not yet been constructed or realized and its existence is presently evidenced solely by the following, which is hereinafter referred to as "the Document":

Peter Ballantine has construction information.

If the Document listed above consists of more than one item, all of the items taken together shall constitute the Document.

I hereby grant Dr. Panza, his successors and assigns the right to have the work constructed or realized, provided that this is done by reference to and in strict and exact compliance with the Document and all of the details and instructions set forth therein and provided further that I, or my personal representatives or my Estate, am notified in writing of the realization.

17   18.

19   (19/A.)

20.

15/A.

JENE HIGHSTEIN

1. *Human Scale Black*, 1975. JH 3

2. *Fresno Aluminium Casting no. 3*, 1974.
   JH 6, The Solomon R. Guggenheim
   Foundation (Panza Gift)

3. *Fresno Aluminium Casting no. 2*, 1974.
   JH 5, The Solomon R. Guggenheim
   Foundation (Panza Gift)

4. *Two Horizontals*, 1974. JH 2

5. *Black Eliptical Cone*, Varese 1976. JH 7,
   The Solomon R. Guggenheim Foundation
   (Panza Gift)

1.

2.

4.

3.

5.

RICHARD SERRA

1. *One Cut Bisected Corners*, 1973. RS 10,
   The Solomon R. Guggenheim Foundation
2. *Shafrazi*, 1974. RS 11,
   The Solomon R. Guggenheim Foundation
3. *Zadikians*, 1974. RS 12,
   The Solomon R. Guggenheim Foundation
4. *Sign Board Prop*, 1969. RS 7,
   The Solomon R. Guggenheim Foundation
5. *Untitled*, 1969. RS 6,
   The Solomon R. Guggenheim Foundation

1.

2.

4.

3.

5.

6. *Unequal Elevations*, 1975. RS 14,
   The Solomon R. Guggenheim Foundation

7. *Untitled*, 1967. RS 2,
   The Solomon R. Guggenheim Foundation

8. *Angle Slabs*, 1967. RS 3,
   The Solomon R. Guggenheim Foundation

9. *Tearing Lead from 1:00 to 1:47*, 1968. RS 4,
   The Solomon R. Guggenheim Foundation

6.

7.

8.

9.

CARL ANDRE

1. *Steel Piece*, 1967. CA 2,
   The Solomon R. Guggenheim Foundation
2. *Finely Divided Square Piece*, May 1970. CA 9
3. *Brass Square Piece*, March 1972. CA 8
4. *Reef*, 1966. CA 1,
   The Solomon R. Guggenheim Foundation
5. *Copper Square*, 1973. CA 10,
   The Solomon R. Guggenheim Foundation

FINELY DIVIDED SQUARE PIECE
FOR MARIANNE*
882 COLD-ROLLED STEEL CHIPS
1/64" X 9/32" X 9/16" EACH
1/64" X 11 13/16" X 11 13/16"
21 LONG X 42 WIDE ARRAY
NEW YORK
MAY 1970
©
*ONLY MARIANNE HAD THE PERSISTENCE OF VISION
NECESSARY TO FINISH THE PIECE
BE WELL & LOVE
Carl

BRASS SQUARE PIECE
100 BRASS UNITS
1/16" X 1/16" X 1/64" EACH
7/8" X 7/8" X 1/64" OVERALL
WINDHAM COLLEGE
MARCH 1972
©

6. *2001 Slope*, 1968. CA 11,
   The Solomon R. Guggenheim Foundation

7. *Zinc Ribbon Piece*, 1969-1971. CA 7,
   The Solomon R. Guggenheim Foundation

8. *Third Copper Triode, October* 1975. CA 15
   Fifth Copper Triode, October 1975. CA 14,
   The Solomon R. Guggenheim Foundation

9. *Seventeenth Copper Triode*, October 1975. CA 13,
   The Solomon R. Guggenheim Foundation

10. *Brass Piece*, 1969. CA 6,
    The Solomon R. Guggenheim Foundation

6.

7.

8.

9.

10.

210

JOEL SHAPIRO

1. *Untitled (Chair)*, 1973-1974. JS 4
2. *Untitled (Table)*, 1974. JS 6
3. *Untitled (Coffin)*, 1971-1973. JS 2
4. *Untitled*, 1974. JS 7
5. *Untitled (Maquette for table)*, 1974. JS 6A
6. *Untitled (Maquette for coffin)*, 1971. JS 2A
7. *Untitled*, 1971. JS 1

2.

3.

4.

5.

6.

7.

DAN FLAVIN

1. *Untitled (to Jan and Ron Greenberg)*, 1972-1973. DF 21
2. *Untitled 1/3*, 1973. DF 1
3. *Untitled 1/3*, 1963-1966. DF 3
4. *Gold, Pink and Red, Red 1/3*, 1964. DF 5
5. *The Nominal Three (to William of Ockham) 2/3*, 1963. DF 2
6. *Ursual's One and Two Picture 1/3*, 1964. DF 6
7. *Untitled (Seven 20 watt fictures form the arc) 1/3*, 1964. DF 7
8. *Monument on the Survival of Mrs. Reppin 1/3*, 1966. DF 8
9. *Untitled 1/3*, 1966. DF 9
10. *Untitled 6 B*, 1968. DF 13
11. *Untitled 1/3*, 1966. DF 10
12. *Kunsthalle, Koln, Installation (with circular lights)*, 1972. DF 22

1, 3, 5, 7, 8, 9, 11, 12:
The Solomon R. Guggenheim Foundation
2, 4 ,6, 10:
The Solomon R. Guggenheim Foundation (Panza Gift)

8.

9.

11.

10.

12

13. *An Artificial Barrier of Blue Red and Blue Fluorescent Light (to Flavin Starbuck Judd)*, 1968. DF 20

14. *Untitled (Diagonal on the wall)*, 1966. DF 12

15. *Green Crossing Green (to Piet Mondrian who lacked green)*, 1966. DF 16

16. *Untitled (to Henri Matisse) 2/3* 1964. DF 4

17. *Untitled (to Barbara Nüsse) 8/50*, 1971. DF 14

18. *Varese Corridor*, 1976. DF 19

13, 14, 15:
The Solomon R. Guggenheim Foundation
16, 17, 18:
The Solomon R. Guggenheim Foundation (Panza Gift)

13.

14.

15.

16.

17.

18.

RICHARD NONAS

1. *The Venus of the South*, Bari, January 1975. RN 1
2. *Southern Boundry*, Bari, January 1975. RN 2
3. *Southern Shortline*, New York 1974. RN 3
4. *Untitled*, Bari, January 1975. RN 4
5. *Great Eastern*, 1972. RN 7
6. *Salita Nord no. 1 (1 down)*, 1974. RN 14

7.

11.

8.

12.

9.

13.

10.

14.

15.

16.

18.

17.

19.

20.

21.

22.

23.

55

Richard Nonas sold or gave his sculpture to:

CONTE PANZA

'H' BEAM SHORTLINE 1974 Steel
6" X 6" X 4 FEET
(made IN ONE SECTION)

Richard Nonas Oct. 1975.

24.

25.

56

Richard Nonas sold or gave his sculpture to:

CONTE PANZA

INLET 1973 (wood)
(MADE IN 9 SECTIONS)
13' X 6½' X 6"

END PIECE OVERLAPS ABOUT ONE INCH

flat platform of 3"X8" planks with another 3X8" plank leaned on each edge forming a sort of sloping side to the platform

END PIECE OVERLAP ABOUT ONE INCH

Richard Nonas Oct. 1975.

26.

53

Richard Nonas sold or gave his sculpture to:

CONTE PANZA

SHORTLINE SERIES (WALL) MOSKUTZ' BROW
1974 steel
75" X 6" X 1"
(MADE IN ONE SECTION)
(WALL)

NAIL NAIL NAIL

WALL SCULPTURE RESTING ON THREE NAILS TO BE HUNG AT ABOUT EYE-LEVEL

Richard Nonas Oct. 1975.

218

27.

28.

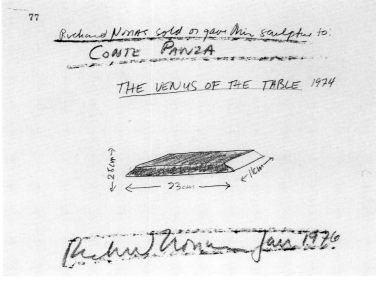

77

Richard NONAS sold or gave this sculpture to:

CONTE PANZA

THE VENUS OF THE TABLE 1974

←25cm→ →1cm←
←23cm→

Richard Nonas Jan 1976

29.

30.

31.

32.

1.

2.

3.

4.

5.

6.

BRUCE NAUMAN

1. *Piece in Which One Can Stand*, 1966.
   BN 4

2. *Lighted Centerpiece*, 1968. BN 7,
   The Solomon R. Guggenheim Foundation
   (Panza Gift)

3. *Hologram (Full Figure Poses)*, 1969. BN 10

4. *Untitled*, 1965 - 1966. BN 2

5. *Hologram (Making Faces)*, 1968. BN 9

6. *Device for a Left Armpit*, 1967. BN 5

7. *Sound Breaking Wall*, 1969. BN 14,
   The Solomon R. Guggenheim Foundation
   (Panza Gift)

8. *Touch and Sound Walls*, December 1969.
   BN 15, The Solomon R. Guggenheim
   Foundation (Panza Gift)

9. *Two Fans Corridor*, January 1970. BN 22,
   The Solomon R. Guggenheim Foundation
   (Panza Gift)

10. *Untitled*, 1965 - 1966. BN 3

7.

8.

9.

10.

11.

14.

12.

15.

13.

16

17.

(can't find my blue pencil)

when I first drew
this piece, I was
thinking of a space
about 40 to 60
feet square, but I
think it can be con-
siderably smaller
if I again give some
thought to it and have
some idea of the space
available in case some one
wants to build it.

18.

19.

20.

21.

22.

23.

24.

25.

26.

27.

28.

29.

32.

30.

31.   33.

1.

4.

2.

5.

3.

6.

7.

ROBERT MORRIS

1. *Untitled (4 wedges)*, 1967. RM 5
   Untitled (4 round wedges), 1967. RM 5A
   Untitled (Piece with battered sides),
   1966. RM 32
   The Solomon R. Guggenheim Foundation

2. *Untitled (Alluminium grating)*, 1969. RM 9,
   The Solomon R. Guggenheim Foundation

3. *Untitled (Door stop)*, 1965. RM 4,
   The Solomon R. Guggenheim Foundation

4. *Untitled (Long wedge)*, 1966. RM 2,
   The Solomon R. Guggenheim Foundation

5. *Untitled (Square donut)*, 1968. RM 33,
   The Solomon R. Guggenheim Foundation

6. *Untitled (Corner piece)*, 1964. RM 1,
   The Solomon R. Guggenheim Foundation

7. *Untitled (16 steel boxes)*, 1967. RM 7,
   The Solomon R. Guggenheim Foundation

8. *Untitled (Steel grating)*, 1967. RM 8,
   The Solomon R. Guggenheim Foundation

9. *Untitled (Five timbers)*, 1969. RM 18,
   The Solomon R. Guggenheim Foundation

10. *Untitled (Brown felt)*, 1973. RM 14,
    The Solomon R. Guggenheim Foundation

11. *War Memorial*, 1970. RM 31,
    The Solomon R. Guggenheim Foundation

8.

10.

9.

11.

227

12.

13.

14.

15.

16.

17.

18.

19.

20.

21.

228

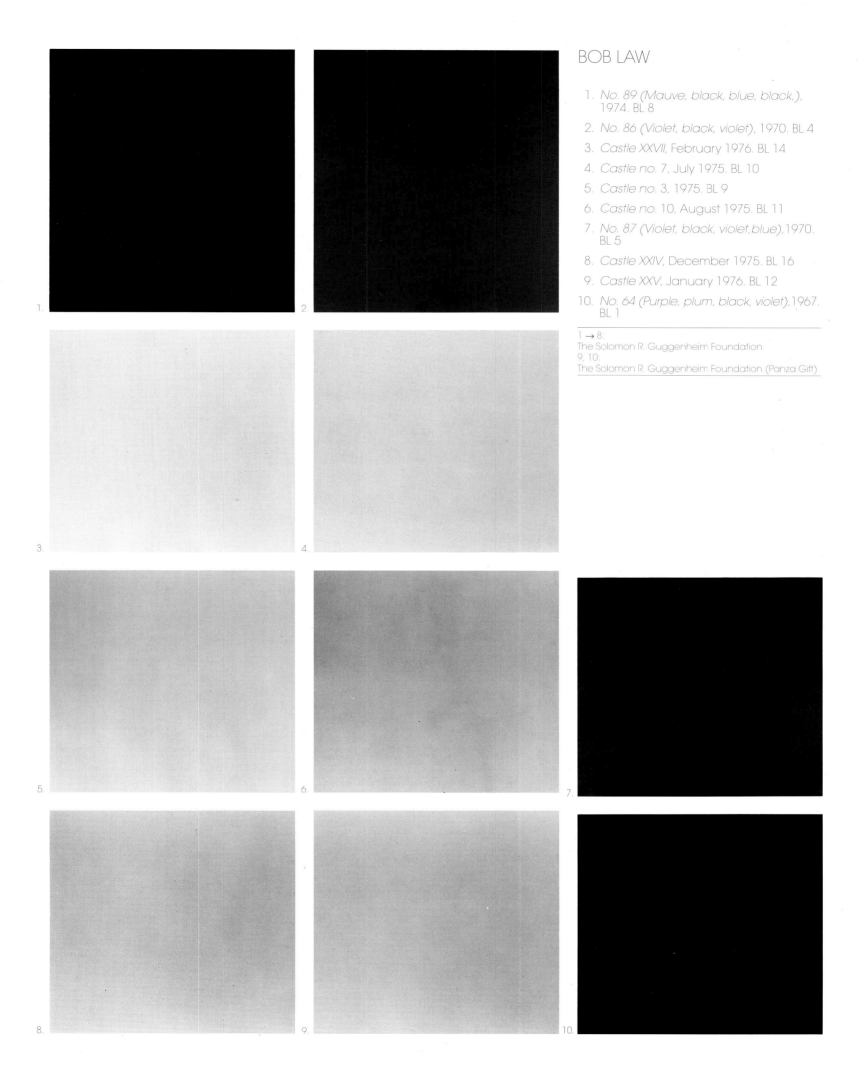

1 → 8:
The Solomon R. Guggenheim Foundation
9, 10:
The Solomon R. Guggenheim Foundation (Panza Gift)

13.

11.

14.

12.

15.

230

1.

ALAN CHARLTON

1. *82 in. Square, 1970 - 1972. AC 4,*
   The Solomon R. Guggenheim Foundation (Panza Gift)

2. *82 in. Square, 1970 - 1972. AC 1,*
   The Solomon R. Guggenheim Foundation (Panza Gift)

3. *Outer piece 90 x 174 in., each inner piece*
   74 1/2 in. square, channel 1 3/4 in.,
   November-December 1972. AC 18,
   The Solomon R. Guggenheim Foundation (Panza Gift)

4. *58 x 180 in.,* June 1970. AC 6, The Solomon R.
   Guggenheim Foundation (Panza Gift)

5. *82 in. Square, 1970 - 1972. AC 2,*
   The Solomon R. Guggenheim Foundation (Panza Gift)

4.

2.

OUTER PIECE 90". 174".
EACH INNER PIECE 74½" SQUARE.
'CHANNEL', EDGE 1¾".

ALAN CHARLTON NOV/DEC. 72.

3.   5.

6. *90 x 90 in., slit 78 in., August 1971.*
   AC 9

7. *90 x 90 in., slit 44 in., September 1971.*
   AC 12

8. *Outer piece 144 x 66 in., inner*
   piece 98 ½ x 50 ½ in., channel 1 ¾
   in., May-August 1972. AC 16

9. *90 x 78 in., slit 66 in., August 1971.*
   AC 10

10. *No. 4/8 Outer piece 84 in. square,*
    inner piece 68 ⁶⁄₁₀ in.
    square, channel 1 ⁵⁄₁₀ in.,
    December 1972 - May 1973. AC 22

11. *Outer piece 51 ½ in. square, inner*
    piece 24 in. square, channel 1 ¾
    in., August 1973. AC 27

12. *No. 1/8 Outer piece 84 in. square,*
    inner piece 68 ⁶⁄₁₀ in. square,
    channel 1 ⁵⁄₁₀ in., December 1972 -
    May 1973. AC 19

13. *No. 6/8 Outer piece 84 in. square,*
    inner piece 68 ⁶⁄₁₀ in. square,
    channel 1 ⁴⁄₁₀ in., December 1972 -
    May 1973. AC 24

14. *No. 5/6 91 x 80 ½ in.,*
    January 1975. AC 33
    No. 3/6 Each piece 98 x 66 ½ in.,
    January 1975. AC 34
    No. 2/6 Each piece 101 x 59 ½ in.,
    January 1975. AC 35

15. *90 x 102 in., each slit 90 in.,*
    January 1972. AC 15

16. *Outer piece 66 in. square, inner*
    piece 55 ½ in. square, channel 1 ¾
    in., October 1973. AC 29

17. *82 in. Square, 1970 - 1972. AC 5*

6.

8.

7.

9.

10.

11.

21. *No. 2/8 Outer piece 84 in. square, inner piece 68 ⁴/₁₀ in.
    square, channel 1 ⁸/₁₀ in.*, December 1972-May 1973.
    AC 20, The Solomon R. Guggenheim Foundation

22. *Outer piece 50 in. square, inner piece 39 ¹/₂ in. square,
    channel 1 ³/₄ in.*, January 1974. AC 32,
    The Solomon R. Guggenheim Foundation

23. *No. 3/8 Outer piece 84 in. square, inner piece 68 ⁴/₁₀ in.
    square, channel 1 ⁸/₁₀ in.*, December 1972-May 1973.
    AC 21, The Solomon R. Guggenheim Foundation

24. *Outer piece 56 in square, inner piece 49 in. square,
    channel 1 ³/₄ in.*, January 1974. AC 31,
    The Solomon R. Guggenheim Foundation

22.

19.

20.

23.

21.

24.

234

PETER JOSEPH

1. *Grey with Ochre Border*, May 1976. PJ 13
2. *Cream with Ochre Border*, June 1976. PJ 14
3. *Untitled (Dark cream with blue border)*, 1975. PJ 9,
   Untitled (Cream colour with black border), May 1975. PJ 5
4. *Untitled (Tan colour with dark blue border) I*, June 1974. PJ 2
   Untitled (Cream colour with black border) II, June 1974. PJ 3
5. *Cream with Brown Border*, February 1976. PJ 12
6. *Cream with Maroon Border*, January 1976. PJ 11
7. *Untitled (Dulled cream with black border)*, October 1975. PJ 10

1 → 7.
The Solomon R. Guggenheim Foundation

235

1.

2/10.

2/9.

2/2.

2/1.

2/8.

2/11.

2/3.

2/4.

ROBERT RYMAN

1. *Allied*, 1966. RRY 1,
   The Solomon R. Guggenheim Foundation

2. *Standard nos. 1-2-3-4-6-8-9-10-11-12-13*, 1967. RRY 2,
   The Solomon R. Guggenheim Foundation

3. *Aacon*, 1968. RRY 3,
   The Solomon R. Guggenheim Foundation

4. *Five Units (nos. 1-2-3-4-5)*, 1969. RRY 13,
   The Solomon R. Guggenheim Foundation

5. *Three Units (nos. 1-2-3)*, 1969. RRY 12,
   The Solomon R. Guggenheim Foundation

6. *Classico II*, 1968. RRY 6,
   The Solomon R. Guggenheim Foundation

7. *Classico 20*, 1968. RRY 10,
   The Solomon R. Guggenheim Foundation

3.

2/13.

2/12.

4/1.

6.

2/6.

5/1.

7.

8.

5/3.

10.

9.

4/2.

5/2.

8. *Lenox*, 1971. RRY 25,
   The Solomon R. Guggenheim Foundation

9. *Surface Veil III*, 1971. RRY 24,
   The Solomon R. Guggenheim Foundation

10. *Capitol*, 1973. RRY 29,
    The Solomon R. Guggenheim Foundation

11. *Aacon*, 1968. RRY 3,
    Impex, 1968. RRY 4,
    Capitol, 1973. RRY 29,
    Empire, 1973. RRY 30,
    The Solomon R. Guggenheim Foundation

12. *Classico I*, 1968. RRY 5,
    The Solomon R. Guggenheim Foundation

13. *Surface Veil I*, 1970. RRY 19,
    Surface Veil II, 1971. RRY 23,
    Surface Veil III, 1971. RRY 24,
    The Solomon R. Guggenheim Foundation

11.

4/4.

12.

4/3.

13.

14.

19/1.

4/5.

15.

17/2.

17/1.

16.

18.

20.

21.

20. *General Painting*, 1971. RRY 22,
The Solomon R. Guggenheim Foundation

21. *Standard nos. 1-2-3-4-5-6-8-9-10-11-12-13*,
1967. RRY 2,
The Solomon R. Guggenheim Foundation

22. *Lithograph*, 1971. RRY 31

23. *Impex*, 1968. RRY 4,
The Solomon R. Guggenheim Foundation

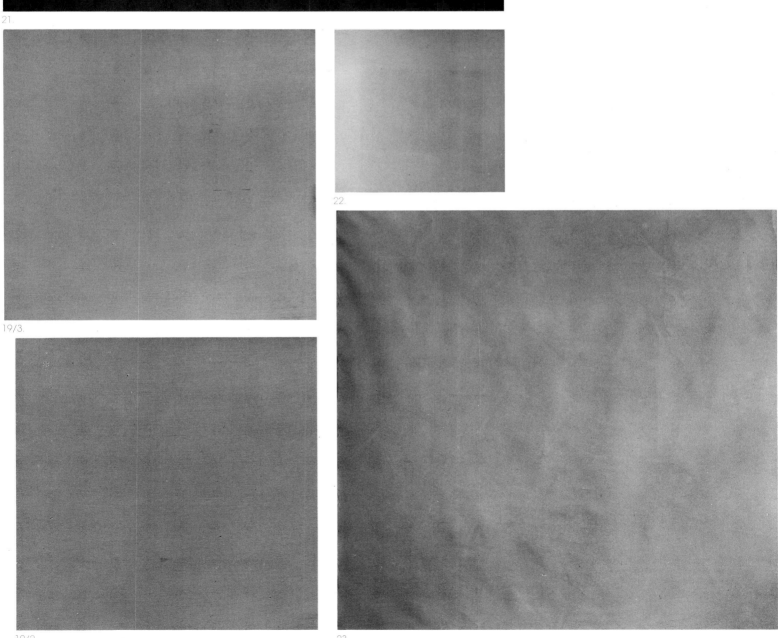

19/3.

22.

19/2

23

241

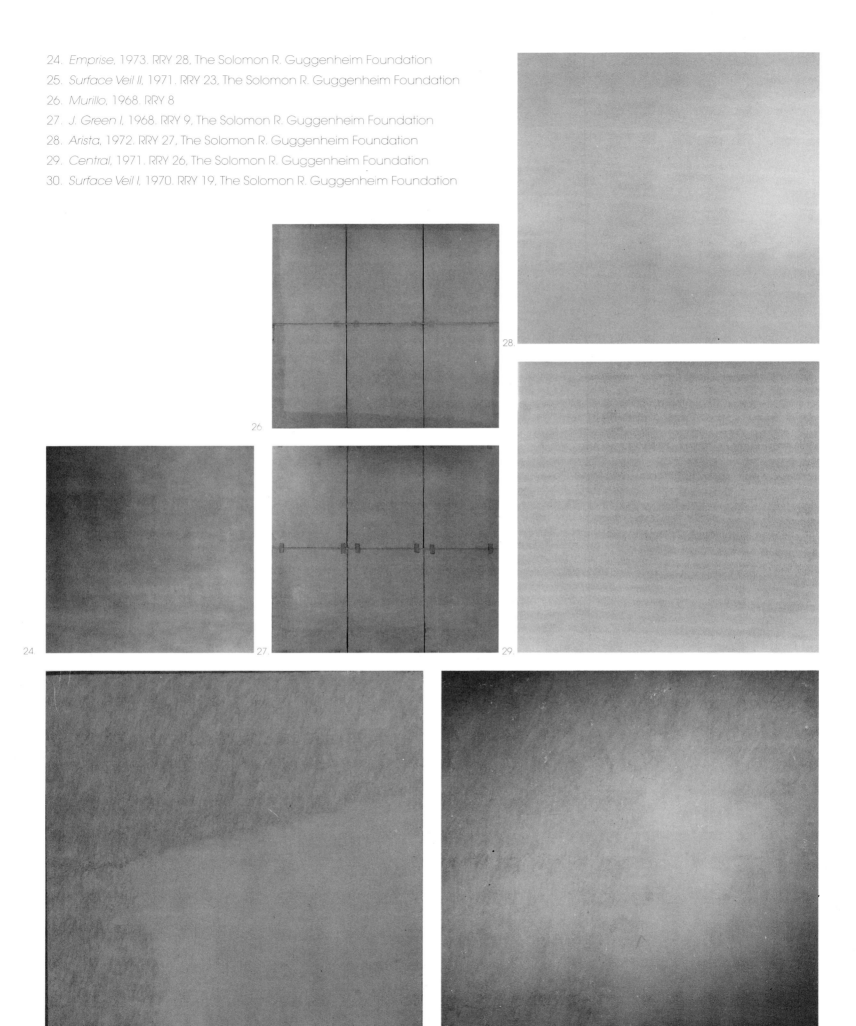

24. *Emprise*, 1973. RRY 28, The Solomon R. Guggenheim Foundation
25. *Surface Veil II*, 1971. RRY 23, The Solomon R. Guggenheim Foundation
26. *Murillo*, 1968. RRY 8
27. *J. Green I*, 1968. RRY 9, The Solomon R. Guggenheim Foundation
28. *Arista*, 1972. RRY 27, The Solomon R. Guggenheim Foundation
29. *Central*, 1971. RRY 26, The Solomon R. Guggenheim Foundation
30. *Surface Veil I*, 1970. RRY 19, The Solomon R. Guggenheim Foundation

BRICE MARDEN

1. *Paris Painting*, 1969. BM 2
2. *To May Madness*, 1972. BM 5
3. *Tour*, 1970 - 1971. BM 4
4. *Passage*, 1973 - 1974. BM 9
5. *Sea Study (Blue-grey)*, 1972 - 1973. BM 6
6. *Private Title*, 1966. BM 1
7. *Untitled*, 1973. BM 8, The Solomon R. Guggenheim Foundation

ROBERT MANGOLD

1. *Circle Painting 6 (Dark-red)*, 1973. RMA 8
2. *Square Within a Square (Warm-green)*, 1974. RMA 28
3. *Distorted Square Circle 7 (Green)*, 1972. RMA 13
4. *Square Within a Rectangle (Blue-Grey)*, 1974. RMA 27
5. *Incomplete Circle no. 1 (Yellow)*, 1972. RMA 3
6. *Untitled (Brown)*, 1973. RMA 16.
7. *Square Within a Rectangle I (Orange)*, 1974. RMA 26
8. *Incomplete Circle no. 2 (Brown)*, 1972. RMA 4
9. *Distorted Square Circle 10 (Grey-blue)*, 1973. RMA 12
10. *Circle In and Out of a Polygon II (Blue)*, 1973. RMA 17
11. *Circle Painting 2 (Grey-violet)*, 1973. RMA 6
12. *Distorted Square Within a Circle 2 (Violet)*, 1973. RMA 30
13. *Distorted Square Within a Circle 3 (Grey-green)*, 1973. RMA 31
14. *Square Within a Square (Yellow)*, 1974. RMA 25

1, 2, 4 → 8, 10, 11, 14
The Solomon R. Guggenheim Foundation

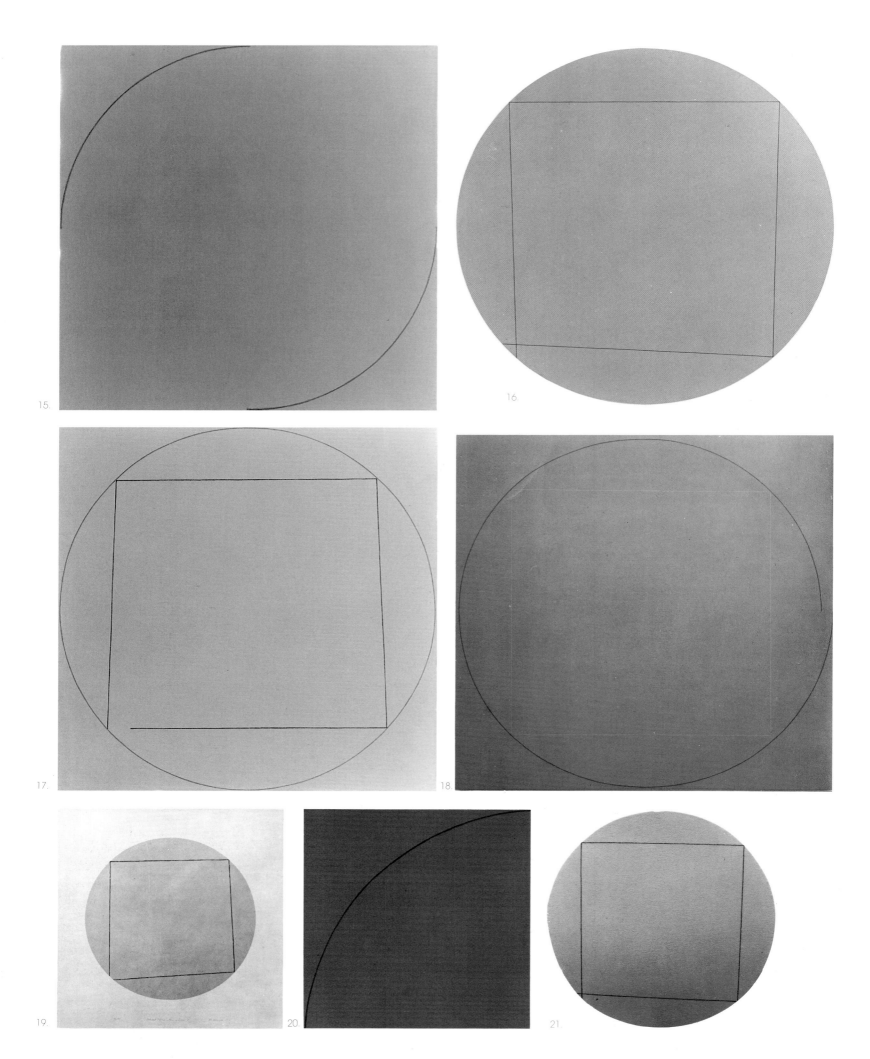

15.

16.

17.

18.

19.

20.

21.

22.

23.

24.

25.

16 → 18, 20, 22 → 28:
The Solomon R. Guggenheim Foundation

26.

27.

28.

29.

30.

LOUIS CANE

1. *Dark Blue Canvas*, March 16, 1973. LC 7
2. *Red Canvas*, May 15-16, 1973. LC 8

BERNARD JOUBERT

1. *Work*, 1974. BJ 1
2. *Work*, 1974. BJ 2
3. *Work*, 1974. BJ 3

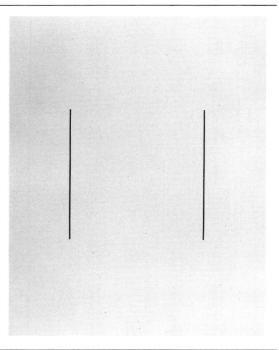

ENEA FERRARI

Untitled, 1945. EF 1

Site Sculpture Project
Times Square Circle Shape
New York City

8 sites (A through H) were located approximately

4000' from central point (Y) so as to describe the

shape of a circle. A 1" diameter self adhering paper

sticker was placed at each site as a marker.

I

Locations

A.   West 57th Street at Seventh Avenue

B.   Park Avenue near 53rd Street

C.   East 42nd Street at Third Avenue

D.   East 32nd Street near Park Avenue

E.   West 28th Street at Seventh Avenue

F.   West 32nd Street at Tenth Avenue

G.   West 42nd Street near Eleventh Avenue

H.   Tenth Avenue near 53rd Street

Y.   West 42nd Street at Seventh Avenue

December, 1968

1.

Duration Piece #14

Salisbury, New Hampshire

On October 7, 1968 four markers (styrofoam: 4" X 4" X 60")

were carried off into the Atlantic Ocean off Salisbury, New Hampshire

by the outgoing tide.

Twelve photographs taken at one minute intervals documented

the event and join with this statement to constitute the form of the

piece.

October, 1968

2

DOUGLAS HUEBLER

1. *Site Sculpture Project, Times Square Circle Shape*, New York City, December 1968. DH 1

2. *Duration Piece no. 14*, Salisbury, New Hampshire, October 1968. DH 2, The Solomon R. Guggenheim Foundation (Panza Gift)

3. *Variable Piece no. 4*, New York City, November 1968. DH 3

3/1.

3/2.

Location Piece # 6

Los Angeles, California

During late February, 1969 two persons, visiting California on other business, assisted the artist in making this piece by placing markers (1" diameter self adhering paper stickers) at eight different locations..and documenting each "marking" by photographing the site.

No structuring system was used other than that the markers were placed wherever and whenever it occured to either one of the two persons to do so.

The eight photographs of the locations, not identified otherwise, join with this statement to constitute the form of this piece.

Douglas Huebler

March, 1969   Douglas Huebler

4.

3/3.

Variable Piece #4

New York City

On November 23, 1968 ten photographs were made with the camera pointed west on 42nd Street in New York City.

With his eyes completely closed the photographer sat on the corner of Vanderbilt Avenue ; each photograph was made at the instant that the sound of traffic approaching 42nd Street stopped enough to suggest that pedestrians could cross the street.

This statement and the ten photographs join together to constitute the form of this piece.

November, 1968   Douglas Huebler

3.

3/4.

Duration Piece #12

Venice, California - Plum Island, (Newburyport) Massachusetts

In March, 1969 a small quantity of sand was removed from the ocean beach at Venice, California and taken to the ocean beach at Plum Island, Massachusetts.

There it was placed where it would be carried into the Atlantic Ocean by the outgoing tide. A similar quantity of sand was, at that time, removed from the Plum Island location and taken (May 1969) to Venice where it, in turn, was carried into the Pacific Ocean.

Another exchange will mark the same sites in 1979 and so on: once every ten years until a total of eleven markings have been made at which time (2069) the piece will be complete. (It will be the responsibility of the owner to arrange for the next ten such exchanges).

One photograph of each site and this statement constitute the form of this piece.

May, 1969   Douglas Huebler

5.

Location Piece #9

New England

On Sunday afternoon March 23, 1969, eleven photographs were made to document a ten mile drive through the New England landscape.

The "cue" for each photograph was taken from the mileage shown on the speedometer (regardless of the speed of the automobile) as the ten miles were traveled.

Six photographs were made at even mileage numbers (the camera being directed "into" the landscape) and five photographs were at uneven numbers (the camera being directed at an angle of approximately 45° to the side of the automobile window).

The photographs with no further identification join with this statement to constitute the form of this piece.

Douglas

March, 1969

6.

Location Piece #1

New York - Los Angeles

In February, 1969 the airspace over each of the thirteen states between New York and Los Angeles was documented by a photograph made as the camera was pointed more or less straight out the airplane window (with no "interesting" view intended).

The photographs join together the east and west coast of the United States as each serves to "mark" one of the thirteen states flown over during that particular flight.

The photographs are not, however, "keyed" to the state over which they were made, but only exist as documents that join with an American Airlines System Map and this statement to constitute the form of this piece.

Douglas Huebler

February, 1969

7.

LE POINT REPRÉSENTÉ CI-DESSUS SEMBLE POUR UN INSTANT ATTIRER ET FIXER CHAQUE ET TOUT AUTRE POINT SITUÉ DANS L'ESPACE "PHYSIQUE" DE CETTE SALLE. CETTE IMPRESSION CONTINUE A ÉVOLUER EN SÉQUENCES RÉGULIÈRES PENDANT TOUTE LA DURÉE DE LA PRÉSENCE DE L'OBSERVATEUR DANS LA SALLE MAIS CESSE IMMÉDIATEMENT D'EXISTER LORSQUE CE DERNIER EST PARTI.

THE POINT REPRESENTED ABOVE DRAWS ONTO ITSELF AND FIXES, FOR AN INSTANT, EACH AND EVERY OTHER POINT LOCATED WITHIN THE PHYSICAL SPACE OF THIS ROOM AND CONTINUES TO DO SO, IN A SEQUENTIAL PROCESS FOR THE ENTIRE TIME THAT THE PERCIPIENT REMAINS IN THE ROOM BUT IMMEDIATELY CEASES TO EXIST AT ALL WHEN THE PERCIPIENT HAS DEPARTED.

15.

16.

17.

18.

CETTE SURFACE REFLÈTE À CET INSTANT MÊME LE CHANGEMENT IMPERCEPTIBLE DE L'ESSENCE PHYSIQUE DE L'OBSERVATEUR.

THIS SURFACE IS, AT THIS INSTANT, REFLECTING THE IMPERCEPTIBLY CHANGING PHYSICAL ESSENCE OF ITS PERCIPIENT.

20.

Variable Piece #19

Bradford, Massachusetts - New York City

On March 13, 1971 over 650 photographs were made that, altogether, document the entire visual appearance in the particular path of travel taken by the artist on a trip between his house in Bradford and the Castelli Gallery in New York.

In each case the photograph was made at the 'point' (on the highway or road) in the direction of travel that was as far as his eye could see; when that point was reached another photograph was made, etc.

For this work one view has been selected as the most 'boring' and its enlargement joins 20 proof prints, a map and this statement to constitute the form of this piece. (The owner may select an alternative 'boring' view for enlargement if he prefers.)

Douglas Huebler

March 1971

19.

Duration Piece # 5
Amsterdam, Holland

12 photographs were made as the documentation of a system of "time" in which each successive stage is a reduction, by one half, of the previous time; one full hour of Greenwich mean time is approached, but impossible to be reached, at the same time that linear distance is described to the extent that physical, not theoretical, possibilities for further stages of documentation of the system are exhausted.

The first photograph was made on January 12, 1970 at the randomly selected intersection of Haarstraat, ter 14, and Bilderdijkstraat 14, with the camera directed towards infinity along Bilderdijkstraat 14. That direction was then walked for 30 minutes and then a 90° right turn was made. Another photograph was taken towards "infinity" and that direction walked for 15 minutes, after which another right turn was made. Another photograph was taken towards "infinity" and that direction was walked for 7 minutes and 30 seconds; the next after 3 minutes, 45 seconds and so on through .0087 seconds. At that time, (at a location in Vondel Park), 58.3877 minutes having passed, the final photograph was made, thereby completing the piece.

(Obviously it was possible to increase or decrease the speed of the "walks" in order not to confront a physical obstacle at the instant of the "right turn.")

The 12 photographs and this statement constitute the form of this piece.

January 1970

Douglas Huebler

16/A.

SOL LEWITT

1. *Wall Drawing no. 265*, Varese, July 1975. SL 11, The Solomon R. Guggenheim Foundation (Panza Gift)

2. *Wall Drawing no. 54*, July 1970. SL 9

3. *Wall Drawing no. 264*, Varese, July 1975. SL 4, The Solomon R. Guggenheim Foundation (Panza Gift)

4. *Wall Drawing no. 24*, September 1969. SL 20

5. *Wall Drawing no. 3*, April 1969. SL 1

6. *Wall Drawing no. 20*, September 1969. SL 2

1.

2.

3.

4.

5.

6.

253

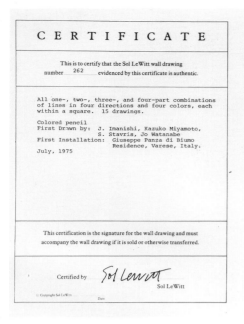

CERTIFICATE

This is to certify that the Sol LeWitt wall drawing
number 262 evidenced by this certificate is authentic.

All one-, two-, three-, and four-part combinations
of lines in four directions and four colors, each
within a square. 15 drawings.

Colored pencil
First Drawn by: J. Imanishi, Kazuko Miyamoto,
S. Stavris, Jo Watanabe
First Installation: Giuseppe Panza di Biumo
Residence, Varese, Italy.
July, 1975

This certification is the signature for the wall drawing and must
accompany the wall drawing if it is sold or otherwise transferred.

Certified by *Sol LeWitt*
Sol LeWitt

© Copyright Sol LeWitt   Date

7.

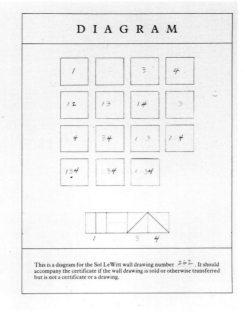

DIAGRAM

This is a diagram for the Sol LeWitt wall drawing number 262. It should
accompany the certificate if the wall drawing is sold or otherwise transferred
but is not a certificate or a drawing.

8.

CERTIFICATE

This is to certify that the Sol LeWitt wall drawing
number 264 evidenced by this certificate is authentic.

A wall divided into 16 equal parts with all
one-, two-, three-, and four-part combinations
of lines and color in four directions.

Colored pencil
First Drawn by: J. Imanishi, Kazuko Miyamoto,
S. Stavris, Jo Watanabe
First Installation: Giuseppe Panza di Biumo
Residence, Varese, Italy.
July, 1975

This certification is the signature for the wall drawing and must
accompany the wall drawing if it is sold or otherwise transferred.

Certified by *Sol LeWitt*
Sol LeWitt

© Copyright Sol LeWitt   Date

3/A.

DIAGRAM

This is a diagram for the Sol LeWitt wall drawing number 264. It should
accompany the certificate if the wall drawing is sold or otherwise transferred
but is not a certificate or a drawing.

CERTIFICATE

This is to certify that the Sol LeWitt wall drawing
number 38 evidenced by this certificate is authentic.

Tissue paper cut into 1.5" (4 cm) squares
rolled and inserted into holes in gray pegboard
walls. All holes in the walls are filled
randomly.
1st wall: White;
2nd wall: White, yellow;
3rd wall: White, yellow, red;
4th wall: White, yellow, red, blue.

Colored tissue papers, gray pegboard walls
First Installation: Tokyo Biennial, Tokyo, Japan
April, 1970

This certification is the signature for the wall drawing and must
accompany the wall drawing if it is sold or otherwise transferred.

Certified by *Sol LeWitt*
Sol LeWitt

© Copyright Sol LeWitt   Date

9.

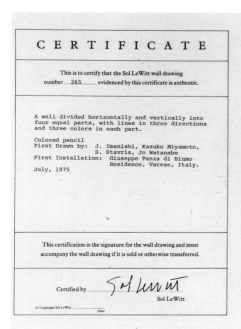

CERTIFICATE

This is to certify that the Sol LeWitt wall drawing
number 265 evidenced by this certificate is authentic.

A wall divided horizontally and vertically into
four equal parts, with lines in three directions
and three colors in each part.

Colored pencil
First Drawn by: J. Imanishi, Kazuko Miyamoto,
S. Stavris, Jo Watanabe
First Installation: Giuseppe Panza di Biumo
Residence, Varese, Italy.
July, 1975

This certification is the signature for the wall drawing and must
accompany the wall drawing if it is sold or otherwise transferred.

Certified by *Sol LeWitt*
Sol LeWitt

© Copyright Sol LeWitt   Date

1/A.

DIAGRAM

This is a diagram for the Sol LeWitt wall drawing number 265. It should
accompany the certificate if the wall drawing is sold or otherwise transferred
but is not a certificate or a drawing.

10.

7. *Wall Drawing no. 262*, Varese, July 1975. SL 3, The Solomon R. Guggenheim Foundation (Panza Gift)

8. *Wall Drawing no. 272*, Varese, July 1975. SL 14

9. *Wall Drawing no. 38*, April 1970. SL 6

10. *Wall Drawing no. 271*, Varese, July 1975. SL 10, The Solomon R. Guggenheim Foundation (Panza Gift)

11. *Wall Drawing no. 146*, September 1972. SL 15, The Solomon R. Guggenheim Foundation (Panza Gift)

12. *Wall Drawing nos. 267-268-269-270*, July 1975. SL 13

11

12/1.

12/2.

12/3.

12/4.

4/A.

DIAGRAM

This is a diagram for the Sol LeWitt wall drawing number 151. It should accompany the certificate if the wall drawing is sold or otherwise transferred but is not a certificate or a drawing.

DIAGRAM

This is a diagram for the Sol LeWitt wall drawing number 271. It should accompany the certificate if the wall drawing is sold or otherwise transferred but is not a certificate or a drawing.

DIAGRAM

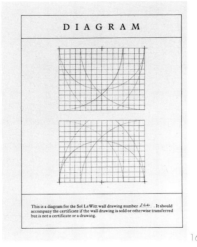

This is a diagram for the Sol LeWitt wall drawing number 266. It should accompany the certificate if the wall drawing is sold or otherwise transferred but is not a certificate or a drawing.

DIAGRAM

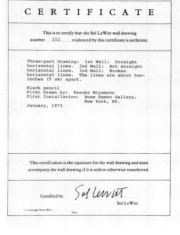

This is a diagram for the Sol LeWitt wall drawing number 152. It should accompany the certificate if the wall drawing is sold or otherwise transferred but is not a certificate or a drawing.

DIAGRAM

This is a diagram for the Sol LeWitt wall drawing number 176. It should accompany the certificate if the wall drawing is sold or otherwise transferred but is not a certificate or a drawing.

DIAGRAM

This is a diagram for the Sol LeWitt wall drawing number 54. It should accompany the certificate if the wall drawing is sold or otherwise transferred but is not a certificate or a drawing.

17.

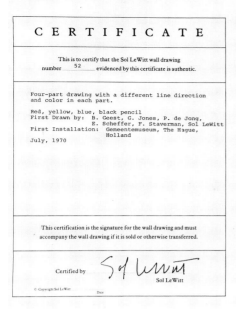

CERTIFICATE

This is to certify that the Sol LeWitt wall drawing number 52 evidenced by this certificate is authentic.

Four-part drawing with a different line direction and color in each part.

Red, yellow, blue, black pencil
First Drawn by: B. Geest, G. Jones, P. de Jong, E. Scheffer, F. Staverman, Sol LeWitt
First Installation: Gemeentemuseum, The Hague, Holland
July, 1970

This certification is the signature for the wall drawing and must accompany the wall drawing if it is sold or otherwise transferred.

Certified by Sol LeWitt

© Copyright Sol LeWitt   Date

DIAGRAM

This is a diagram for the Sol LeWitt wall drawing number 52. It should accompany the certificate if the wall drawing is sold or otherwise transferred but is not a certificate or a drawing.

18.

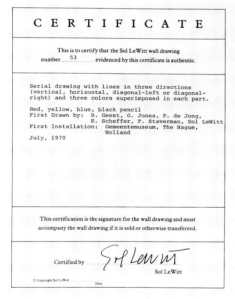

CERTIFICATE

This is to certify that the Sol LeWitt wall drawing number 53 evidenced by this certificate is authentic.

Serial drawing with lines in three directions (vertical, horizontal, diagonal-left or diagonal-right) and three colors superimposed in each part.

Red, yellow, blue, black pencil
First Drawn by: B. Geest, G. Jones, P. de Jong, E. Scheffer, F. Staverman, Sol LeWitt
First Installation: Gemeentemuseum, The Hague, Holland
July, 1970

This certification is the signature for the wall drawing and must accompany the wall drawing if it is sold or otherwise transferred.

Certified by Sol LeWitt

© Copyright Sol LeWitt   Date

DIAGRAM

This is a diagram for the Sol LeWitt wall drawing number 53. It should accompany the certificate if the wall drawing is sold or otherwise transferred but is not a certificate or a drawing.

19.

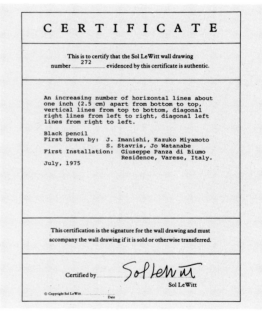

CERTIFICATE

This is to certify that the Sol LeWitt wall drawing number 272 evidenced by this certificate is authentic.

An increasing number of horizontal lines about one inch (2.5 cm) apart from bottom to top, vertical lines from top to bottom, diagonal right lines from left to right, diagonal left lines from right to left.

Black pencil
First Drawn by: J. Imanishi, Kazuko Miyamoto, S. Stavris, Jo Watanabe
First Installation: Giuseppe Panza di Biumo Residence, Varese, Italy.
July, 1975

This certification is the signature for the wall drawing and must accompany the wall drawing if it is sold or otherwise transferred.

Certified by Sol LeWitt

© Copyright Sol LeWitt   Date

8/A.

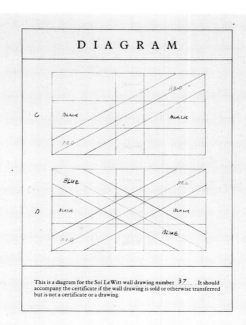

CERTIFICATE

This is to certify that the Sol LeWitt wall drawing number 37 evidenced by this certificate is authentic.

Intersecting symmetrical bands of parallel lines 36" (90 cm) wide, in four directions and colors, on four walls progressively.

Red, yellow, blue, black pencil
First Drawn by: Betts and others
First Installation: La Jolla Museum of Contemporary Art, La Jolla, CA.
April, 1970

This certification is the signature for the wall drawing and must accompany the wall drawing if it is sold or otherwise transferred.

Certified by Sol LeWitt

© Copyright Sol LeWitt   Date

20.

DIAGRAM

This is a diagram for the Sol LeWitt wall drawing number 37. It should accompany the certificate if the wall drawing is sold or otherwise transferred but is not a certificate or a drawing.

DIAGRAM

This is a diagram for the Sol LeWitt wall drawing number 37. It should accompany the certificate if the wall drawing is sold or otherwise transferred but is not a certificate or a drawing.

LEO CASTELLI INC

4 EAST 77 ST • NEW YORK 100?

Dr. Giuseppe Panza
Milan, Italy

17 April 1973

NO.

ROBERT BARRY	9	IT CAN ONLY BE KNOWN AS SOMETHING ELSE 1969	
			$1,800.00
	33	UNTITLED SLIDE PIECE 1972	
		81 35mm slides	
		40 slides with text	
		41 blank slides	$1,800.00
		total:	$3,600.00

BUTTERFIELD 8-4820

A part of a piece.

It could be with other things, or it could be alone. It could be part of something else and be dependent on it. It can be distinguished from other things and it could effect them.

It has some variety and an origin.

It has been arranged, but it could be changed. It is interrelated. It has some continuity, possibilities and limitations.

It can be appreciated, defended and repeated. It can also be avoided, isolated, restricted, removed, replaced and destroyed.

It has been influenced. So far it has been preserved.

It may seem familiar or strange or uncertain. It might be discussed, being rejected or accepted. It is vulnerable.

Robert Barry

1972

BASIC FORMAT FOR
WIRE INSTALLATION
FLOOR TO CEILING
90° ANGLE
SIDE VIEW
R. BARRY '68

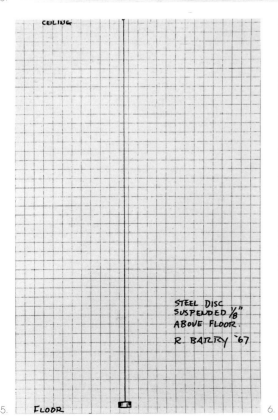

STEEL DISC
SUSPENDED ⅛"
ABOVE FLOOR.
R. BARRY '67

RADIATION INSTALLATION; CESIUM-137
1969

MUST BE INSTALLED OUTSIDE.
(EXAMPLE: ON ROOF
IN PARK
BURIED UNDERGROUND
IN FOREST, MOUNTAIN
IN THE RO...)

R.B.

BASIC FORMAT FOR
HANGING STRING
PIECE.
R. BARRY '68

ROBERT BARRY

1. *It Can Only Be Known as Something Else*, 1969. RB5
2. *A Part of a Piece*, 1972. RB 13
3. *Untitled*, 1975. RB 21
4. *Wire Installation*, 1968. RB 3
5. *Steel Disc Suspended* 1/8 *in. Above Floor*, 1967. RB 1
6. *Radiation Installation; Cesium 137*, 1969. RB 4
7. *String Piece*, 1968. RB 2
8. *It Is Always Changing*, 1970. RB 17
9. *Untitled*, 1967. RB 9
10. *360°*, 1968. RB 16
11. *It Can Seem to Be...*, 1971 - 1972. RB 10
12. *It Has Variety. It Can Change....*,1969-1971. RB 7
13. *F.M. Carrier Wave (Approx. 98 MC)*, 1968. RB 8

Leo Castelli

8 July 1976

Dr. Giuseppe Panza
Corso di Porta Romana 78-1
Milano 20122
Italy

Dear Dr. Panza,

Robert Barry has asked me to respond to your letter to him of 7 June. He has been out of town for several weeks and just now received it.

The following Barry pieces were sent to you in Zurich in March of this year:
Refrain (LC#45)
Appearances (LC # 40)
Untitled drawing (LC#D-10)

The "It is always changing piece" is titled <u>Art Work</u>, 1970 (LC # 36) and the complete text is
It is always changing.
It has order.
It doesn't have a specific place.
It affects other things.
It may be accessible but go unnoticed.
Part of it may also be part of something else.
Some of it is familiar.
Some of it is strange.
Knowing of it changes it.

The documentation for the piece is a framed page from the catalogue of the "Information" show at the Museum of Modern Art, New York, 1970. It was sent to you along with the other works to Zurich.

The two other works you ask about - "Something which is unknown to me" and "Something that is searching for me" belong to Paul Maenz. When this was discovered, you took the slide piece "Refrain" and the untitled drawing instead.

I hope this clears up your questions. If you need any further information, let me know.

Sincerely,

Janelle Reiring
420 West Broadway   New York 10012   Telephone (212) 431-5160

8.

9.

10.

11.

12.

13.

17.

14.

18.

15.

16.

19.

HANNE DARBOVEN

1. *45 Drawings*, 1971 - 1972. HD 6

2. *51 Drawings*, 1971 - 1972. HD 4

3. *43 Drawings*, 1971 - 1972. HD 5

4. *Drawings nos. 1-2-3*, 1972. HD 3,
   The Solomon R. Guggenheim Foundation
   (Panza Gift)

5. *Index: 17k - 58k*, 1969. HD 7

6. *27k - No 8 - No 26*, 1968 - 1969. HD 9

1.

2.

3.

4.

5.

6/1.

6/2.

7/1.

7/2.

7/3.

8/1.

9/1.

8/2.

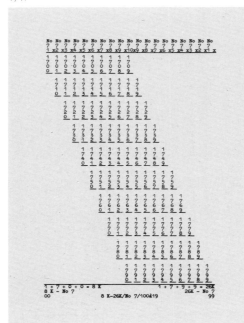

9/2.

10/1.

10/2.

11/1.

11/2

12/1

13/1.

11/3.

12/2

13/2.

15/1.

14.

15/2.

16/1.

17.

18.

19.

16/2.

20/1.

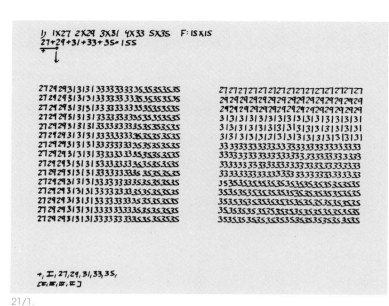

1) 1×27 2×29 3×31 4×33 5×35   F:15×15
27+29+31+33+35=155

+,I,27,29,31,33,35,
[II,III,IV,V]

21/1.

index-zeichnungen: ↓→ /①→45/②/③/④

(3×5=15)   K: 15×15=225:5= 45   (1+2+3+4+5=15)

indices: zeichnungen: ①→45

K:5 / zahl ①   K:225 / zahl 45

Ⅰ abschnitt 0→15   Ⅱ abschnitt 16→30   Ⅲ abschnitt 31→45

mamme darborn / 1972/1973 / (ordner: 4)

20/2.

1) 1×12 2×14 3×16 4×18 5×20   F:15×15
12+14+16+18+20=80

+,I,12,14,16,18,20,
[II,III,IV,V]

16/3.

zeichnungen: ↓→ /31(ã3)→45(ã3)/Ⅲ.abschnitt

1	1	1	1	1	1	1	1	1	1	1	1	1	1	1
2	2	2	2	2	2	2	2	2	2	2	2	2	2	2
3	3	3	3	3	3	3	3	3	3	3	3	3	3	3
K:155	K:160	K:165	K:170	K:175	K:180	K:185	K:190	K:195	K:200	K:205	K:210	K:215	K:220	K:225
31	32	33	34	35	36	37	38	39	40	41	42	43	44	45

mamme darborn / 1972/1973 / (ordner: 3)

21/2.

Varianten-aufzeichnungen
1 ⟶ 99

(ordner: 5)

mamme darborn / 1972/1973

22/1.

Varianten-aufzeichnungen
1 ⟶ 99

(ordner: 6)

mamme darborn / 1972/1973

23/1.

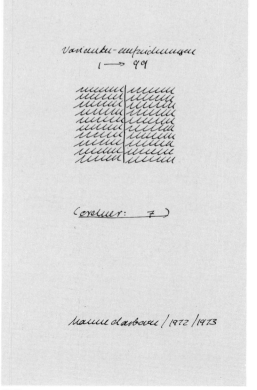

Varianten-aufzeichnungen
1 ⟶ 99

(ordner: 7)

mamme darborn / 1972/1973

24/1.

266

25/1.

25/2.

26/1.

22/2.

23/2.

24/2.

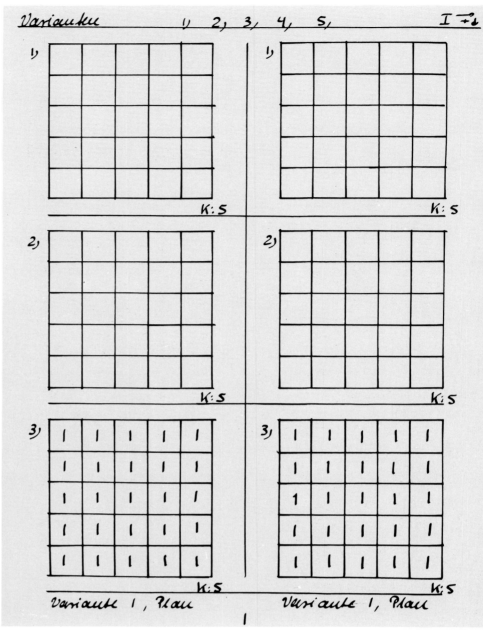

Varianten   1) 2, 3, 4, 5,   I →↓

1)   1)

K: 5   K: 5

2)   2)

K: 5   K: 5

3)

1	1	1	1	1
1	1	1	1	1
1	1	1	1	1
1	1	1	1	1
1	1	1	1	1

3)

1	1	1	1	1
1	1	1	1	1
1	1	1	1	1
1	1	1	1	1
1	1	1	1	1

K: 5   K: 5

Variante 1, Plan   Variante 1, Plan

1

27.   26/2.

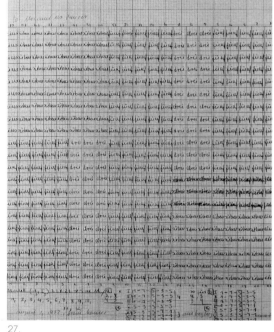

Varianten—Pläne

zahlen:

1 ⟶ 99

(Ordner: 10)

Hummelsborn 1972/1973

28/1.

[→↓   1) 2, 3, 4, 5,   Varianten

1)
46	48	50	52	54
46	48	50	52	54
46	48	50	52	54
46	48	50	52	54
46	48	50	52	54
K: 250

1)
46	46	46	46	46
48	48	48	48	48
50	50	50	50	50
52	52	52	52	52
54	54	54	54	54
K: 250

2)
48	49	50	51	52
48	49	50	51	52
48	49	50	51	52
48	49	50	51	52
48	49	50	51	52
K: 250

2)
48	48	48	48	48
49	49	49	49	49
50	50	50	50	50
51	51	51	51	51
52	52	52	52	52
K: 250

3)
50	50	50	50	50
50	50	50	50	50
50	50	50	50	50
50	50	50	50	50
50	50	50	50	50
K: 250

3)
50	50	50	50	50
50	50	50	50	50
50	50	50	50	50
50	50	50	50	50
50	50	50	50	50
K: 250

28/2.

29.

1.

2.

ON KAWARA

1. *Oct. 24. 1971*, New York 1971. OK 1
2. *One Millions Years*, 1970 - 1971. OK 3
3. *Oct. 26. 1971*, New York 1971. OK 2
4. *Oct. 29. 1971*, New York 1971. OK 4

3.

4.

ROMAN OPALKA

460.260-464.052, 1965. RO 1

VINCENZO AGNETTI

No, March 30, 1973. VA 1

LAWRENCE WEINER

4.

THE RESIDUE OF A FLARE
IGNITED UPON A BOUNDARY

1.

A STONE LEFT UNTURNED

5.

A STAKE SET IN THE GROUND IN DIRECT LINE
WITH A STAKE SET IN THE GROUND
ON AN ADJACENT COUNTRY

2.

OVER AND OVER . OVER AND OVER
AND OVER AND OVER . AND OVER AND OVER

6.

ONE KILOGRAM OF LACQUER
POURED UPON A FLOOR

3.

SMUDGED

7.

FLUSHED

JAN DIBBETS

1. *The Sperone Gallery Photographed from Wall A to Wall B,*
   Torino 1971. JD 4

2. *The Shortest Day of 1970 Photographed in My House Every 6*
   Minutes, Amsterdam 1970. JD 1
   Tide, 1969. JD 2

3. *0°-135° Cross,* 1972. JD 9

4. *Horizon Up and Down (Land),* 1971. JD 6

5. *A White Wall,* Amsterdam 1971. JD 5

6. *Shadows in the Sperone Gallery,* Torino, March 10, 1971.
   JD 3

2.

5.

3.

6.

4.

7.

9.

10.

11.

8.

12.

1/1.

2/1.

2/2.

1/2.

1. *CDBF - Ritorno ai campi d'azione abbandonati, 1974 - 1975. CC 9*

2. *Trasfigurazione/Separazione Due, 1966 - 1974. CC3*

3. *L'opera che continua a porsi..., 1974. CC1*

4. *Sehspass 01 (Sequoia Semper Virens), 1976. CC 13*

3.

4.

273

1.

5.

2.

19 MAY 1970

MR. GUISEPPE PANZA
CORSO DI PORTA ROMANA 78/1
MILANO, ITALY

DEAR MR. PANZA:

THANK YOU FOR YOUR CABLE INQUIRY REGARDING THE WORK OF JOSEPH KOSUTH.

I HAVE ONE WORK CURRENTLY AVAILABLE FOR SALE. THE WORK IS ENTITLED "TWENTY-FIVE WORKS IN A CONTEXT AS ONE WORK"
    A. CONCEPT AS ART (AS IDEA)
    B. INFORMATION AS ART (AS IDEA)
    C. VISUAL EXPERIENCE AS ART (AS IDEA)
    D. INVESTIGATION OF CHANCE FOR NON-COMPOSITIONAL
        PRESENTATION.
    (THIS IS THE FOURTH INVESTIGATION IN THE SERIES
     ART AS IDEA AS IDEA, BEGUN IN 1965.)

THE ACTUAL WORK CONSISTS OF TWENTY-NINE STICKERS WITH LOCATIONS, NOTES AND DIRECTIONS TYPED ON THE STICKERS. THE STICKERS ARE ON PLASTIC, AND CAN BE ADHERED TO ANY SURFACE, WALL, OR NOTE-BOOK.

THE PURCHASE PRICE OF THE WORK IS $1200.00.

PROJECT FOR SEVEN SQUARE GREY PAINTINGS ON CANVAS WITH WORDS AS ART, DRAWING, 8" X 10". FRAMED IN PLEXIGLASS FRAME.

PURCHASE PRICE, $300.00.

I WILL LOOK FORWARD TO HEARING FROM YOU.

EUGENIA BUTLER

3.

ONE TWO THREE FOUR FIVE
SIX SEVEN EIGHT NINE TEN
ELEVEN TWELVE THIRTEEN FOURTEEN FIFTEEN
SIXTEEN SEVENTEEN EIGHTEEN NINETEEN TWENTY
TWENTY-ONE TWENTY-TWO TWENTY-THREE TWENTY-FOUR TWENTY-FIVE

4.

THREE COLOR SENTENCE

ART

6/9.

NINE

6/1.

GREY

6/2.

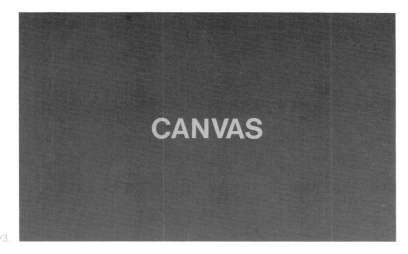

JOSEPH KOSUTH

1. *One and Eight - a Description (Green)*, 1965. JK 4
   One and Eight - a Description (Blue), 1965. JK 5
   One and Eight - a Description (Red), 1965. JK 6

2. *Clear, Square, Glass, Leaning*, 1965. JK 8

3. *Twenty - Five Works in a Contest as One Work (Special investigation)*, New York 1968 - Los Angeles 1969. JK 23

4. *Five Five's (to Donald Judd)*, 1965. JK 3

5. *Three Color Sentence*, 1965. JK 1

6. *Nine Paintings with Words as Art*, 1966. JK 27

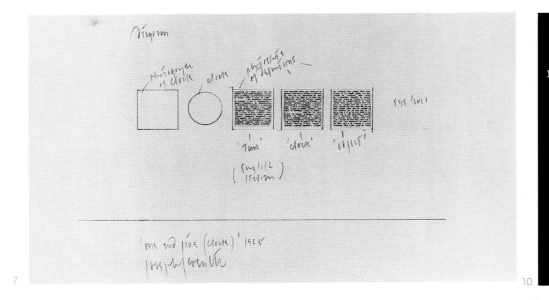

Nothing [ˈnʌθɪŋ], I. *pron. & s.* nichts; das Nichts, die Kleinigkeit; (nought) die Null (also *fig.*); (*pl.*) Nichtigkeiten; — but, — else than, nur, lediglich; no —! rein garnichts, nicht so viel; — of a gentleman, keineswegs ein feiner, gebildeter Herr; **1.** (*with verbs*) be —, an nichts glauben (*Rel.*); there is — in it, das hat nichts auf sich; that is — to me, das ist mir ganz gleichgültig; he is — to us, er steht uns in keiner Beziehung nahe; he does — but . . ., er tut nichts als . . .; it will come to —, daraus wird nichts; (*coll.*) — doing, nichts zu machen, umsonst, nichts los; feel like — on earth, sich hundeelend fühlen; make — of, sich (*Dat.*) nichts aus (einer Sache) machen; nichts mit (einer S.) anfangen können; (*Prov.*) — venture, — have, frisch gewagt ist halb gewonnen.

ul'ti-mate, 1 ul'tɪ-mɪt; 2 ŭl'tĭ-mat, *a.* **1.** Beyond which there is none other; last of a series; final.
As a general rule, no man is able to foretell distinctly the *ulti-mate*, permanent results of any great social change. CHANNING *Works, Laboring Classes* lect. ii, p. 58. [A. U. A. 1883.] **2.** Fundamental or essential; hence, not susceptible of further analysis; elementary; primary; as, *ultimate* truths; an *ultimate* idea. **3.** *Entom.* Last: said of the stage succeeding the scarabæidoid in the larval development of hypermetamorphic beetles, as oil-beetles. **4.** [Rare.] Most distant; farthest. **5.** *Mech.* Designating the maximum strength of a body, or a strain of the least intensity sufficient to cause rupture. [< LL. *ultimatus*, pp. of L. *ultimo*, come to an end.

noth-ing (nuth'ing). [Orig. two words, *no thing.*] **I.** *n.* No thing, not anything, or naught (as, to see, do, or say *nothing*; "I opened wide the door: Darkness there, and *nothing* more!" Poe's "Raven"); no part, share, or trace (*of*: as, the place shows *nothing* of its former magnificence; there is *nothing* of his father about him); also, that which is non-existent (as, to create a world out of *nothing*; to reduce something to *nothing*, as by a process of extinction or annihilation); also, something of no importance or significance (as, "Gratiano speaks an infinite deal of *nothing*," Shakspere's "Merchant of Venice," i. 1. 114; "The defeat itself was *nothing* . . . but the death of the Prince was a blow," Besant's "Coligny," ix.); a trifling action, matter, circumstance, or thing; a trivial remark (as, "In pompous *nothings* on his side, and civil assents on that of his cousins, their time passed": Jane Austen's "Pride and Prejudice," xv.); a person of no importance, or a nobody or nonentity; in *arith.*, that which is without quantity or magnitude; also, a cipher or naught (0).

nothing, *n.* nulla, niente; zero, *m.*; nessuna cosa, *f.* ~ *at all*, niente affatto, nulla a. *make* ~ *of*, non capire affatto. *a mere* ~, una cosa da nulla, una bagattella, un'inezia. ~**ness,** *n.* nullità, *f.*; oblio, *m.*

Nothing [nuth'-ing], *s.* **1.** Nada, ninguna cosa. **2.** Nadería, cosa de poca entidad, friolera. **3.** Estado de lo que no tiene existencia; la nada. **4.** La cifra 0; cero. *That is nothing to me*, Eso nada me importa. *It is good for nothing*, Para nada sirve. *He had nothing to live upon*, No tenía nada con que mantenerse. *It signifies nothing*, Eso no significa nada, nada quiere decir. *He made nothing of his labour*, Nada sacó de su trabajo.

nothing [ˈnʌθiŋ] intet, ikke noget; ubetydelighed, nul; slet ikke, ikke spor af (fx. *I have been fortunate; I've had a number of offers ... Fortunate nothing! They were damned lucky to get you); a mere ~* en ren bagatel; *~ at all* slet intet; *~ (else) but* intet andet end, kun; *~ doing* T der er ikke noget at gøre; du kan tro nej; det bliver der ikke noget af; *the police has ~ on him* politiet har ikke noget på ham (ɔ: intet anklagemateriale); *they have ~ on us* (amr. T) de har ikke noget at lade os høre; *she is ~ if not pretty* hun er meget smuk; smuk det er hun; *~ like as large* ikke nær så stor; langt fra så stor; *make ~ of* ikke regne for noget; ikke få noget ud af; *I can make ~ of it* jeg kan ikke blive klog på det; *~ short of* intet mindre end; *~ venture, ~ have* hvo intet vover, intet vinder.

13.

nothing [ˈnʌθiŋ] pron. Rien ; *nothing but,* rien que ; *to see nothing,* ne rien voir. ‖ Rien de ; *nothing else matters,* rien d'autre n'importe, tout le reste n'est rien ; *nothing much,* pas grand-chose ; *nothing more,* rien de plus ; *nothing new,* rien de nouveau ; *there is nothing for it but to,* il n'y a rien d'autre à faire qu'à. ‖ Loc. *Nothing doing,* rien à faire ; *to be nothing if not intelligent,* être intelligent avant tout ; *to do nothing of the sort,* n'en faire rien.
— n. Rien *m.; as if nothing had happened,* comme si de rien n'était ; *for nothing,* gratuitement (free of charge) ; pour rien (in vain) ; sans raison (groundlessly) ; *for next to nothing,* pour trois fois rien. ‖ Rien, objet (*m.*) d'indifférence ; *to be nothing to,* n'être rien pour, être indifférent à ; *to make nothing of,* ne pas se soucier de (not to care about) ; ne rien comprendre à (not to understand) ; ne pas faire cas de (not to value). ‖ Rien, néant *m.; to come to nothing,* aboutir à zéro, faire fiasco, venir à rien. ‖ Rien *m.,* vétille *f.; a mere nothing,* un zéro (person) ; une bagatelle, une broutille (thing).
— adv. Pas du tout, aucunement, en rien ; *nothing less than,* rien moins que.

14.

mēaning, s.: disegno, *m.,* intenzione, *f.,* intento, *m.;* significazione, *f.,* significato, senso, sentimento, *m.*

15.

Silen-ce; silènzo *m.* Dead —, silenzio mortale. To —, far tacere; spegner il fuoco di. Keep —, tacére. Keep — about, tacere. Pass over in —, passare sotto silenzio. — gives consent, chi tace acconsente. —! zitti! **-cer**; bariletto di scaricamento, camera di scarico, marmitta *f.* **-t**; tácito, taciturno. **-tly**; tacitaménte, pian piano.

16.

277

DANIEL BUREN

*White and Green Papers Collage,
Varese, December 1968. DB 1*

1/A.

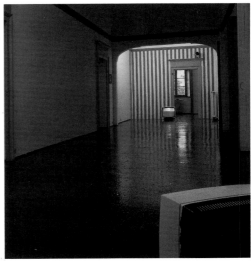

1.

JEAN TINGUELY

1. *La Vittoria (Mille grazia)*, Milano 1970.
   JTI 4
2. *La Vittoria (Vive Panza)*, Milano 1970. JTI 2
3. *La Vittoria (Per Panza)*, Milano 1970. JTI 3
4. *La Vittoria*, Milano 1970. JTI 1

1/1.

2.

1/2.

3.

4.

MARIA NORDMAN

1. *Room Determined by One istant of Light*, New Port Beach 1973. MN 5, FAI (Fondo per l'Ambiente Italiano)

2. *Toselli Room*, Milano 1974. MN 2, The Solomon R. Guggenheim Foundation (Panza Gift)

3. *Varese Room*, 1976. MN 12, The Solomon R. Guggenheim Foundation (Panza Gift)

4. *Irwine Room*, 1973. MN 1, The Solomon R. Guggenheim Foundation (Panza Gift)

5. *Villa Scheibler Prosapal I*, 1976. MN 13

9.

6.

7.

8/1.

8/2.

1. *Dot Painting*, 1963 - 1965. RI 1
2. *Scrim (Ace Gallery)*, Los Angeles 1972. RI 5,
   FAI (Fondo per l'Ambiente Italiano)
3. *Varese Scrim*, 1973. RI 6,
   The Solomon R. Guggenheim Foundation (Panza Gift)
4. *Plastic Disc*, 1968 - 1969. RI 3
5. *12' Acrylic Column*, 1970 - 1971. RI 4

8.

7.

6.

9.

7.

10.

282

JAMES TURRELL

1. *Afruml*, 1967. JT 2, The Solomon R. Guggenheim Foundation (Panza Gift)
2. *Iltar*, 1976. JT 11, The Solomon R. Guggenheim Foundation (Panza Gift)
3. *Argus*, Varese 1976. JT 1, The Solomon R. Guggenheim Foundation (Panza Gift)
4. *Wallen*, Varese 1976. JT 10, The Solomon R. Guggenheim Foundation (Panza Gift)

ERIC ORR

Zero Mass, 1974. EO 1.
The Solomon R. Guggenheim Foundation (Panza Gift)

1.

1/A.   **ZERO MASS**

LARRY BELL

Two Glass Walls, 1971 - 1972. LB 4

MAURIZIO MOCHETTI   Milano, 19 novembre 1976

Specchio con sorgente luminosa

Il lavoro è realizzato con uno specchio di piccole dimensioni
(Ø mm.20) e una fonte luminosa. Lo specchio - autoadesivo -
può essere applicato in qualsiasi posizione (parete, pavimento,
soffitto) in modo tale però da permettere la relazione tra la
fonte luminosa, l'immagine riflessa e l'occhio. Quando la luce
colpisce lo specchio questo diventa fonte di luce.

Il lavoro è in numero di 5 esemplari.
La prima versione è stata realizzata per la collezione Giuseppe
Panza di Biumo.

maurizio mochetti

1

MAURIZIO MOCHETTI   Milano, 19 novembre 1976

Grande specchio con punto opaco

Il lavoro si realizza costruendo un telaio in legno grande quanto
la parete scelta. Sul telaio viene applicata una plastica speciale
perfettamente specchiante. Il punto nero opaco autoadesivo viene
posto al centro della parete-specchio ad una altezza di cm. 160 da
terra (orizzonte ottico).

Il lavoro è un esemplare unico realizzato per la collezione Giuseppe Panza di Biumo.

maurizio mochetti

2

MAURIZIO MOCHETTI   Milano, 19 novembre 1976

Linea di mercurio

L'opera è realizzata con un unico tubo di vetro (Ø esterno mm. 8,
interno mm. 5). La lunghezza è da determinarsi in funzione dello
spazio in cui il lavoro viene installato. Il tubo viene riempito
di mercurio sul posto e sigillato alle estremità. La linea di
mercurio non deve essere vincolata al pavimento.
La sorgente luminosa, esterna al tubo, deve essere posta in modo
che il rapporto tra fonte luminosa, immagine riflessa e occhio sia
possibile per tutta la lunghezza del tubo.

Il lavoro è in numero di 5 esemplari.
La prima versione è stata realizzata per la collezione Giuseppe
Panza di Biumo.

maurizio mochetti

3

CERTIFICATO DI AUTENTICAZIONE -

Io maurizio mochetti' dichiaro di
essere l'unico autore dell'opera
denominata (Contatore digitale
luminoso posto in uno spazio
indica continuamente il numero
crescente e decrescente delle persone
che si trovano in quello spazio)
progettato e costruito nell'anno
1971 in numero di 5 versioni.
Una di proprietà del Sig. Giuseppe
Panza Conte di Biumo -

maurizio mochetti'

Roma 4 maggio 1971

4

5.

6.

CERTIFICATO DI AUTENTICAZIONE-

Io maurizio mochetti dichiaro di
essere l'unico autore dell'opera
denominata "Cilindri luce-suono,,
progettata e realizzata nell'anno
1969.
L'opera è stata eseguita in numero
di 3 versioni differenti - Una di
proprietà del Sig. Giuseppe Panza
Conte di Biumo
                    maurizio mochetti

Dati tecnici:
L'opera consiste in due cilindri
di Alluminio del diametro di cm
30, autonomi, corrispondenti,
disposti l'uno di fronte all'altro
ad una distanza X aventi un
foro centrale di uguale diametro -
Dal cilindro no 1 parte automatica_
mente ogni 15 secondi un impulso
luminoso, al quale corrisponde
nel cilindro no 2 un suono -

                    maurizio mochetti
Roma 26 marzo 1971

7.

Carta di Autenticazione

Io maurizio mochetti dichiaro di essere
l'autore dell'opera denominata Specchio
ø 10 mm. progettata e realizzata nel 1972
L'opera è stata eseguita in numero cinque
versioni identiche - Una di queste opere
è di proprietà del Sig -
Esiste un solo punto da cui l'osservatore può
individuare l'immagine del punto riflessa
nello specchio sul pavimento.

                    maurizio mochetti

Dati tecnici-
Specchio ø 10 mm posto in un punto qualsiasi
del pavimento - punto autoadesivo ø 20 mm.
posto in un punto del soffitto.

                    maurizio mochetti
Milano 16/marzo 1973.

8.

9.

5. *Punto di luce*, 1969 - 1970. MM 6

6. *Elastico estensibile*, 1969. MM 7

7. *Cilindri luce-suono*, 1969. MM5

8. *Specchio Ø 10 mm.*, 1972. MM 11

9. *Generatrice*, 1968. MM 2

10. *Sfera con movimento verticale pseudo perpetuo*, 1968. MM 1

11. *Asse oscillante*, 1968-1969. MM 3

12. *O → X → O*, 1969. MM 4

11.

10.

12.

1.

DIM
TRAILS

3.

5.

FACING BOTH WAYS

4.

6.

288

HAMISH FULTON

1. *Untitled (4 colour photos of Florida wild life)*, 1971. HF 6

2. *Untitled 2/3*, 1972. HF2

3. *Dim Trails 2/3*, 1972. HF 4

4. *Eight Photographic Works*, 1970. HF 1

5. *Facing Both Ways 2/3*, 1972. HF 3

6. *Untitled (Artist in front of a Lake) 2/3*, 1971. HF 5

7. *Goat Fell Mountain, Isle of Arran, Scotland, Spring 1970*. HF 7

8. *Untitled (Iceland 1975) 2/3*, Late Spring 1975. HF 12

9. *Untitled (Landscape with cows)*, 1970. HF 8

10. *Skyline Ridge 2/3, Summer 1974*. HF 13

11. *Untitled (4 photos with eagles)*, 1970. HF 10

12. *Untitled*, 1970. HF 9

13. *France on the Horizon 1/3*, Early Summer 1975. HF 14

14. *Looking at Tomorrow (Scottish North West Highlands)*, 1974.
    HF 15

14/2.

14/3.

14/4.

13.

14/1.

14/5.

1.

DOUG WHEELER

1. *Ace Gallery Installation (Environmental light)*, January 1970. DW 1, The Solomon R. Guggenheim Foundation (Panza Gift)

2. *Amsterdam Stedelijk Museum Installation (Environmental light)*, September 1969. DW 3

3. *PSAD Synthetic Desert III*, 1971. DW 6, The Solomon R. Guggenheim Foundation (Panza Gift)

4. *Luminefepous Space*, 1968 - 1975. DW 8, The Solomon R. Guggenheim Foundation (Panza Gift)

5. *Eindhoven Stedelijk Van Abbemuseum Installation (Environmental light)*, 1969 - 1970. DW 2

2.

3.

4.

5.

13.

14.

WALTER DE MARIA

1. *High energy Bar no. 75*
2. *Calendar no. 1/12, 1961 - 1975. WM 4*
3. *Balldrop,* 1961. DW 1, The Solomon R. Guggenheim Foundation (Panza Gift)

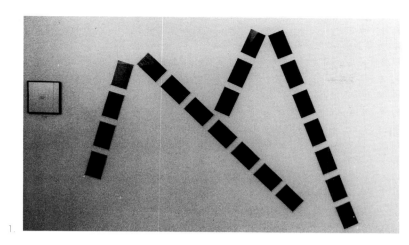

DAVID TREMLETT

1. *Cue*, 1974. DT 1
2. *Watching the Way the Rabbits Run in Milwaukee*, 1975. DT2
3. *Scotland 1/2 (Lock Ness)*, 1975. DT 7
4. *Scotland 1/3 (Lock Ness)*, 1975. DT 8

1.

RICHARD LONG

1. *Square Wood Sculpture*, 1967. RLO 1,
   The Solomon R. Guggenheim Foundation

2. *Sculpture at Galerie Lambert*, Milano 1969. RLO 4,
   The Solomon R. Guggenheim Foundation

3. *Untitled-England*, 1967. RLO 2,
   The Solomon R. Guggenheim Foundation

4. *Line of Lake Stones*, 1983. RLO 19,
   The Solomon R. Guggenheim Foundation

2.

4.

3.

5. *Sculpture at Konrad Fischer*, Dusseldorf, July 1969. RLO 8,
The Solomon R. Guggenheim Foundation

6. *Sculpture Untitled June 1968 England*, 1968. RLO 3,
The Solomon R. Guggenheim Foundation

7. *2¹⁄₂ Mile Walk Sculpture*, 1969. RLO 6,
The Solomon R. Guggenheim Foundation

8. A *Sculpture by Richard Long, Wiltshire*,
12-15 October 1969. RLO 5,
The Solomon R. Guggenheim Foundation

7.

Line 1	55 yards	Walked 32 times	Total distance 1 mile
Line 2	55 yards	Walked 24 times	Total distance ¾ mile
Line 3	55 yards	Walked 16 times	Total distance ½ mile
Line 4	55 yards	Walked 8 times	Total distance ¼ mile

5.

8.

6.

Revised catalogue
of works in the Panza Collection
from the 50s, 60s and 70s

Artists are listed in alphabetical order with essential biographical information. Pages where photographs of works can be found are indicated. Works in the list are preceded by one or more numbers referring to the relevant photographs. Numbers in bold type refer to illustrated plates, those in standard type to the photographic catalogue.

Works are listed in the order laid down by the catalogue code of the Panza Collection, comprising an acronym and a serial number. Each entry records the title, date, technique and dimensions of works, expressed mainly in Imperial units of measurement. Where the artist has used the decimal metric system, the equivalent measurement in Imperial units has been added in brackets.

Works now in the custody of museums or foundations are indicated (see Notes for Readers).

VINCENZO AGNETTI (Milan, Italy, 1926-1981) p. 269

1. *No*, March 30, 1973. Two telegrams and receipts, 100 x 51 cm. (39 ⅝ x 20 in.) VA 1
   Monologue, May 9, 1973. Chrome cassette. VA 2
   Statale Speech, May 5, 1972. Chrome cassette. VA 3

CARL ANDRE (Quincy, Massachusetts, 1935) pp. 92-96, 209-210

53.4. *Reef*, 1966. 80 orange styrofoam planks, lenghtwise from wall to wall, each 20 x 10 x 108 in., overall 20 x 800 x 108 in. CA 1, The Solomon R. Guggenheim Foundation
1. *Steel Piece*, October 1967. 100 hot rolled steel plates, each 0,5 x 50 x 50 cm. (⁵/₁₆ x 19 ⁵/₄ x 19 ⁵/₄ in.), overall 0,5 x 250 x 1000 cm. (⁵/₁₆ x 98 ⁵/₄ x 395 in.) CA 2, The Solomon R. Guggenheim Foundation
47.50. *2 x 18 Aluminium Lock*, 1968. 36 aluminium plates, each 1 x 100 x 100 cm. (⁵/₈ x 39 ½ x 39 ½ in.), overall 1 x 200 x 1800 cm. (⁵/₈ x 79 x 711 in.) CA 3, The Solomon R. Guggenheim Foundation
48. *Hague Steel Piece*, 1968. 36 hot rolled steel plates, each 1 x 100 x 100 cm. (⁵/₈ x 39 ½ x 39 ½ in.), overall 1 x 600 x 600 cm. (⁵/₈ x 237 x 237 in.) CA 4, The Solomon R. Guggenheim Foundation
49.50. *Fall*, 1968. 21 L-shaped hot rolled steel units, against wall, each 1 x 28 x 72 x 72 in., overall 1 x 72 x 72 x 588 in. CA 5, The Solomon R. Guggenheim Foundation
10. *Brass Piece*, 1969. 249 thin brass units, in line on floor, each 6,5 x 8,5 cm. (2 ⅛ x 3 ⅝ in.), overall 8,5 x 1835 cm. (3 ⅝ x 722 ½ in.) CA 6, The Solomon R. Guggenheim Foundation
7. *Zinc Ribbon Piece*, 1969-1971. ¹/₁₆ in. thick zinc ribbon coiled/uncoiled on edge on floor, 9 x 2100 x 0,1 cm. (3 ½ x 826 ⁵/₄ x ¹/₁₆ in.) CA 7, The Solomon R. Guggenheim Foundation
3. *Brass Square Piece*, March 1972. 100 brass units, each ¹/₁₆ x ¹/₁₆ x ¹/₆₄ in., overall ⅞ x ⅞ x ¹/₆₄ in. CA 8
2. *Finely Divided Square Piece (for Marianne)*, May 1970. 882 cold rolled steel chips, each ¹/₆₄ x ⁹/₃₂ x ⁹/₁₆ in., overall ¹/₆₄ x 11 ¹⁵/₁₆ x 11 ¹⁵/₁₆ in. CA 9
52.5. *Copper Square*, 1973. 100 copper plates, each 0,5 x 50 x 50 cm. (⁵/₁₆ x 19 ⁵/₄ x 19 ⁵/₄ in.), overall 0,5 x 500 x 500 cm. (⁵/₁₆ x 197 ½ x 197 ½ in.) CA 10, The Solomon R. Guggenheim Foundation
6. *2001 Slope*, 1968. 6 hot rolled steel plates, extending at angle from base of wall, 5 units each ⅝ x 36 x 36 in., 1 trapezoid unit ⅝ x 36 x 33 in., overall ⅝ x 36 x 216 in. CA 11, The Solomon R. Guggenheim Foundation
46. *Portland Regulus*, 1973-1974. 18 river stones and 17 geological specimens on 35 concrete blocks, each block 2 x 12 x 12 in., overall 6 x 204 x 300 in. CA 12, The Solomon R. Guggenheim Foundation
54.9. *Seventeenth Copper Triode*, October 1975. 25 copper plates in a tee (17 along base wall, 8 extending), each unit 0,5 x 50 x 50 cm. (⁵/₁₆ x 19 ⁵/₄ x 19 ⁵/₄ in.), overall 0,5 x 850 x 450 cm. (⁵/₁₆ x 335 x 177 in.) CA 13, The Solomon R. Guggenheim Foundation

8. *Fifth Copper Triode*, October 1975. 7 copper plates in a tee (5 along base wall, 2 extending), each unit 0,5 x 50 x 50 cm. (⁵/₁₆ x 19 ⁵/₄ x 19 ⁵/₄ in.) CA 14, The Solomon R. Guggenheim Foundation
8. *Third Copper Triode*, October 1975. 4 copper plates in a tee (3 along base wall, 1 extending), each unit 0,5 x 50 x 50 cm. (⁵/₁₆ x 19 ⁵/₄ x 19 ⁵/₄ in.), overall 0,5 x 150 x 100 cm. (⁵/₁₆ x 59 x 39 in.) CA 15, The Solomon R. Guggenheim Foundation

ART AND LANGUAGE (Terry Atkinson, 1939. Michael Baldwin, 1945. David Bainbridge, 1941. Harold Hurrell, 1940. All born in England)

The French Army: 22 Sentences, 1967. Text. AL 1
Hot Warm Cool Cold, 1967. Text. AL 2
Translation Piece I-II-III-IV-V 2/3 1972. Five portfolios with typed sheets. AL 3
Olivet Discourse, 1971. Text. AL 4

ROBERT BARRY (New York City, 1936) pp. 137-139, 258-260

5. *Steel Disc Suspended ⅛ in. Above Floor*, 1967. Nylon string, steel disc 2 in. diameter and ⅝ in. high. RB 1
7. *String Piece*, 1968. String extending floor to ceiling. RB 2
4. *Wire Installation*, 1968. Wire extending floor to ceiling to floor at 90° angle. RB 3
6. *Radiation Installation; Cesium 137*, 1969. Lead container 1 x 1 x 3 in. approx. Must be installed outside. RB 4
1. *It Can Only Be Known as Something Else*, 1969. Text. RB 5
114. *It Is Wholly Indeterminate. It Has No Specific Traits....*, 1970. Text. RB 6
12. *It Has Variety. It Can Change...*, 1969-1971. 60 slides with text. RB 7
13. *F. M. Carrier Wave (Approx 98 MC)*, 1968. Wooden box with radio transmitter, 2 x 5 x 7 in. RB 8
9. *Untitled*, 1967. 4 panels each 2 x 2 in., hung 12 in. diagonally from the corners of a wall. RB 9
11. *It Can Seem to Be....*, 1971-1972. 80 slides, 40 with text and 40 blank. RB 10
15. *It Is and It Can Be*, 1971-1972. 80 slides, 40 with text and 40 blank. RB 11
115.18. *Try. All In Now. Here...*, 1972. 80 slides, 40 with text and 40 blank. RB 12, The Solomon R. Guggenheim Foundation (Panza Gift)
2. *A Part of a Piece*, 1972. Text. RB 13
14. *Speculations*, 1973. 80 slides, 20 with text, 20 with blue spot, 40 blank. RB 14
17. *Right. Ever...*, 1973. 80 slides, 20 with text, 20 with blue spot, 40 blank. RB 15
10. *360°*, 1968. Book, 360 pages, drawn line on paper, 29 x 21,5 x 4 cm. (11 ½ x 8 ½ x 1 ½ in.). RB 16
8. *It Is Always Changing.*, 1970. Text. RB 17
19. *Refrain*, 1975. 81 slides, 27 with text and 54 blank. RB 18
16. *Appearances*, 1973. 80 slides, 20 with text, 20 with blue spot, 40 blank. RB 20
3. *Untitled*, 1975. Prestype and pencil on paper, 29 x 37 ¼ in. RB 21

LARRY BELL (Chicago, Illinois, 1939) pp. 164-165, 284

142. *Light Brown Box*, 1968. Coated glass, 51 x 51 x 51 cm. (20 x 20 x 20 in.) LB 1
143. *Two Glass Walls-Diagonal Top*, 1973. 2 coated glass panels, each 72 x 72 in. LB 2
144. *Two Glass Walls*, 1971-1972. 2 coated glass panels, each 96 x 60 in. LB 3
1. *Two Glass Walls*, 1971-1972. 2 coated glass panels, each 72 x 72 in. LB 4

JOSEPH BEUYS (Kleve, West Germany, 1921 - Dusseldorf, West Germany, 1986) p. 199

2. *Fontana Dose,* 1963. Blackboard, 30,5 x 21,5 cm. (12 x 8 ¹/₂ in.) JB 1
1. *Untitled,* 1961. Plastic pail, 16 x 18 x 18 cm. (6 ¹/₄ x 7 ¹/₈ x 7 ¹/₈ in.) JB 2
   Multiple 97/100, 1971. Felt and tape, 16 x 25 x 25 cm. (6 ¹/₄ x 9 ³/₄ x 9 ³/₄ in.) JB 3

STANLEY BROUWN (Paramaribo, Suriname, 1935)

My steps in Torino, 1971. My total number of steps in Torino: 16.827. SB 1
My steps in Milan, 1971. The total number of my steps in Milan in 1971: 168.584. SB 2

DANIEL BUREN (Boulogne, France, 1938) p. 278

1. *White and Green Papers Collage,* Varese, December 1968. Approx. 30 paper sheets. DB 1

VICTOR BURGIN (Sheffield, England, 1941)

Perfomatif Narratif Piece 1/3, 1971. Text with photographs on paper. VB 1
VI 4/9, 1973. Text with photographs on paper. VB 2

PIERPAOLO CALZOLARI (Bologna, Italy, 1943)

Telegram no. 349, April 26, 1976. PC 1
Telegram no. 252, April 27, 1976. PC 2
Telegram no. 20, April 28, 1976. PC 3
Telegram no. 198, April 28, 1976. PC 4
Telegram no. 0705, April 28, 1976. PC 5
Telegram no. 221, April 29, 1976. PC 6

LOUIS CANE (Beaulieu-sur-Mer, France, 1943) p. 248

Red-White Canvas, January 10-1973. Oil on cotton, 505 x 241 cm. (199 ³/₄ x 95 in.) LC 1
Dark Brown Square Canvas, March 18-1973. Oil on cotton, 362 x 344 cm. (142 ¹/₂ x 135 ¹/₂ in.) LC 2
Clear Brown Canvas, November 15-1972. Oil on cotton, 626 x 245 cm. (246 ¹/₂ x 96 ¹/₂ in.) Wall-floor-floor. LC 3
Red Square Canvas, May 1973. Oil on cotton, 440 x 433 cm. (173 ¹/₄ x 171 ¹/₂ in.) LC 4
Yellow Square Canvas, March 25-1973. Oil on cotton, 312 x 321 cm. (123 x 126 ¹/₄ in.) LC 5
Clear Blue Canvas, July 1973. Oil on cotton, 414 x 292 cm. (163 x 115 in.) Wall-floor. LC 6
1. *Dark Blue Canvas,* March 16-1973. Oil on cotton, 618 x 240 cm. (243 ¹/₂ x 94 ¹/₂ in.) LC 7
2. *Red Canvas,* May 15-16, 1973. Oil on cotton, 654 x 243 cm. (257 ¹/₂ x 96 in.) LC 8
Clear Brown Canvas, July 1973. Oil on cotton, 545 x 242 cm. (214 ¹/₂ x 95 ¹/₄ in.) Wall-floor-floor. LC 9
Black-Red Canvas, October 10-1973. Oil on cotton, 402 x 242 cm. (158 ¹/₄ x 95 ¹/₄ in.) Wall-floor. LC 10
Blue Canvas, January 25-1974. Oil on cotton, 547 x 241 cm. (215 ¹/₂ x 95 in.) LC 11
Red Bordeaux Canvas, February 15-1974. Oil on cotton, 495 x 242 cm. (191 x 95 ¹/₂ in.) Wall-floor. LC 12
Drawing, February 4-1973. Coloured pencil and pen on paper, 21 x 27 cm. (8 ¹/₂ X 10 ³/₄ in.) LC 13
Drawing, February 1973. Coloured pencil and pen on paper, 21 x 27 cm. (8 ¹/₂ x 10 ³/₄ in.) LC 14
Drawing, June 1973. Coloured pencil and pen on paper, 21 x 27 cm. (8 ¹/₂ x 10 ³/₄ in.) LC 15
Drawing, May 1974. Coloured pencil and pen on paper, 29,5 x 41,5 cm. (11 ¹/₂ x 16 ¹/₄ in.) LC 16
Imperatrice de Chine no.17, 1975. Oil on cotton, 410 x 460 cm. (161 ¹/₂ x 181 in.) LC 17
No.11, 1974. Oil on cotton, 310 x310 cm. (122 x122 in.) LC 18

CIONI CARPI (Milan, Italy, 1923) p. 273

3. *L'opera che continua a porsi...,* 1974. Drawing, 29,5 x 19,5 cm. (11 ⁵/₈ x 7 ³/₄ in.) CC 1
Trasfigurazione/Sparizione Uno, 1966-1974. Text and

photographs on paper, 2 sets, each 44 x 99 cm. (17 ¹/₄ x 39 in.). Edition 7/15. CC 2
2. *Trasfigurazione/Sparizione Due,* 1966-1974. Text and photographs on paper, 5 sets, each 39 x 81 cm. (15 ¹/₂ x 32 in.). Edition 1/3. CC 3
Trasfigurazione/Sparizione Quattro, 1966-1974. Text and photographs on paper, 5 sets, each 37 x 80 cm. (14 ¹/₂ x 31 ¹/₂ in.). Edition 1/3. CC 4
Trasfigurazione/Sparizione Cinque, 1966-1974. Text and photographs on paper, 4 sets, each 37 x 79 cm. (14 ¹/₂ x 31 in.). Edition of 2. CC 5
55 cm. sul livello del mare 1/5, 1972. 16 mm. film. CC 6
Trasfigurazione Zero, 1966 1974. 16 mm. film. CC 7
Abbiamo creato atipici sistemi 1963-1974. Text and photographs on paper, 9 sets, each 50 x 40 cm. (19 ³/₄ x 15 ⁵/₈ in.). Edition of 9. CC 8
1. *CDFB Ritorno ai campi d'azione abbandonati,* 1974-1975. 100 slides and tape. CC 9
CDFB Whole cello improsession, 1975. Tape. Edition 3/15. CC 10
Per un otto coricato, 1977. 100 slides and tape. CC 11
Sehspass 001 (Quadro Collage), 1964-1977. Mixed media on masonite, 20,5 x 20,5 x 4 cm. (8 x 8 x ¹/₂ in.) CC 12
4. *Sehspass 01 (Sequoia semper virens),* 1976. Mixed media on paper, 40 x 50 cm. (15 ³/₄ x 19 ³/₄ in.) CC 13
Palinsesto 8 stadi, 1963. Mixed media, 50 x 68 cm. (19 ³/₄ x 27 ⁵/₄ in.) CC 14

ALAN CHARLTON (Sheffield, England, 1948) pp. 130-131, 231-234

2. *82 in. Square,* 1970-1972. 2 square holes left side. Acrylic on canvas, 82 x 82 in. AC 1, The Solomon R. Guggenheim Foundation (Panza Gift)
5. *82 in. Square,* 1970-1972. 2 square holes in diagonal. Acrylic on canvas, 82 x 82 in. AC 2, The Solomon R. Guggenheim Foundation (Panza Gift)
104. *82 in. Square,* 1970-1972. 4 square holes. Acrylic on canvas, 82 x 82 in. AC 3, The Solomon R. Guggenheim Foundation (Panza Gift)
1. *82 in. Square,* 1970-1972. 3 square holes. Acrylic on canvas, 82 x 82 in. AC 4, The Solomon R. Guggenheim Foundation (Panza Gift)
17. *82 in. Square.* 1970-1972. 1 square hole. Acrylic on canvas, 82 x 82 in. AC 5, The Solomon R. Guggenheim Foundation (Panza Gift)
4. *58 x 180 in.,* June 1970. Acrylic on canvas, 58 x 180 in. AC 6, The Solomon R. Guggenheim Foundation (Panza Gift)
101. *112 x 56 in., slit 100 in.,* March 1971. Acrylic on canvas, 112 x 56 in. AC 7, The Solomon R. Guggenheim Foundation (Panza Gift)
101. *90 x 180 in., slit 156 in.,* August-November 1971. Acrylic on canvas, 90 x 180 in. AC 8, The Solomon R. Guggenheim Foundation (Panza Gift)
6. *90 x 90 in., slit 78 in.,* August 1971. Acrylic on canvas, 90 x 90 in. AC 9, The Solomon R. Guggenheim Foundation
9. *90 x 78 in., slit 66 in.,* August 1971. Acrylic on canvas, 90 x 78 in. AC 10, The Solomon R. Guggenheim Foundation
102. *90 x 56 in., slit 44 in.,* September 1971. Acrylic on canvas, 90 x 56 in. AC 11, The Solomon R. Guggenheim Foundation
7. *90 x 90 in., slit 44 in.,* September 1971. Acrylic on canvas, 90 x 90 in. AC 12, The Solomon R. Guggenheim Foundation
19. *90 x 180 in., each slit 78 in.,* January 1972. Acrylic on canvas, 90 x 180 in. AC 13, The Solomon R. Guggenheim Foundation
103. *90 x 78 in., each slit 78 in.,* January 1972. Acrylic on canvas, 90 x 78 in. AC 14, The Solomon R. Guggenheim Foundation
15. *90 x 102 in., each slit 90 in.,* January 1972. Acrylic on canvas, 90 x 102 in. AC 15, The Solomon R. Guggenheim Foundation (Panza Gift)
8. *Outer piece 114 x 66 in., inner piece 98 ¹/₂ x 50 ¹/₂ in., channel 1 ³/₄ in.,* May-August 1972. Acrylic on canvas, 114 x 66 in. AC 16, The Solomon R. Guggenheim Foundation (Panza Gift)
101. *Outer piece 84 x 144 in., inner piece 68 ¹/₂ x 128 ¹/₂ in., channel 1 ³/₄ in.,* May-August 1972. Acrylic on canvas, 84 x144 in. AC 17, The Solomon R. Guggenheim Foundation (Panza Gift)
3. *Outer piece 90 x 174 in., each inner piece 74 ¹/₂ in. square, channel 1 ³/₄ in.,* November-December 1972. Acrylic on canvas, 90 x 174 in. AC 18, The Solomon R. Guggenheim Foundation (Panza Gift)
12. *No. 1/8: outer piece 84 in. square, inner piece 68 ⁶/₁₀ in. square, channel 1 ⁸/₁₀ in.,* December 1972-May 1973. Brown plus blue added to the grey acrylic on canvas, 84 x 84 in. AC 19, The Solomon R. Guggenheim Foundation

21. *No. 2/8: outer piece 84 in. square, inner piece 68 $^4/_{10}$ in. square, channel 1 $^8/_{10}$ in.* (16 $^1/_2$ x 11 $^5/_8$ in.), December 1972-May 1973. Green plus brown added to the grey acrylic on canvas, 84 x 84 in. AC 20, The Solomon R. Guggenheim Foundation

23. *No. 3/8: outer piece 84 in. square, inner piece 68 $^4/_{10}$ in. square, channel 1 $^8/_{10}$ in.*, December 1972-May 1973. Green added to the grey acrylic on canvas, 84 x 84 in. AC 21, The Solomon R. Guggenheim Foundation

10. *No. 4/8: outer piece 84 in. square, inner piece 68 $^4/_{10}$ in. square, channel 1 $^8/_{10}$ in.*, December 1972-May 1973. Black added to the white acrylic on canvas, 84 x 84 in. AC 22, The Solomon R. Guggenheim Foundation

18. *No. 5/8: outer piece 84 in. square, inner piece 68 $^4/_{10}$ in. square, channel 1 $^8/_{10}$ in.*, December 1972-May 1973. Brown added to the grey acrylic on canvas, 84 x 84 in. AC 23, The Solomon R. Guggenheim Foundation

13. *No. 6/8: outer piece 84 in. square, inner piece 68 $^4/_{10}$ in. square, channel 1 $^8/_{10}$ in.*, December 1972-May 1973. Brown plus blue added to the grey acrylic on canvas, 84 x 84 in. AC 24, The Solomon R. Guggenheim Foundation

20. *No. 8/8: outer piece 84 in. square, inner piece 68 $^4/_{10}$ in. square, channel 1 $^8/_{10}$ in.*, December 1972-May 1973. Black added to the white acrylic on canvas, 84 x 84 in. AC 25, The Solomon R. Guggenheim Foundation

106. *Outer piece 58 in. square, inner piece 18 in. square, channel 1 $^5/_8$ in.*, September 1973. Acrylic on canvas, 58 x 58 in. AC 26, The Solomon R. Guggenheim Foundation

11. *Outer piece 51 $^1/_2$ in. square, inner piece 24 in. square, channel 1 $^3/_4$ in.*, August 1973. Acrylic on canvas, 51 $^1/_2$ x 51 $^1/_2$ in. AC 27, The Solomon R. Guggenheim Foundation

107. *Outer piece 63 $^1/_2$ in. square, inner piece 12 in. square, channel 1 $^3/_4$ in.*, September 1973. Acrylic on canvas, 63 $^1/_2$ x 63 $^1/_2$ in. AC 28, The Solomon R. Guggenheim Foundation

16. *Outer piece 66 in. square, inner piece 55 $^1/_2$ in. square, channel 1 $^3/_4$ in.*, October 1973. Acrylic on canvas, 66 x 66 in. AC 29, The Solomon R. Guggenheim Foundation

105. *Outer piece 60 in. square, inner piece 38 $^1/_2$ in. square, channel 1 $^3/_4$ in.*, December 1973. Acrylic on canvas, 60 x 60 in. AC 30

24. *Outer piece 56 in. square, inner piece 49 in. square, channel 1 $^3/_4$ in.*, January 1974. Acrylic on canvas, 56 x 56 in. AC 31, The Solomon R. Guggenheim Foundation

22. *Outer piece 50 in. square, inner piece 39 $^1/_2$ in. square, channel 1 $^3/_4$ in.*, January 1974. Acrylic on canvas, 50 x 50 in. AC 32, The Solomon R. Guggenheim Foundation

14. *No. 5/6: each piece 91 x 80 $^1/_2$ in.*, January 1975. 2 pieces. Acrylic on canvas, overall 91 x 162 $^3/_4$ in. AC 33, The Solomon R. Guggenheim Foundation (Panza Gift)

14. *No. 3/6: each piece 98 x 66 $^1/_2$ in.*, January 1975. 2 pieces. Acrylic on canvas, overall 98 x 134 $^3/_4$ in. AC 34, The Solomon R. Guggenheim Foundation (Panza Gift)

14. *No. 2/6: each piece 101 $^1/_2$ x 59 $^1/_2$ in.*, January 1975. 2 pieces. Acrylic on canvas, overall 101 $^1/_2$ x 120 $^3/_4$ in. AC 35, The Solomon R. Guggenheim Foundation (Panza Gift)

HANNE DARBOVEN (Munich, West Germany, 1941)
pp. 176-179, 261-268

27. *August 1*, 1972. Ink on paper, 59 x 42 cm. (23 $^1/_4$ x 16 $^1/_2$ in.) HD 1, The Solomon R. Guggenheim Foundation (Panza Gift)

29. *August 1*, 1972. Typewritting and ink on paper, 59 x 44 cm. (23 $^1/_4$ x 17 $^3/_8$ in.) HD 2, The Solomon R. Guggenheim Foundation (Panza Gift)

4. *Drawings nos 1-2-3*, 1972. Ink on paper, 3 sheets, each 29 x 20,5 cm. (11 $^3/_8$ x 8 $^1/_8$ in.) HD 3, The Solomon R. Guggenheim Foundation (Panza Gift)

5. *Index 17K-58K*, 1969. Typewritting on paper, 42 sheets, each 41 x 29 in. (16 $^1/_8$ x 11 $^3/_8$ in.) HD 7

6. *27K - No 8 - No 26*, 1968-1969. Typewritting on paper, 146 sheets, each 29,5 x 21 cm. (11 $^5/_8$ x 8 $^1/_4$ in.) HD 9

159.7. *00 ►99=No 1► 2K► 20K*, 1969-1970. Pen on paper, 138 sheets, each 29,5 x 21 cm. (11 $^5/_8$ x 8 $^1/_4$ in.) HD 10
Form a work of 6 parts:

161.13. *101 Drawings*, 1971-1972. Pen on paper, 101 sheets, each 42 x 29,5 cm. (16 $^1/_2$ x 1l $^5/_8$ in.) HD 16

162.2. *51 Drawings*, 1971-1972. Ink on paper, 51 sheets, each 41,5 x 29 cm. (16 $^3/_8$ x 11 $^3/_8$ in.) HD 4

1. *45 Drawings*, 1971-1972. Ink on paper,45 sheets, each 41,5 x 29 cm. (16 $^3/_8$ x 11 $^3/_8$ in.) HD 6

3. *43 Drawings*, 1971-1972. Ink on paper, 43 sheets, each 41,5 x 29 cm. (16 $^3/_8$ x 11 $^3/_8$ in.) HD 5

14. *85 Drawings*, 1971-1972. Pen on paper, 85 sheets, each 42 x 29,5 cm. (16 $^1/_2$ x 11 $^5/_8$ in.) HD 17

160.17. *49 Drawings*, 1971-1972. Pen on paper, 49 sheets, each 42 x 29,5 cm. (16 $^1/_2$ x 11 $^5/_8$ in.) HD 18
Form a work of 5 parts:

8. *I/II/III*, 1970-1971. Typewritting on paper, 96 sheets, each 29,5 x 21 cm. (11 $^5/_8$ x 8 $^1/_4$ in.) HD 11

9. *IV/V/VI*, 1970-1971. Typewritting on paper, 96 sheets, each 29,5 x 21 cm. (11 $^5/_8$ x 8 $^1/_4$ in.) HD 12

10. *VII/VIII/IX*, 1970-1971. Typewritting on paper, 96 sheets, each 29,5 x 21 cm. (11 $^5/_8$ x 8 $^1/_4$ in.) HD 13

12. *X/XI/XII*, 1970-1971. Typewritting on paper, 96 sheets, each 29,5 x 21 cm. (11 $^5/_8$ x 8 $^1/_4$ in.) HD 14

11. *365 x 100 + 1 x 25 = 36525, Index*, 1970-1971. Typewritting on paper, 202 sheets, each 29,5 x 21 cm. (11 $^5/_8$ x 8 $^1/_4$ in.) HD 15
Form a work of 2 parts:

18. *Erstes Buch 2-61-43*, 1972. Typewritting on paper, 138 sheets, each 29,5 x 21 cm. (11 $^5/_8$ x 8 $^1/_4$ in.) HD 19

19. *Zweiundzwanzigstes Buch 23-40-22*, 1972. Typewritting on paper, 128 sheets, each 29,5 x 21 cm. (11 $^5/_8$ x 8 $^1/_4$ in.) HD 20
Form a work of 10 parts:

15. *K: 15 x 15–F: 15 x 15 (ordner: 1)*, 1972-1973. Ink on paper, 46 sheets, each 42 x 30 cm. (16 $^1/_2$ x 11 $^3/_4$ in.) HD 21

16. *K: 15 x 15–F: 15 x 15 (ordner: 2)*, 1972-1973. Ink on paper, 46 sheets, each 42 x 30 cm. (16 $^1/_2$ x 11 $^3/_4$ in.) HD 22

21. *K: 15 x 15–F: 15 x 15 (ordner: 3)*, 1972-1973. Ink on paper, 46 sheets, each 42 x 30 cm. (16 $^1/_2$ x 11 $^3/_4$ in.) HD 23

20. *K: 15 x 15 (ordner: 4)*, 1972- 1973. Ink on paper, 46 sheets, each 42 x 30 cm. (16 $^1/_2$ x 11 $^3/_4$ in.). HD 24

22. *Varianten-aufzichungen 1► 99 (ordner: 5)*, 1972-1973. Ink on paper, 51 sheets, each 42 x 30 cm. (16 $^1/_2$ x 11 $^3/_4$ in.) HD 25

23. *Varianten-aufzichungen 1► 99 (ordner: 6)*, 1972-1973. Ink on paper, 51 sheets, each 42 x 30 cm. (16 $^1/_2$ x 11 $^3/_4$ in.) HD 26

24. *Varianten-aufzichungen 1► 99 (ordner: 7)*, 1972-1973. Ink on paper, 46 sheets, each 42 x 30 cm. (16 $^1/_2$ x 11 $^3/_4$ in.) HD 27

25. *Varianten-Pläne-Kurven zahlen: 1► 99 (ordner: 8)*, 1972-1973. Ink on paper, 45 sheets, each 42 x 30 cm. (16 $^1/_2$ x 11 $^3/_4$ in). HD 28

26. *Varianten-Pläne zahlen: 1► 99 (ordner: 9)*, 1972-1973. Ink on paper, 50 sheets, each 42 x 30 cm. (16 $^1/_2$ x 11 $^3/_4$ in.) HD 29

28. *Varianten-Pläne zahlen: 1► 99 (ordner: 10)*, 1972-1973. Ink on paper, 51 sheets, each 42 x 30 cm. (16 $^1/_2$ x 11 $^3/_4$ in.) HD 30

DOUGLAS DAVIS (Washington D.C., 1933)

Studies in Myself II, 1973. Color videotape, 30 mins. DD 1
Studies in Color Videotape II, 1972. Color videotape, 30 mins. DD 2
Talk-Out, 1972. Color videotape, 65 mins. DD 3
The Santa Clara Tapes, 1973. Color videotape, 30 mins. DD 4
The Austrian Tapes, 1974. Color videotape, 15 mins. DD 5
Fragment for a New Art of the Seventies, 1975. Color videotape, 30 mins. DD 6
The Last Videotape, 1975. Color videotape, 10 mins. DD 6A
The Florence Tapes, 1974. Bl/wh videotape, 18 mins. DD 7
Three Silent and Secret Acts, 1976. Color videotape, 30 mins. DD8
The Last Nine Minutes, 1977. Color videotape, 9 mins. DD 9
Reading Marx Box, 1976. Documentation of multimedia performance held in Bologna 1976. 2 Books and videotape presented in a plexiglass box, 33 x 51 x 10 cm. (13 x 20 x 4 in.) DD 10
Seven Thoughts, 1976. Documentation of perfomance held in Huston Astronome Dec. 26, 1976 presented in a wooden box, 17 x 22 x 23 cm. (6 $^3/_4$ x 8 $^3/_4$ x 9 in.).DD.11
Double Entendre, 1981. Color videotape, 30 mins. DD 12
Double Entendre Double Print, 1981. 3 printed sheets, each 48 x 42 cm. (19 x 16 $^1/_2$ in.) DD 13

WALTER DE MARIA (Albany, California, 1935) pp. 147, 293-294

123.3. *Balldrop*, 1961. Plywood box with pencil wording and solid wood ball, 76 x 24 x 6 $^5/_8$ in. Edition of 6. WM 1, The Solomon R. Guggenheim Foundation (Panza Gift)

1. *High Energy Bar no. 75*, 1966. Stainless steel, 3,7 x 35,7 x 3,7 cm. (1 $^1/_2$ x 14 x 1 $^1/_2$ in.) WM 2
Hard Core no. 3/100, 1969. 16 mm. film. WM 3

fluorescent light, 192 in. high in corner. DF 53, FAI (Fondo per l'Ambiente Italiano) on permanent loan to Guggenheim

Untitled (Fondly to Margo) 1/5, 1986. Yellow and pink fluorescent light, 96 in. high in corner. DF 54, FAI per l'Ambiente Italiano) on permanent loan to Guggenheim

Untitled (Fondly to Margo) 1/3, 1986. Yellow and pink fluorescent light, 102 in. high, 96 in. wide in corner. DF 55, FAI (Fondo per l'Ambiente Italiano) on permanent loan to Guggenheim

Untitled (to Eugenia) 3/5, 1987. Cool white, daylight and warm white fluorescent light, 6 units 48 in. each, 96 in. high. DF 56, FAI (Fondo per l'Ambiente Italiano) on permanent loan to Guggenheim

HAMISH FULTON (London, England, 1946) pp. 167, 288-290

4. *Eight Photographic Works,* 1970. 8 sets of photographs on paper, each 30 x 39,5 cm. (12 x 15 1/2 in.) HF 1
2. *Untitled 2/3,* 1972. 2 photographs on paper, 50 x 60 cm. (19 5/8 x 23 5/8 in.) HF 2
5. *Facing Both ways 2/3,* 1972. 2 photographs wiht text on paper, 50 x 60 cm. (19 5/8 x 23 5/8 in.) HF 3
3. *Dim Trails 2/3* 1972. 2 photographs with text on paper, 50 x 60 cm. (19 5/8 x 23 2/3 in.) HF 4
6. *Untitled (Artist in front of a Lake) 2/3,* 1971. 6 photographs on paper, 30 x 51 cm. (12 x 20 in.) HF 5
1. *Untitled (4 colour photos of Florida wild life),* 1971. 4 photographs on paper, 23 x 30 cm. (9 x 12 in.) HF 6
148.149.7. *Goat Fell Mountain, Isle of Arran, Scotland,* Spring 1970. 10 sets of photographs on paper, 1 drawing and 1 letter concerning the work presented in a loose leaf binder, 2 x 8 1/2 x 11 in. HF 7
9. *Untitled (Landscape with cows),* 1970. 2 photographs on paper, 31 x 43,5 cm. (12 1/4 x 17 in.) HF 8
12. *Untitled,* 1970. 2 photographs on paper, 29 x 39,5 cm. (11 1/2 x 15 1/2 in.) HF 9
11. *Untitled (4 photos with eagles),* 1970. 4 photographs on paper, 31 x 43,5 cm. (12 1/4 x 17 in.) HF 10
147. *Untitled (4 photos with land of stones),* 1970. 4 photographs on paper, 29,5 x 39,5 cm. (11 1/2 x 15 1/2 in.) HF 11
8. *Untitled (Iceland 1975) 2/3,* Late Spring 1975. 3 photographs with text on paper, 39 1/2 x 109 1/8 in. HF 12
10. *Skyline Ridge 2/3,* Summer 1974. Photograph with text on paper, 104,5 x 121,5 cm. (41 x 48 in.) HF 13
13. *France on the Horizon 1/3,* Early Summer 1975. Photograph with text on paper, 101 x 121 cm. (40 x 47 1/4 in.) HF 14
14. *Looking at Tomorrow (Scottish North West Highlands),* 1974. 5 photographs with text on paper, each 61 x 85,5 cm. (24 x 33 1/2 in.) HF 15

GILBERT AND GEORGE (Gilbert Proesch, Dolomite Mountains, Austria, 1943. George Passmore, Totnes Devon, England, 1942) p. 199

1. *We Are Only Human Sculptors,* London 1970. Text on paper, 37 x 56 cm. (14 1/2 x 22 in.) Work in edition. GG 1

RAYMOND HAINS (Saint-Brieuc, France, 1926) p. 199

1. *Untitled,* 1960. Paper on zinc plate, 32 x 40 cm. (12 5/8 x 15 3/4 in.) H 1

JENE HIGHSTEIN (Baltimore, Maryland, 1942) pp. 169, 206

151.152. *Untitled,* 1974. Seamless steel pipe, 1229 cm. (484 in.) long, 32,39 cm. (12 3/4 in.) inside diameter. JH 1, The Solomon R. Guggenheim Foundation (Panza Gift)
4. *Two Horizontals,* 1974. Seamless steel pipe, 2 units, each 420 in. long and 16 in. diameter. JH 2
1. *Human Scale Black,* 1975. Steel armature and black cement, 660 and 600 in. base diameters, 78 in. high. JH 3
2. *Fresno Aluminium Casting no. 2,* 1974. Unique casting, 3 x 14 x 41 in., 100 lbs. JH 5, The Solomon R. Guggenheim Foundation (Panza Gift)
3. *Fresno Aluminium Casting no. 3,* 1974. Unique casting, 5 x 14 x 41 in., 200 lbs. JH 6, The Solomon R. Guggenheim Foundation (Panza Gift)
5. *Black Eliptical Cone,* Varese 1976. Wood armature and black cement, 230 cm. (90 1/2 in.) and 253 cm. (99 5/8 in.) base diameters, 195 cm. (76 5/4 in.) high. JH 7, The Solomon R. Guggenheim Foundation (Panza Gift)

Twelve Part Vertical Pipe Piece, 1973. 12 seamless steel pipes, each 216 in. high by 6 in. diameter, overall 216 x 936 x 6 in. JH 8
Black Mound(Turtle), 1976. Wood, wire, concrete, 78 x 237 x 147 in., room: 144 x 468 x 344 in. JH 9

DOUGLAS HUEBLER (Ann Arbor, Michigan, 1924 - Truro, Massachusetts, 1997) pp. 152, 182-183, 249-252

1. *Site Sculpture Project, Times Square Circle Shape,* New York City, December 1968. 1 statement 41 x 34 cm. (16 1/8 x 13 3/8 in.), 1 map 33 x 40 cm. (13 x l5 3/8 in.), 9 photographs each 32 x 37 cm. (12 5/8 x 14 5/8 in.) DH 1
2. *Duration Piece no. 14,* Salisbury, New Hampshire, October 1968. 1 statement (4 styrofoam markers) 40 x 33 cm. (15 5/8 x 13 in.), 3 sets of 4 photographs each 44,5 x 58 cm. (17 1/2 x 23 in.) DH 2, The Solomon R. Guggenheim Foundation (Panza Gift)
3. *Variable Piece no. 4,* New York City, November 1968. 1 statement (Closed eyes photographs) 40 x 34 cm. (15 5/8 x 13 5/8 in.), 10 photographs each 31,5 x 36,5 cm. (12 1/4 x 14 3/8 in.) DH 3
130.7. *Location Piece no. 1,* New York - Los Angeles, February 1969. 1 statement (Thirteen States airspace) 40,5 x 34 cm. (16 x 13 3/8 in.), 1 map 40,5 x 70 cm. (16 x 27 5/8 in.), 13 photographs each 31 x 36 cm. (12 1/4 x 14 3/8 in.) DH 4
6. *Location Piece no. 9,* New England, March 1969. 1 statement (Ten mile drive) 40 x 34 cm. (15 5/8 x 13 5/8 in.), 11 photographs each 34 x 30 cm. (13 3/8 x 11 7/8 in.) DH 5, The Solomon R. Guggenheim Foundation (Panza Gift)
4. *Location Piece no. 6,* Los Angeles, March 1969. 1 statement (Paper stickers) 40 x 33 cm. (15 5/8 x 13 in.), 8 photographs each 30 x 36 cm. (11 7/8 x 14 1/4 in.) DH 6, The Solomon R. Guggenheim Foundation (Panza Gift)
5. *Duration Piece no. 12,* Venice, California - Plum Island, Massachusetts, May 1969. 1 statement (Sand exchange) 40 x 34 cm. (15 5/8 x 13 3/8 in.), 2 photographs each 36 x 31 cm. (14 1/8 x 12 1/4 in.) DH 7
165.166.10. *Location Piece no. 8,* Bradford, Massachusetts, May 1969. 1 statement (Secret) 40 x 33 cm. (15 5/8 x 13 in.), 1 text 31 x 38,5 cm. (12 1/4 x 15 1/4 in.) DH 8
9. *Location Piece no. 23,* Los Angeles - Cape Cod, August 1969. 1 statement (Ace Gallery transposition) 40 x 33 cm (15 5/8 x l3 in.), 1 map 33 x 40 cm. (13 x l5 3/8 in.), 6 photographs each 37 x 42 cm. (14 5/8 x l6 1/2 in.) DH 9, The Solomon R. Guggenheim Foundation (Panza Gift)
14. *Duration Piece no. 9,* Berkeley, California - Hull, Massachusetts, January-October 1969. 1 statement (Mail sending) 40 x 33 cm. (15 5/8 x 13 in.), 1 map 39,5 x 50 cm. (15 1/2 x 19 5/8 in.), 9 mail receipts framed 57,5 x 49 cm. (22 5/8 x 19 1/4 in.), 1 box 8,5 x 13 x 7 cm. (3 3/8 x 5 1/8 x 2 3/4 in.) DH 10, The Solomon R. Guggenheim Foundation (Panza Gift)
13. *Location Piece no. 10,* Bradford, Massachusetts - Los Angeles, California, December 1969. 1 statement (Currency) 40 x 33 cm. (15 5/8 x 13 in.), 1 envelope with 5 $ bill 24 x 35 cm. (9 1/2 x 13 3/4 in.), 1 xerox copy 33 x 39 cm. (13 x 15 3/8 in.) DH 11, The Solomon R. Guggenheim Foundation (Panza Gift)
8. *Duration Piece no. 16, Global,* December 1969. 1 statement (Spermatozoid) 40,5 x 34 cm. (16 x 13 3/8 in.) DH 12
12. *Variable Piece no. 4,* Paris, France, January 1970. 1 statement (Place Kossuth) 33 x 40 cm. (13 x 15 5/8 in.), 1 map 71 x 90 cm. (28 x 35 1/2 in.), 1 photograph 38 x 43 cm. (15 x 17 in.) DH 13, The Solomon R. Guggenheim Foundation (Panza Gift)
130.11. *Duration Piece no. 4,* Paris, France, January 1970. 1 statement (One half previous time) 41 x 31 cm. (16 1/8 x 12 1/4 in.), 12 photographs each 31 x 36 cm. (12 1/4 x 14 1/8 in.) DH 14, The Solomon R. Guggenheim Foundation (Panza Gift)
16. *Duration Piece no. 5,* Amsterdam, Holland, January 1970. 1 statement (One half previous time) 40,5 x 34 cm. (16 x 13 3/8 in.), 12 photographs each 31,5 x 36 cm. (12 1/2 x 14 1/8 in.) DH 15, The Solomon R. Guggenheim Foundation (Panza Gift)
20. *Variable Piece no. 49,* Bradford, Massachusetts-New York City, March 1971. 1 statement (Home-Castelli Gallery trip) 40,5 x 34 cm. (16 x 13 3/8 in.), 1 map 34,5 x 32,5 cm. (13 1/2 x 12 3/4 in.), 5 sets of 36 x 4 proof prints each 53 x 63 cm. (21 x 24 1/2 in.), 1 photograph 33 x 38 cm. (13 x 15 in.) DH 16
15. *Drawing,* 1970. (Sequencial process), 14 1/8 x 12 5/8 in. DH 17
19. *Drawing,* 1970. (Reflecting essence), 14 1/8 x l2 1/8 in. DH 18
17. *Variable Piece no. 44, Global,* March 1971. Work in process, Giuseppe Panza no. 6/100. Cardboard sheet 18 x 24 in.

with spaces for photographs and statement, 10 x 8 ½ in. DH 19

18. *Variable Piece no. 44, Global,* March 1971. Work in process, Giovanna Panza no. 5/100. Cardboard sheet 18 x 24 in. with spaces for photographs and statement, 10 x 8 ½ in. DH 20

ROBERT IRWIN (Long Beach, California, 1928) pp. 153-155, 281-282

1. *Dot Painting,* 1963-1965. One of a series of ten each unique. Acrylic on canvas on board, 82 x 84 in. RI 1
131. *Disc Coloured Pale Grey Green Pink Violet,* 1966-1967. Painted steel disc 152 cm. (60 in.) diameter and 4 placed lamps. RI 2
4. *Plastic Disc,* 1968-1969. One of a series of 18 each unique. Cast acrylic disc with acryl colour coating 135 cm. (53 in.) diameter and 4 placed lamps. RI 3
5. *12' Acrylic Column,* 1970-1971. One of a series of 8 each unique. Poured optical acrylic material, 144 in. high, cross section triangular with 5 facets. RI 4
2. *Scrim (Ace Gallery),* Los Angeles 1972. Transparent nylon material and light, room: 200 x 324 x 336 in. Rl 5, FAI (Fondo per l'Ambiente Italiano) on permanent loan to Guggenheim
3. *Varese Scrim,* 1973. Transparent nylon material, room: 350 x 410 x 1400 cm. (138 x 161 x 551 in.) RI 6, The Solomon R. Guggenheim Foundation (Panza Gift) on permanent loan to FAI
10. *Dividing Wall (The Pace Gallery),* New York, December 1973. Wall height 69 ½ in., room: 120 x 660 x 264 in. RI 7, FAI (Fondo per l'Ambiente Italiano) on permanent loan to Guggenheim
132. 7. *Varese Window Room,* 1973. Environment, room: 350 x 500 x 410 cm. (138 x 197 x 161 in.) RI 8, The Solomon R. Guggenheim Foundation (Panza Gift) on permanent loan to FAI
133. 6. *Varese Portal Room,* 1973. Environment, room: 350 x 450 x 1120 cm. (138 x 177 x 441 in.) RI 10, The Solomon R. Guggenheim Foundation (Panza Gift) on permanent loan to FAI
8. *Soft Wall-Scrim Piece (The Pace Gallery),* New York, November 1974. Transparent nylon material and light, room: 120 x 660 x 264 in. RI 11, FAI (Fondo per l'Ambiente Italiano) on permanent loan to Guggenheim
9. *Scrim-Fractured Light (Museum of Modern Art),* New York, November 1970 - March 1971. Transparent nylon material and light, room: 144 x 180 x 360 in. RI 17, The Solomon R. Guggenheim Foundation (Panza Gift)
Full Room Skylight - Scrim V (Fog Museum, Harvard University), 1972. Nylon scrim forming V volume next to ceiling approx. 60 in. from floor, natural light, room: 192 x 336 x 216 in. RI 26
Illuminated Scrim Wall (University of Kansas), 1974. Two floor to ceiling scrim walls with opening light, room: 134 x 472 x 197 in. RI 40, The Solomon R. Guggenheim Foundation (Panza Gift)
Eye Level Scrim (Fort Worth Museum), 1975. Scrim from ceiling to approx. 68 in. from floor, light, room: 134 x 472 x 197 in. RI 41, The Solomon R. Guggenheim Foundation (Panza Gift)
Three Primarys (Chicago Art Institute), 1975. Three spaces 24 in. wide each determined by blue, red and yellow fluorescent light. RI 42, The Solomon R. Guggenheim Foundation (Panza Gift)
Varese Horizontal Scrim, 1973. Scrim approx. 96 in. from floor, light with gradation from warm white to daylight. RI 43, The Solomon R. Guggenheim Foundation (Panza Gift)

PETER JOSEPH (London, England, 1929) pp. 132-133, 235

109. *Untitled (Cream colour with brown border),* March 1974. Oil on canvas, 60 x 105 in. PJ 1, The Solomon R. Guggenheim Foundation (Panza Gift)
4. *Untitled (Tan colour with dark blue border) I,* June 1974. Oil on canvas, 105 x 60 in. PJ 2, The Solomon R. Guggenheim Foundation (Panza Gift)
4. *Untitled (Cream colour with black border) II,* June 1974. Oil on canvas, 105 x 66 in. PJ 3, The Solomon R. Guggenheim Foundation (Panza Gift)
109. *Untitled (Grey-blue colour with black border),* November 1974. Oil on canvas, 74 x 62 in. PJ 4, The Solomon R. Guggenheim Foundation (Panza Gift)
108. 3. *Untitled (Cream colour with black border),* May 1975. Oil on

canvas, 79 x 66 in. PJ 5, The Solomon R. Guggenheim Foundation (Panza Gift)
110. *Untitled (Grey with blue border),* 1975. Acrylic on canvas, 80 x 56 in. PJ 7, The Solomon R. Guggenheim Foundation (Panza Gift)
108. *Untitled (Cream colour with dark blue border),* 1976. Acrylic on canvas, 76 x 61 ½ in. PJ 8, The Solomon R. Guggenheim Foundation (Panza Gift)
3. *Untitled (Dark cream with blue border),* 1975. Acrylic on canvas, 75 x 53 in. PJ 9, The Solomon R. Guggenheim Foundation (Panza Gift)
7. *Untitled (Dulled cream with black border),* October 1975. Acrylic on canvas, 60 ½ x 106 in. PJ 10, The Solomon R. Guggenheim Foundation (Panza Gift)
6. *Cream with Maroon Border,* January 1976. Acrylic on canvas, 59 ½ x 90 in. PJ 11, The Solomon R. Guggenheim Foundation (Panza Gift)
5. *Cream with Brown Border,* February 1976. Acrylic on canvas, 76 x 54 in. PJ 12, The Solomon R. Guggenheim Foundation (Panza Gift)
1. *Grey with Ochre Border,* May 1976. Acrylic on canvas, 60 x 85 in. PJ 13, The Solomon R. Guggenheim Foundation (Panza Gift)
2. *Cream with Ochre Border,* June 1976. Acrylic on canvas, 59 x 92 in. PJ 14, The Solomon R. Guggenheim Foundation

BERNARD JOUBERT (Paris, France, 1946) p.248

1. *Work,* 1974. Three red vertical strips, 120 x 240 cm. (47 ¼ x 94 ½ in.) BJ 1
3. *Work,* 1974. Two red vertical strips, 240 x 240 cm. (94 ½ x 94 ½ in.) BJ 2
2. *Work,* 1974. Three strips, blue, red and yellow, 200 x 600 cm. (78 ¾ x 236 ¼ in.) BJ 3

DONALD JUDD (Excelsior Springs, Missouri, 1928 - New York City, 1994) pp. 118-123, 202-205

13. *Untitled,* 1965. Brown painted aluminium, 22 x 50 x 37 in. DSS 122 2/2. DJ 1, The Solomon R. Guggenheim Foundation (Panza Gift)
10. *Untitled,* 1965. Ramp, perforated steel, 8 x 120 x 66 in. DSS 131 1/3. DJ 2, The Solomon R. Guggenheim Foundation
83. *Untitled,* 1969. Large stack, solid copper with mirror finish, 10 units, each 9 x 40 x 31 in. DSS 204. DJ 3, The Solomon R. Guggenheim Foundation
87. *Untitled,* 1970. Perforated cold rolled steel, 12 x 138 x 117 in. DSS 240. DJ 4, The Solomon R. Guggenheim Foundation
5. *Untitled,* 1970. 21' Fibronacci progression, anodized aluminium tube with blue aluminium boxes, 8 ¼ x 253 x 8 in. DSS 223 1/3. DJ 5, The Solomon R. Guggenheim Foundation
Untitled, 1970. Round front progression, copper, 5 x 69 x 8 ½ in. DSS 233 3/3. DJ 6, The Solomon R. Guggenheim Foundation
85. *Untitled,* 1966-1972. Large round front progression, brass, 14 x 78 x 25 ½ in. DSS 267 3/3. DJ 7, The Solomon R. Guggenheim Foundation
82. 8. *Untitled,* 1971. 8 orange painted cold rolled steel boxes, each 48 x 48 x 48 in. DSS 243. DJ 8, The Solomon R. Guggenheim Foundation
81. 1. *Untitled,* 1972. 6 brass with red fluorescent plexiglass boxes, each 34 x 34 x 34 in. DSS 282. DJ 9, The Solomon R. Guggenheim Foundation
12. *Untitled,* 1973. Rectangular hot rolled steel tube, 33 x 48 x 68 in. DSS 292. DJ 10, The Solomon R. Guggenheim Foundation
85. *Untitled,* 1973. Brass and blue plexiglass, 33 x 48 x 68 in. DSS 291. DJ 11, The Solomon R. Guggenheim Foundation
88. 4. *Untitled,* 1972-1973. 7 plywood open boxes, each 72 x 72 x 72 in. DJ 12, The Solomon R. Guggenheim Foundation
7. *Untitled,* May 1972. 5 plywood 26,5° open boxes, each 72 x 72 x 42 in. DSS 265. DJ 13, The Solomon R. Guggenheim Foundation
18. *Untitled,* 1974. 8 plywood closed back boxes, each 72 x 72 x 72 in. DJ 19, The Solomon R. Guggenheim Foundation
17. *Untitled,* 1974. 8 plywood open back boxes, each 48 x 48 x 48 in. DJ 20, The Solomon R. Guggenheim Foundation
19. *Double Closed Copper Wall,* 1974. Against existing wall, 15 in. apart, 60 x 15 in., lenght according to room size. DJ 21, The Solomon R. Guggenheim Foundation
16. *Single Steel Wall Bent,* 1974. ³⁄₈-¹⁄₂ in. thick hot rolled steel plates,

along 3 existing walls, 15 in. apart, 15 in. bent, 60 in. high, lenght according to room size. DJ 22, The Solomon R. Guggenheim Foundation

3. *Bern Piece no. 2*, Bern 1976. $^1/_2$ -1 in. thick hot rolled steel box to fill room, 72 in. approx from walls, 48 in. high. DJ 23, The Solomon R. Guggenheim Foundation

80.9. *Straight Single Tube*, 1974. Hot rolled steel, 60 x 144 x 84 in. DJ 24, The Solomon R. Guggenheim Foundation

20. *Wall of Boxes*, 1974. $^1/_8$ in. thick galvanized iron boxes with closed back hung on wall, each 50 x 100 x 50 cm. (19 $^3/_4$ x 39 $^3/_8$ x 19 $^3/_4$ in.) DJ 25, The Solomon R. Guggenheim Foundation

86. *Eight Hot Rolled Steel Boxes*, 1974. 8 hot rolled steel boxes, each 60 x 60 x 60 in. DJ 26, The Solomon R. Guggenheim Foundation

84. *Galvanized Iron Wall*, 1974. $^1/_4$ in. thick galvanized iron plates, along 3 existing walls, 8 in. apart, 60 in. high, lenght according to room size. DJ 27, The Solomon R. Guggenheim Foundation (Panza Gift)

2. *Bern Piece no. 1*, Bern 1976. $^1/_2$ -1 in. thick hot rolled steel box to fill room, 72 in. approx from walls, 48 in. high. DJ 28, The Solomon R. Guggenheim Foundation

11. *Raised Top Plywood Piece (Lisson 1)*, 1974. $^3/_4$ in. thick plywood box against one existing wall, 49 x 94 in., lenght according to room size. DJ 29, The Solomon R. Guggenheim Foundation

6. *Bern Piece no. 3*, Bern 1976. $^1/_2$ -1 in. thick hot rolled steel box to fill room, 72 in. approx from walls, 48 in. high. DJ 30, The Solomon R. Guggenheim Foundation

14. *Large Tube, Parallelogram Inside*, 1974. 3 cm. (1 $^5/_{16}$ in.) thick hot rolled steel, 60 x 180 x 96 in. DJ 31, The Solomon R. Guggenheim Foundation

15. *Wall of Boxes*, 1974. $^1/_8$-$^1/_4$ in. thick cold rolled steel boxes with end recessed 12,5 cm. (5 in.) hung on wall, each 50 x 100 x 50 cm. (19 $^3/_4$ x 39 $^3/_8$ x 19 $^3/_4$ in.) DJ 32, The Solomon R. Guggenheim Foundation

ON KAWARA (Aichi Prefecture,Japan, 1933) p. 269

1. *Oct. 24. 1971*, New York 1971. Today series no. 95. Cardboard box with piece of newspaper and liquitex painted canvas, 25,6 x 33,2 cm. (10 x 13 in.) OK 1

3. *Oct. 26. 1971*, New York 1971. Today series no. 97. Cardboard box with piece of newspaper and liquitex painted canvas, 25,2 x 32,7 cm. (10 x 12 $^7/_8$ in.) OK 2

2. *One Millions Years*, 1970-1971. 10 books each 29,5 x 23,4 x 8 cm. (11 $^5/_8$ x 9 $^5/_8$ x 3 $^1/_8$ in.) Edition of 12. OK 3

4. *Oct. 29. 1971*, New York 1971. Today series no. 98. Carboard box with piece of newspaper and liquitex painted canvas, 20 x 25,5 cm. (8 x 10 in.) OK 4

FRANZ KLINE (Wilkes - Barre, Pennsylvania, 1910 New York City, 1962) pp. 35, 75, 196-198

8. *Tower*, 1953. Oil on canvas, 81 x 52 in. FK 1 MOCA
2. *Thorpe*, 1954. Oil on canvas, 62 x 43 $^1/_4$ in. FK 2 MOCA
17. *Ilza*, 1955. Oil on canvas, 41 $^1/_4$ x 33 in. FK 3 MOCA
4.1. *Monitor*, 1956. Oil on canvas, 78 $^3/_4$ x 115 $^3/_4$ in. FK 4 MOCA
5. *Buttress*, 1956. Oil on canvas, 46 $^1/_4$ x 55 $^1/_2$ in. FK 5 MOCA
4. *Hazelton*, 1957. Oil on canvas, 41 $^1/_4$ x 78 in. FK 6 MOCA
7. *Black and White*, 1957. Oil on canvas, 32 x 24 in. FK 7 MOCA
15. *Alva*, 1958. Oil on canvas, 40 $^1/_2$ x 36 $^1/_2$ in. FK 8 MOCA
11. *Line Through White Oblong*, 1959. Oil on canvas, 60 $^1/_4$ x 81 in. FK 9 MOCA
4.13. *Orleans*, 1959. Oil on canvas, 101 x 76 in. FK 10
12. *Sabro II*, 1959-1960. Oil on canvas, 62 x 79 in. FK 11 MOCA
6. *Black Iris*, 1961. Oil on canvas, 108 $^1/_4$ x 79 $^1/_2$ in. FK 12 MOCA
3. *Drawing*, 1957. Oil on paper, 51 x 72 cm. (20 x 28 $^1/_4$ in.) FK 13
9. *Drawing*, 1957. Oil on paper, 31 x 41 cm. (12 $^1/_2$ x 16 $^1/_8$ in.) FK 14
14. *Drawing*, 1957. Oil on paper, 47 x 39 cm. (18 $^1/_2$ x 15 $^1/_8$ in.) FK 15
10. *Drawing*, 1957. Oil on paper, 28 x 20 cm. (11 x 7 $^7/_8$ in.) FK 16

JOSEPH KOSUTH (Toledo, Ohio, 1945) pp. 148-151, 274-277

5. *Three Color Sentence*, 1965. Red, blue and green neon tubing, 119 cm. (46 $^7/_8$ in.) long. JK 1
127. *Self-defined*, 1965. White neon tubing, 30 in. approx. long. JK 2
4. *Five Five's (to Donald Judd)*, 1965. White neon tubing, 338 cm. (133 in.) long. JK 3

1. *One and Eight - a Description (Green)*, 1965. Green neon tubing, 310 cm. (122 in.) long. JK 4
1. *One and Eight - a Description (Blue)*, 1965. Blue neon tubing, 306 cm. (120 $^1/_2$ in.) long. JK 5
1. *One and Eight - a Description (Red)*, 1965. Red neon tubing, 304 cm. (119 $^3/_4$ in.) long. JK 6
124. *Box, Cube, Empty, Clear, Glass - a Description*, 1965. 5 glass cubes with black lettering, each 100 x 100 x 100 cm. (40 x 40 x 40 in.) JK 7
2. *Clear, Square, Glass, Leaning*, 1965. 4 glass plates with black lettering, each 36 or 60 in. square. JK 8
7. *One and Five (Clock)*, 1965. 1 clock, 1 photograph of clock and 3 photographs of definitions (time, clock, object), each 50 x 50 cm. (20 x 20 in.) JK 10
125. *Titled (Art as idea as idea)*, 1966. Definition of paint in a set of 8 parts printed on cardboard, each 120 x 120 cm. (47 $^1/_2$ x 47 $^1/_2$ in.) JK 11
8. *Titled (Art as idea as idea)*, 1967. Definition of ultimate (english) printed on cardboard, 145 x 145 cm. (57 x 57 in.) JK 13
126. *Titled (Art as idea as idea)*, 1967. Definition of idea (english) printed on cardboard, 145 x 145 cm. (57 x 57 in.) JK 14
15. *Titled (Art as idea as idea)*, 1967. Definition of meaning (italian) printed on cardboard, 120 x 120 cm. (47 $^1/_2$ x 47 $^1/_2$ in.) JK 15
16. *Titled (Art as idea as idea)*, 1967. Definition of silence (italian) printed on cardboard, 120 x 120 cm. (47 $^1/_2$ x 47 $^1/_2$ in.) JK 16
9. *Titled (Art as idea as idea)*, 1967. Definition of nothing (italian) printed on cardboard, 120 x 120 cm. (47 $^1/_2$ x 47 $^1/_2$ in.) JK 17
11. *Titled (Art as idea as idea)*, 1967. Definition of nothing (english) printed on cardboard, 120 x 120 cm. (47 $^1/_2$ x 47 $^1/_2$ in.) JK 18
10. *Titled (Art as idea as idea)*, 1967. Definition of nothing (german) printed on cardboard, 120 x 120 cm. (47 $^1/_2$ x 47 $^1/_2$ in.) JK 19
12. *Titled (Art as idea as idea)*, 1967. Definition of nothing (spanish) printed on cardboard, 120 x 120 cm. (47 $^1/_2$ x 47 $^1/_2$ in.) JK 20
14. *Titled (Art as idea as idea)*, 1967. Definition of nothing (french) printed on cardboard, 120 x 120 cm. (47 $^1/_2$ x 47 $^1/_2$ in.) JK 21
13. *Titled (Art as idea as idea)*, 1967. Definition of nothing (danish) printed on cardboard, 120 x 120 cm. (47 $^1/_2$ x 47 $^1/_2$ in.) JK 22
3. *Twenty-five Works in a Contest as One Work (Special investigation)*, New York 1968-Los Angeles 1969. 29 stikers. JK 23
128. *The Eighth Investigation, proposition 3*, 1971. Installation, various material. JK 24
129. *The Tenth Investigation, proposition 4*, 1974. Installation, various material. JK 26
6. *Nine Paintings with Words as Art*, 1966. 9 grey canvas with white word, each 56 x 95 cm. (22 x 37 $^1/_2$ in.) JK 27

DAVID LAMELAS (Buenos Aires,Argentina, 1946)

Reading of an Extract from "Labyrinths" by J.L. Borges, 1970. 16 mm. bl/wh film. DL 1

BOB LAW (Brentford, England, 1934) pp. 135-136, 229-230

113.10. *No. 64 (Purple, plum, black, violet)*, 1967. Ink on canvas, 66 x 69 in. BL 1, The Solomon R. Guggenheim Foundation (Panza Gift)
11. *No. 84 (Blue, black, black, violet)*, 1970. Ink on canvas, 66 x 69 in. BL 2, The Solomon R. Guggenheim Foundation (Panza Gift)
14. *No. 85 (Violet, violet, black, violet)*, 1970. Ink on canvas, 66 x 69 in. BL 3, The Solomon R. Guggenheim Foundation (Panza Gift)
2. *No. 86 (Violet, black,violet)*, 1970. Ink on canvas, 66 x 69 in. BL 4, The Solomon R. Guggenheim Foundation
7. *No. 87 (Violet, black,violet, blue)*, 1970. Ink on canvas, 66 x 69 in. BL 5, The Solomon R. Guggenheim Foundation
13. *No. 82 (Violet, black)*, 1971. Ink on canvas, 66 x 69 in. BL 6, The Solomon R. Guggenheim Foundation
112. *No. 83 (Crimson, blue, violet, black)*, 1971. Ink on canvas, 66 x 69 in. BL 7, The Solomon R. Guggenheim Foundation
1. *No. 89 (Mauve, black, blue, black)*, 1974. Ink on canvas, 66 x 69 in. BL 8, The Solomon R. Guggenheim Foundation
5. *Castle no. 3*, 1975. Acrylic on canvas, 60 x 63 in. BL 9, The Solomon R.Guggenheim Foundation

4. *Castle no.7,* July 1975. Acrylic on canvas, 60 x 63 in. BL 10, The Solomon R. Guggenheim Foundation
6. *Castle no. 10,* August 1975. Acrylic on canvas, 60 x 63 in. BL 11, The Solomon R. Guggenheim Foundation
9. *Castle XXV,* January 1976. Acrylic on canvas, 60 x 63 in. BL 12, The Solomon R. Guggenheim Foundation (Panza Gift)
15. *Castle XXVI,* January 1976. Acrylic on canvas, 60 x 63 in. BL 13, The Solomon R. Guggenheim Foundation (Panza Gift)
3. *Castle XXVII,* February 1976. Acrylic on canvas, 60 x 63 in. BL 14, The Solomon R. Guggenheim Foundation
Castle XXVIII, February 1976. Acrylic on canvas, 60 x 63 in. BL 15, The Solomon R. Guggenheim Foundation
8. *Castle XXIV,* December 1975. Acrylic on canvas, 60 x 63 in. BL 16, The Solomon R. Guggenheim Foundation
12. *Castle XXIX,* March 1976. Acrylic on canvas, 60 x 63 in. BL 17, The Solomon R. Guggenheim Foundation

SOL LEWITT (Hartford, Connecticut, 1929) pp. 144-147, 180-181, 253-257

122.5. *Wall Drawing no. 3,* April 1969. A 40 in. (100 cm.) band of vertical and both sets of diagonal lines superimposed, centered top to bottom, running the lenght of the wall. Black pencil. SL 1
6. *Wall Drawing no. 20,* September 1969. Lines in four directions, each with a different color, superimposed on a wall. Red, yellow, blue, black pencil. SL 2
123.7. *Wall Drawing no. 262,* Varese, July 1975. All one, two, three, and four part combinations of lines in four directions and four colors, each within a square. 15 drawings. Red, yellow, blue, black pencil. SL 3, The Solomon R. Guggenheim Foundation (Panza Gift)
3. *Wall Drawing no. 264,* Varese, July 1975. A wall divided into 16 equal parts with all one, two, three, and four-part combinations of lines and color in four directions. Red, yellow, blue, black pencil. SL 4, The Solomon R. Guggenheim Foundation (Panza Gift)
20. *Wall Drawing no. 37,* April 1970. Intersecting symmetrical bands of parallel lines 36 in. (90 cm.) wide, in four directions and colors, on four walls progressively. Red, yellow, blue, black pencil. SL 5
9. *Wall Drawing no. 38,* April 1970. Tissue paper cut into 1 $^1/_2$ in. (4 cm.) squares rolled and inserted into holes in gray pegboard walls. All holes in the walls are filled randomly. First wall: white. Second wall: white, yellow. Third wall: white, yellow, red. Fourth wall: white, yellow, red, blue. SL 6
18. *Wall Drawing no. 52,* July 1970. Four-part drawing with a different line direction and color in each part. Red, yellow, blue, black pencil. SL 7
19. *Wall Drawing no. 53,* July 1970. Serial drawing with lines in three directions (vertical, horizontal, diagonal-left or diagonal-right) and three colors superimposed in each part. Red, yellow, blue, black pencil. SL 8
2. *Wall Drawing no. 54,* July 1970. Six part serial drawing with lines in two directions (vertical, horizontal, diagonal-left or diagonal-right) and two color superimposed in each part. Red, yellow, blue, black pencil. SL 9
10. *Wall Drawing no. 271,* Varese, July 1975. Black circles, red grid, yellow arcs from four corners, blue arcs from the midpoints of four sides (ACG 195). Colored pencil. SL 10, The Solomon R. Guggenheim Foundation (Panza Gift)
1. *Wall Drawing no. 265,* Varese, July 1975. A wall divided horizontally and vertically into four equal parts, with lines in three directions and three colors in each part. Red, yellow, blue pencil. SL 11, The Solomon R. Guggenheim Foundation (Panza Gift)
121.14. *Wall Drawing no. 266,* Varese, July 1975. Two-part drawing. Grid and arcs from two adjacent corners and the midpoint of one side, between (ACG 118). One drawing has arcs from the bottom. The second drawing has arcs from the top. Black pencil. SL 12, The Solomon R. Guggenheim Foundation (Panza Gift)
12. *Wall Drawing no. 267-268-269-270,* July 1975. Arcs from four corners and the midpoints of three sides (ACG 47-96-145-194). One room. Black pencil. SL 13
8. *Wall Drawing no. 272,* Varese, July 1975. An increasing number of horizontal lines about 1 in. (2,5 cm.) apart from bottom to top, vertical lines from top to bottom, diagonal right lines from left to right, diagonal left lines right to left. Black pencil. SL 14
120.11. *Wall Drawing no. 146,* September 1972. All two-part combinations of blue arcs from corners and sides and blue straight, not straight and broken lines. Blue crayon. SL 15, The Solomon R. Guggenheim Foundation (Panza Gift)

17. *Wall Drawing no. 150,* October 1972. Ten thousand 1 in. (2,5 cm.) lines evenly spaced on each of six walls. Black pencil. SL 16
13. *Wall Drawing no. 151,* January 1973. All combinations of a single line in four directions (15 parts). Black crayon. SL 17
16. *Wall Drawing no. 152,* January 1973. Three-part drawing. First wall: straight horizontal lines. Second wall: not straight horizontal lines. Third wall: broken horizontal lines. Lines about 2 in. (5 cm.) apart. Black pencil. SL 18
15. *Wall Drawing no. 176,* May 1973. A horizontal line from left side (more than half way, less than all the way). Red crayon. SL 19
4. *Wall Drawing no. 24,* September 1969. Drawing Series B on aluminum box. One series on each face. Black pencil and white painted aluminum box, 72 x 48 in. (180 x 120 cm.) SL 20
Wall Drawing no. 17, September 1969. Four-part drawing with different line direction in each part. Black pencil. SL 34
Wall Drawing no. 18, September 1969. Four-part serial drawing. A wall divided vertically into four equal parts, with three of the four different kinds of line direction (vertical, horizontal, diagonal-left, diagonal-right) superimposed in each part. Black pencil. SL 35
Wall Drawing no. 19, September 1969. Six-part serial drawing. A wall divided vertically into six equal parts, with two of the four kinds of line direction(vertical, horizontal, diagonal-left, diagonal-right) superimposed in each part. Black pencil. SL 36

ROY LICHTENSTEIN (NewYork City, 1923-1997) pp. 80, 201

1. *Cézanne,* 1962. Acrylic on canvas, 70 x 48 $^1/_2$ in. RL 1 MOCA
29. *Desk Calendar,* 1962. Acrylic on canvas, 48 $^1/_2$ x 68 in. RL 2 MOCA
28. *Meat,* 1962. Acrylic on canvas, 21 $^1/_4$ x 25 $^1/_4$ in. RL 3 MOCA
2. *The Grip,* 1962. Acrylic on canvas, 30 x 30 $^1/_4$ in. RL 4 MOCA

RICHARD LONG (Bristol, England, 1945) pp.172-175, 297-298

157.1. *Square Wood Sculpture,* 1967. 420 twig pieces, each 15 cm. (6 in.) long, 210 x 210 cm. (83 x 83 in.) RLO 1, The Solomon R. Guggenheim Foundation
3. *Untitled-England,* 1967. 2 photographs, 51 x 101 cm. (20 x 40 in.) RLO 2, The Solomon R. Guggenheim Foundation
6. *Sculpture Untitled, June 1968 England,* 1968. 2 photographs, 37 x 63 cm. (14 $^1/_2$ x 25 in.) RLO 3, The Solomon R. Guggenheim Foundation
157.2. *Sculpture at Galerie Lambert,* Milano 1969. Pine needles, 443 x 335 cm. (175 x 132 in.) RLO 4, The Solomon R. Guggenheim Foundation
8. *A sculpture by Richard Long,* Wiltshire, 12-15 October 1969. Map with text, 35 x 33 cm. (14 x 13 in.) RLO 5, The Solomon R. Guggenheim Foundation
7. *2 $^1/_2$ Mile Walk Sculpture,* 1969. Photograph and text on paper, 18 x 20 cm. (7 x 8 in.) RLO 6, The Solomon R. Guggenheim Foundation
5. *Sculpture at Konrad Fischer,* Dusseldorf, July 1969. Pine needles, 850 x 280 cm. (335 x 110 $^1/_4$ in.) RLO 8, The Solomon R. Guggenheim Foundation
156. *Stone Circle,* Roma 1976. About 305 stones, 218 cm. (86 in.) radius. RLO 9, The Solomon R. Guggenheim Foundation
155. *Stone Circle,* Roma 1976. About 182 stones, 220 cm. (87 in.) radius. RLO 10, The Solomon R. Guggenheim Foundation
158. *Arizona Circle,* 1987. 83 stones, 94 $^1/_2$ in. diameter. RLO 14
158. *Cross of Sticks,* 1983. Wood, 900 x 900 cm. (354 x 354 in.). RLO 15
Wood Line, Dusseldorf, March 1978. About 400 pieces of wood, 1430 x 20 cm. (563 x 780 $^1/_2$ in.). RLO 17
158. *Madrid Circle,* 1986. Stones, 1160 cm. (456 $^3/_4$ in.) diameter, 290 cm. (114 in.) and 580 cm. (228 $^3/_8$ in.) radii. RLO 18
4. *Line of Lake Stones,* 1983. Lake stones, 2180 x 150 cm. (858 x 59 in.). RLO 19, The Solomon R. Guggenheim Foundation

ROBERT MANGOLD (North Tonawanda, NewYork, 1937) pp. 124-125, 244-247

90.25. *Neutral Pink Area,* 1966. 2 panels, oil on masonite, 48 x 96 in. RMA 1, The Solomon R. Guggenheim Foundation
27. *Ellipse Within a Square (Grey),* 1972. Acrylic on canvas, 72 x 72 in. RMA 2, The Solomon R. Guggenheim Foundation
5. *Incomplete Circle no. 1 (Yellow),* 1972. Acrylic on canvas, 60 x 60 in. RMA 3, The Solomon R. Guggenheim Foundation

BRICE MARDEN (Bronxville, New York, 1938) pp. 129, 243

MAURIZIO MOCHETTI (Rome, Italy, 1940) pp. 285-287

ROBERT MORRIS (Kansas City, Missouri, 1931) pp. 39, 81-91, 226-228

(11 ³/₄ x 267 ³/₄ in.). RM 15, The Solomon R. Guggenheim Foundation

18. *Untitled (Pink felt)*, 1970. 63 felt pieces of different size piled on floor. RM 16, The Solomon R. Guggenheim Foundation

30.9. *Untitled (Five timbers)*, 1969. 5 timbers, each 12 x 144 x 12 in. RM 18, The Solomon R. Guggenheim Foundation

34.41. *Untitled (¹/₂ round piece)*, 1967. Grey painted plywood, 48 x 144 x 144 in. RM 19, The Solomon R. Guggenheim Foundation

17. *Untitled (Grey wedge)*, 1966. Grey painted plywood, 72 x 120 x 72 in. RM 20, The Solomon R. Guggenheim Foundation

13. *Untitled (Steel plate on granite column)*, 1969. Steel plate:120 x 120 x 3 in., red granite column: 120 in. long and 18 in. diameter. RM 21, The Solomon R. Guggenheim Foundation

19. *Untitled (4 steel plate piece)*, 1969. Inverted U-shape of steel plates, each 60 x 120 x 2 in., overall 62 x 120 x120 in. RM 22, The Solomon R. Guggenheim Foundation

39.41.16. *Untitled (4 steel plate piece)*, 1969. Square of vertical steel plates, each 36 x 120 x 2 in., overall 36 x 122 x 122 in. RM 23, The Solomon R. Guggenheim Foundation

37.15. *Untitled (3 steel plate piece)*, 1969. Wedge- shape of steel plates, 2 plates each 60 x 120 x 2 in.,1 plate 54 x 120 x 2 in., overall 56 x 106 x 120 in. RM 24, The Solomon R. Guggenheim Foundation

37.39. *Untitled (5 steel plate piece)*, 1969. H-shape of steel plates, each 60 x 120 x 2 in., overall 64 x120 x 120 in. RM 26, The Solomon R. Guggenheim Foundation

38.43.75. *Untitled (Aluminum I-beams)*, 1967. Aluminium, 66 x 306 x 402 in. RM 27, The Solomon R. Guggenheim Foundation

36. *Philadelphia Labyrinth*, 1974. Plywood, 96 in. high, 360 in. diameter. RM 28, The Solomon R. Guggenheim Foundation

12. *Triangular Labyrinth*, 1973. Plywood, each side 200 x 1440 cm. (79 x 491 in.) RM 29, The Solomon R. Guggenheim Foundation

14. *War Memorial*, 1970. Large cross-shaped trench with steam, cross:1950 x 1950 cm. (768 x 768 in.), trench:100 cm. (40 in.) deep. RM 30, The Solomon R. Guggenheim Foundation

11. *War Memorial*, 1970. Steel ball in trench, ball:300 cm. (118 in.) diameter, trench:150 cm. (60 in.) deep. RM 31, The Solomon R. Guggenheim Foundation

32.35.1. *Untitled (Piece with battered sides)*, 1966. Grey painted plywood, 48 x 96 x 96 in. RM 32, The Solomon R. Guggenheim Foundation

40.5. *Untitled (Square donut)* ,1968. Fiberglass, 72 x 96 x 18 ¹/₂ in. RM 33, The Solomon R. Guggenheim Foundation

BRUCE NAUMAN (Fort Wayne, Indiana, 1941) pp. 108-117, 220-225

20. *Untitled*, 1964-1965. Oil on shaped canvas, 168 x 32 cm. (66 x 12 ¹/₂ in.) BN 1

4. *Untitled*, 1965-1966. Latex rubber with cloth backing, 96 x 50 x 3 ¹/₂ in. BN 2

10. *Untitled*, 1966. Black fiberglass, 211 x 9 x 5 cm. (83 x 3 ¹/₂ x 2 in.) BN 3

1. *Piece in Which One Can Stand*, 1966. Laquered metal, 22 x 69 x 44 cm. (8 ³/₄ x 27 ¹/₄ x 17 ¹/₄ in.) BN 4

6. *Device for a Left Armpit*, 1967. Copper painted plaster, 14 x 7 x 10 in. BN 5

73. *My Last Name Exaggerated Fourteen Times Vertically*, 1967. Pale purple neon tubing, 63 x 33 in. BN 6

2. *Lighted Centerpiece*, 1968. 4 lamps each 1000 watts on aluminium plate, 107 x 107 cm. (42 x 42 in.) BN 7, The Solomon R. Guggenheim Foundation (Panza Gift)

11. *Hologram (Making Faces)*, 1968. Holographic image on glass, 8 x 10 in. BN 8

5. *Hologram (Making Faces)*, 1968. Holographic image on glass, 8 x 10 in. BN 9

3. *Hologram (Full Figure Poses)*, 1969. Holographic image on glass, 8 x 10 in. BN 10

16. *Lighted Performance Box*, 1969. Aluminium box with 1000 watts spot light, 78 x 20 x 20 in. BN 11, The Solomon R. Guggenheim Foundation
Art Make Up, 1967-1968. Four 16 mm color films. BN 12

22. *Performance Corridor*, 1968-1970. Wallboard, 96 x 240 x 20 in. BN 13, The Solomon R. Guggenheim Foundation (Panza Gift)

7. *Sound Breaking Wall*, 1969. Wallboard, tape and speakers, 108 x 288 in. BN 14, The Solomon R. Guggenheim Foundation (Panza Gift)

8. *Touch and Sound Walls*, December 1969. Wallboard, microphons and speakers, one wall:108 x 192 and one wall:108 x 240 in. BN 15, The Solomon R. Guggenheim Foundation (Panza Gift)

78.14. *Sound Wedge (Double wedge)*, 1969-1970. Wallboard and acoustic material, 104 x 334 x 72 in. BN 16, The Solomon R. Guggenheim Foundation

22. *Live-Taped Video Corridor*, 1969-1970. Wallboard, camera, videotape and 2 monitors, ceiling high, 384 x 20 in. BN 17, The Solomon R. Guggenheim Foundation (Panza Gift)

22. *Paralax Corridor*, 1969 1970. Wallboard, 96 x 144 x 2 in. BN 18, The Solomon R. Guggenheim Foundation (Panza Gift)

26. *Video Surveylance Piece (Public room-private room)*, 1969-1970. 2 rooms with camera and monitor each. BN 19, The Solomon R. Guggenheim Foundation (Panza Gift)

19. *Diagonal Sound Wall*, February 1970. Wallboard and acoustic material, 96 in. high, 420 in. long approx. BN 20, The Solomon R. Guggenheim Foundation (Panza Gift)

24. *Video Corridor (for San Francisco)*, January 1970. 2 cameras and 2 monitors, 480 in. minimum apart. BN 21, The Solomon R. Guggenheim Foundation (Panza Gift)

9. *Two Fans Corridor*, January 1970. In an existing room, wallboard and 2 fans, ceiling high, 24 in. wide approx. BN 22, The Solomon R. Guggenheim Foundation (Panza Gift)

15. *Four Fans Room (Enclosed)*, 1970. Wallboard and 4 fans, 118 x 236 x 236 in. BN 23, The Solomon R. Guggenheim Foundation

69. *Green Light Corridor*, 1970. Wallboard and green fluorescent light, 120 x 480 x 12 in. BN 24, The Solomon R. Guggenheim Foundation (Panza Gift)

17. *Performance Parallelogram (Rolling)*, 1970. Plywood basement and 2 mirrors, 33 x 197 x 87 in.. BN 25, The Solomon R. Guggenheim Foundation

18. *Yellow-Blue-Yellow Corridor on Three Sides of a Room*, 1970. Wallboard and yellow and blue fluorescent light, 120 in. high, 12-20-10 in. wide. BN 26, The Solomon R. Guggenheim Foundation

31. *None Sing Neon Sign*, 1970. Ruby-red and cool white neon tubing, 13 x 24 ¹/₄ in. Edition of 6. BN 27, The Solomon R. Guggenheim Foundation
Violin-Jumping Ball, 1971. Film. BN 28

74.75.30. *Triangle Room*, 1978-1980. Wallboard and 3 yellow sodium vapor lamps, cadmium-red painted inside, one side 144 x 360 in. and two sides 144 x 240 in. each, 144 x 360 x 158 in. BN 29, The Solomon R. Guggenheim Foundation

13. *Parallax Room with Three Horizontal Bars*, 1971. Plasterwalls and 3 in. square steel plate bars, white painted inside, 300 x 800 x 400 cm. (118 x 316 x 158 in.) BN 30, The Solomon R. Guggenheim Foundation

71.72. *Pink and Yellow Light Corridor (Variable Lights)*, 1972. Pink and yellow fluorescent light, 4 rows of double tube fixtures, dimensions according to room size. BN 31, The Solomon R. Guggenheim Foundation

79.29. *Double Wedge Corridor (with mirror)*, 1970-1974. Wallboard and mirror, white painted inside, 104 x 334 x 72 in. BN 32, The Solomon R. Guggenheim Foundation

32. *Spinning Spheres (Film installation)*, 1970. Colour film and 4 continous projectors. BN 33, The Solomon R. Guggenheim Foundation

28. *Compression and Disappearance*, 1974. 3,8 cm. (1 ¹/₂ in.) tape stuck on floor up to wall, space required 224,5 x 460 x 822 cm. (88 ¹/₂ x 181 x 324 in.) BN 34, The Solomon R. Guggenheim Foundation

27. *Floating Room (Light outside, dark inside)*, 1972. Wallboard and fluorescent light inside existing room, 96 x 192 x 192 in., 5 in. off the floor. BN 35, The Solomon R. Guggenheim Foundation

21. *Elliptical Space (Kassel Corridor)*, 1972. Wallboard, 177 x 563 x 102 in. BN 36, The Solomon R. Guggenheim Foundation

25. *Acoustic Corridor (Castelli Gallery)*, 1973. Wallboard and acoustic material, 95 in. high, 708 in. long approx. BN 37, The Solomon R. Guggenheim Foundation

70. *Yellow Room (Triangular)*, 1973. Wallboard and yellow fluorescent light, each sides 120 x 216 in. BN 38, The Solomon R. Guggenheim Foundation

77.23. *Double Doors - Projection and Dispacement*, 1973. Wallboard, 360 x 800 x 400 cm. (142 x 316 x 158 in.) BN 39, The Solomon R. Guggenheim Foundation

33. *False Silence*,1975. Wallboard and tape. Corridor with 2 triangular rooms. Corridor: ceiling high, 792 in. long and 15 in. wide. Top triangle: base 216 in. and height 132 in. Bottom triangle: base 264 in. and height 108 in. BN 40, The Solomon R. Guggenheim Foundation

76.12. *Forced Perspectives: Open Mind, Closed Mind, Parallel Mind, Equal Mind (allegory and symbolism)*, 1975. 64 stone blocks (rhomboids) of four different sizes, x 372 x 120 in. BN 42, The Solomon R. Guggenheim Foundation

RICHARD NONAS (New York, 1936) pp. 170-171, 215-219

1. *The Venus of the South*, Bari, January 1975. Steel, 12 x 120 x 17 cm. (4 ³/₄ x 47 ¹/₄ x 6 ³/₄ in.) RN 1
2. *Southern Boundry*, Bari, January 1975. Steel, 2 pieces, each 7 x 240 x 3,5 cm. (2 ³/₄ x 94 ¹/₂ x 1 ³/₈ in.) RN 2
3. *Southern Shortline*, New York 1974. Steel, 2 pieces, each 5 ¹/₁₆ x 24 x ⁵/₃₂ in. RN 3
4. *Untitled*, Bari, January 1975. Wood, 15,5 x 128 x 20 cm. (6 ¹/₈ x 50 ³/₈ x 7 ⁷/₈ in.) RN 4
8. *Boundry Man*, 1974. Steel, 2 bars in 2 adjacent rooms, one 684 in. long (6 sections) and one 570 in. long (5 sections), each section 2 ¹/₂ x 114 x 1 ¹/₂ in. RN 5
5. *Great Eastern*, 1972. Wood, 4 sections, 16 x 50 x 60 in. RN 7
7. *Jaw Bone*, 1973. Wood, 3 sections, one 12 x 312 x 8 in. and two 12 x 204 x 8 in. each. RN 8
9. *Fresno Shortline*, 1974. Wood, 5 sections, 24 x 600 x 14 in. RN 9
12. *Stopped Bar (Down)*, 1974. Steel, 3 sections, 3 ¹/₂ x 49 ¹/₂ x 2 ¹/₂ in. RN 10
15. *Pia-Oik*, 1975. Wood, 2 sections, each 18 x 96 x 18 in., placed 240 in. apart. RN 11
13. *Edge*, 1975. Steel, 2 sections, each 2 x 42 x 6 in., placed 42 in. apart. RN 12
Untitled, 1975. Brass, 0,5 x 12 x 0,45 cm. (⁵/₁₆ x 4 ³/₄ x ⁵/₁₆ in.) RN 13
6. *Salita Nord no.1 (1 down)*, 1974. Steel, 4 sections, 4 x 160 x 160 cm. (1 ³/₄ x 63 x 63 in.) RN 14
11. *Salita Nord no. 2 (Fault line)*, 1974. Steel, 3 sections, 4 x 113 x 200 cm. (1 ³/₄ x 44 ¹/₂ x 79 in.) RN 15
16. *Genoa Flat (Stopped bar series)*, 1974. Steel, 3 sections, 6 x 160 x 20 cm. (2 ³/₈ x 63 x 7 ⁷/₈ in.) RN 16
10. *Down in Front*, 1974. Steel, 2 sections, 6 x 70 x 20 cm. (2 ³/₈ x 27 ¹/₂ x 7 ⁷/₈ in.) RN 17
16. *Genoa Slot Series (2 down 2 up)*, 1974. Wall sculpture. Steel, 4 sections, 5,4 x 100 x 7,5 cm. (2 ¹/₈ x 39 ³/₈ x 2 ¹/₂ in.) RN 18
14.16. *Genoa Slot Series (1 up 1 down)*, 1974. Wall sculpture. Steel, 3 sections, 5,4 x 100 x 7,5 cm. (2 ¹/₈ x 39 ³/₈ x 2 ¹/₂ in.) RN 19
16. *Genoa Slot Series (2 up)*, 1974. Wall sculpture. Steel, 3 sections, 3,6 x 100 x 7,5 cm. (1 ³/₄ x 39 ³/₈ x 2 ¹/₂ in.) RN 20
16. *Salita Nord no. 3 (2 down)*, 1974. Steel, 5 sections, 4 x 180 x 160 cm. (1 ³/₄ x 70 ⁷/₈ x 63 in.) RN 22
16. *Southern Flats*, 1974. Wall sculpture. Wood, 0,75 x 75 x 9 cm. (⁵/₁₆ x 29 ¹/₂ x 3 ¹/₂ in.) RN 23
19. *Southern Cork*, Bari, January 1975. Steel, 2 pieces in a corner, each 17 x 12 x 12 cm. (6 ³/₄ x 4 ³/₄ x ³/₄ in.) RN 24
17. *Bari Shortline*, Bari, January 1975. Wood, 3 sections, 33 x 257 x 21 cm. (13 x 101 x 8 ¹/₄ in.) RN 25
20. *Scarp*, 1975. Steel, 2 sections, 6 x 48 x 48 in. RN 26
18. *Shortline Flats*, 1974. Steel, ¹/₈ x 144 x 6 in. RN 27
21. *Stopped Bar Series (Straight up)*, 1975. Steel, 3 sections, 6 ¹/₂ x 54 ¹/₂ x 5 in. RN 28
26. *Shortline Series, Moskutz' Brow*, 1974. Wall sculpture. Steel, 1 x 75 x 6 in. RN 29
25. *Blue Line*, 1974. Blue coloured steel, 3 sections, 2 ¹/₂ x 83 x 1 ¹/₂ in. RN 30
24. *H Beam Shortline*, 1974. Steel, 6 x 48 x 6 in. RN 31
22. *Inlet*, 1973. Wood, 9 sections, 6 x 156 x 72 ¹/₂ in. RN 32
23. *Mound*, 1975. Wood, 10 sections, 4 x 80 x 76 in. RN 34
29. *The Venus of the Table*, 1974. Steel, 2,5 x 23 x 11 cm. (1 x 9 x 4 ³/₄ in.) RN 35
153.28. *Drive (Shortline series)*, 1976. Steel, 4 sections forming 2 units, 8 x 1640 x 20 cm. (3 ¹/₈ x 642 x 7 ⁷/₈ in.) RN 36
31. *The Circle of Giotto (San Francisco's Dance)*, Spoleto 1976. Steel, 4 sections, 5 x 125 x 60 cm. (2 x 49 ¹/₄ x 23 ¹/₄ in.) RN 39
32. *The Death of San Francisco (Giotto's Hat)*, Spoleto 1976. Steel, 3 sections, 5 x 125 x 125 cm. (2 x 49 ¹/₄ x 49 ¹/₄ in.) RN 40
27. *Cesarino 's Bone (Maria's Mirror)*, 1976. Steel, 5 units, 8 x 740 x 1090 cm. (3 ¹/₈ x 291 ³/₈ x 429 ¹/₈ in.) RN 41
Varese Cut-Off (House Pets), 1976. Steel, 2 pieces each in 2 units, each unit 5 x 20 x 5 cm. (2 x 7 ⁷/₈ x 2 in.) RN 42
30. *House Pet (Varese Cut-Off)*, 1976. Steel, 2 sections, 3 x 36,5 x 11 cm. (1 ¹/₈ x 14 ³/₈ x 4 ³/₈ in.) RN 43

MARIA NORDMAN (Goerlitz, Germany, 1943) pp. 168, 279-280

4. *Irwine Room*, 1973. An existing room with a current entry made for the person, the light, the sound. Entering at ground level with 51 feet entrance, begining 22 inches wide opening to 5 feet, with a floor to ceiling mirror (second image of entry) dividing the room in two diagonal light room touching a dark room. MN 1, The Solomon R. Guggenheim Foundation (Panza Gift)

2. *Toselli Room*, Milano 1974. With the given light and with the given sound in a city dark entry way (280 x 880 x 480 cm.) light entrance area not directly lighted (880 x 309 x 480 cm.) MN 2, The Solomon R. Guggenheim Foundation (Panza Gift)
8. *June 22 Azimuth*, 1974. With the given daylight and with the given sound at the edge of a city, 112 x 441 x 149 in. MN 3, The Solomon R. Guggenheim Foundation (Panza Gift)
7. *Open White Room - Closed Dark Room*, 1974. With the given light and with the given sound at the edge of a city, each room 144 x 324 x 324 in. MN 4, The Solomon R. Guggenheim Foundation (Panza Gift)
1. *Room Determined by One Istant of Light*, New Port Beach 1973. Negative light extensions with the given daylight and with the given sound in a city. MN 5, FAI (Fondo per l'Ambiente Italiano) on permanent loan to Guggenheim
6. *Room with 1 ¹/₂ in. Opening to Skylight*, Pasadena 1972. 154 ¹/₂ to 156 in. high, 312 x 156 in. MN 6, The Solomon R. Guggenheim Foundation (Panza Gift)
150.3. *Varese Room*, 1976. With the given daylight and the given sound for one or two people. Two antirooms with doors (door dimensions 77 x 206 cm. each with transparent mirror at eye level). Each antiroom opens in a larger (given) room which warries two bodies of daylight entering parallel with the antirooms. Between both is an area without direct light from outside (579 x 303 x 428 cm.) MN 12, The Solomon R. Guggenheim Foundation (Panza Gift) on permanent loan to FAI
5. *Villa Scheibler Proposal I*, 1976. A room open to changing condition from the west, changing condition from the east. 1550 x 480 cm. (610 ¹/₂ x 189 in.) MN 13
9. *Villa Scheibler Proposal II*, 1976. Two equal sized rooms (using existing doors and windows). East room with direct sun light and sound: 810 x 620 cm. (319 x 244 in.) /antiroom without; south room without: 610 x 670 cm. (240 x 264 in.) /antiroom with direct sun light and sound. MN 14

CLAES OLDENBURG (Stockholm, Sweden, 1929) pp. 35, 38-39, 79, 188-189

8.25.22. *Mu Mu*, 1961: Enamel on plaster, 64 x 41 ¹/₂ x 4 in. CO 1 MOCA
8. *Pentecostal Cross*, 1961. Enamel on plaster, 52 ³/₄ x 40 ¹/₂ x 6 in. CO 2 MOCA
8.12. *Fragment of Candies in a Box*, 1961. Enamel on plaster, 44 x 32 x 6 in. CO 3 MOCA
3. *Bride*, 1961. Enamel on plaster, 61 x 37 ¹/₂ x 35 ¹/₂ in. CO 4 MOCA
13. *Blue and Pink Panties*, 1961. Enamel on plaster, 62 ¹/₄ x 34 ³/₄ x 6 in. CO 5 MOCA
9. *Cigarette Fragment*, 1961. Enamel on plaster, 32 ³/₄ x 30 ³/₄ x 6 ³/₄ in. CO 6 MOCA
8.26.23. *Pepsi-Cola*, 1961. Enamel on plaster, 58 ¹/₄ x 46 ¹/₂ x 7 ¹/₂ in. CO 7 MOCA
10. *A Brown Shoe*, 1961. Enamel on plaster, 23 ¹/₂ x 43 ¹/₄ x 5 in. CO 8 MOCA
11. *Green Stocking*, 1961. Enamel on plaster, 43 ¹/₄ x 18 x 4 in. CO 9 MOCA
1. *White Shirt on Chair*, 1962. Enamel on plaster and mixed media, 39 ³/₄ x 30 x 25 ¹/₄ in. CO 10 MOCA
5.4. *Umbrella and Newspaper*, 1962. Enamel on mixed media, 38 ¹/₂ x 19 ¹/₂ x 6 in. CO 11 MOCA
5. *Hamburger*, 1962. Enamel on plaster, 7 x 9 x 9 in. CO 12 MOCA
6. *Pie à la Mode*, 1962. Enamel on plaster, 22 x 18 ¹/₂ x 11 ³/₄ in. CO 13 MOCA
2. *Blue Pants on Chair*, 1962. Enamel on plaster and wood, 37 x 17 x 26 ³/₄ in. CO 14 MOCA
7. *Tennis Shoes*, 1962. Enamel on plaster, 24 x 24 x 10 in. CO 15 MOCA
27. *Breakfast Table*, 1962. Enamel on plaster and wood, 34 ¹/₂ x 35 ¹/₂ x 34 ¹/₂ in. CO 16 MOCA

ROMAN OPALKA (Abbeville, France, 1931) p. 269

1. *460.260 - 484.052*, 1965. Acrylic on canvas, 195x145 cm. (77 x 57 in.) RO 1

DENNIS OPPENHEIM (Mason City, Washington, 1938)

Various material presented in a paperboard box (38 x 38 x 21 cm. = 15 x 15 x 8 ¹/₄ in.) form one work. DO 1:

Cancelled Crop/Finsterwhode Holland, 1969. Plastic bag with seeds inside, 42 x 27 cm. (16 $^1/_2$ x 10 $^3/_4$ in.)
Exhibit E Calf, 1969. Leather sheet, 85 x 70 cm. (33 $^1/_2$ x 27 $^1/_2$ in.)
Exhibit B l Calf, 1969. Leather sheet, 69 x 51 cm. (27 $^1/_4$ x 20 in.)
Exhibit Calf, 1969. Steel brand, 13 cm. (5 $^1/_8$ in.) diameter and 2 cm. ($^3/_4$ in.) thick.
The Artist View Point, December 4, 1969. Text and tape.
Untitled, 1967-1968. 20 slides of various scuptures.
Gallery Heat in Slowly Replaced by Exterior Temperature Proposal, 1968. Booklet with 4 calendar pages of Jan. 1969, 33 x 28 cm. (13 x 11 in.)
Removal Project, 1968. 6 pages booklet, 25 x 24 cm. (10 x 9 $^1/_2$ in.)
Gallery Art, June 1967. 5 pages booklet, 28 x 29 cm. (11 x 11 $^1/_2$ in.)
Untitled, June 1968. 8 colour photographs on cardboards, each 27 x 27 cm. (10 $^5/_8$ x 10 $^5/_8$ in.)
Untitled, 1968-1970. 37 colour photographs on cardboards, each 34 x 26,5 cm. (13 $^1/_2$ x 10 $^1/_2$ in.)

ERIC ORR (Covington, Kentucky, 1939) p. 284

1. *Zero Mass*, 1974. Seamless paper, plywood panels, light, 144 x 480 x 138 in. EO 1, The Solomon R. Guggenheim Foundation (Panza Gift)

LUCIO POZZI (Milan, Italy, 1935)

Level Group, 1975. Acrylic on canvas, 2 panels, each 17 $^3/_{16}$ x 11 $^1/_2$ in., depth: 3 $^1/_2$ in. (left) and 2 $^3/_4$ in. (right) LP 1
Level Group, 1975. Acrylic on canvas, 2 panels, each 17 $^3/_{16}$ x 11 $^1/_2$ x 5 $^1/_4$ in. LP2
Level Group, 1975. Acrylic on canvas, 2 panels, each 17 $^3/_{16}$ x 11 $^1/_2$ in., depth: 2 $^5/_8$ in. (left) and 3 $^1/_2$ in. (right). LP 3
Level Group, 1975. Acrylic on canvas, 2 panels, each 17 $^3/_{16}$ x 11 $^1/_2$ x 2 $^1/_2$ in. LP 4
Level Group, 1975. Acrylic on canvas, 2 panels, each 17 $^3/_{16}$ x 11 $^1/_2$ x $^1/_2$ in. LP 5

ROYDEN RABINOWITCH (Toronto, Canada, 1943)

Barrel Sculpture, 1964. Wood, 90 x 89 cm. (35 $^1/_2$ x 35 in.) RRA 1

MARIO RADICE (Como, Italy, 1900-1987) p. 195

1. *Untitled*, 1956. Oil on wood, 4 panels, each 146 x 65 x 4 cm. (57 $^1/_2$ x 25 $^1/_2$ x l $^1/_2$ in.) MRA 1

ROBERT RAUSCHENBERG (Port Arthur, Texas, 1925) pp. 35, 77, 200-201

20. *Untitled Combine*, 1955. Mixed media, 86 $^1/_2$ x 37 x 26 $^1/_4$ in. RR 1 MOCA
19. *Interview*, 1955. Mixed media, 72 $^3/_4$ x 49 $^1/_4$ in. RR 2 MOCA
2. *Small Rebus*, 1956. Mixed media, 35 x 46 in. RR 3 MOCA
3. *Factum I*, 1957. Mixed media, 61 $^1/_2$ x 35 $^3/_4$ in. RR 4 MOCA
22. *Coca Cola Plan*, 1958. Mixed media, 26 $^3/_4$ x 25 $^1/_4$ x 4 $^3/_4$ in. RR 5 MOCA
21. *Painting with Grey Wing*, 1959. Mixed media, 31 x 21 in. RR 6 MOCA
7. *Kickback*, 1959. Mixed media, 75 x 32 in. RR 7 MOCA
5.5. *Gift for Apollo*, 1959. Mixed media, 43 $^3/_4$ x 29 $^1/_2$ in. RR 8 MOCA
6. *Inlet*, 1959. Mixed media, 84 $^1/_2$ x 48 $^1/_2$ in. RR 9 MOCA
1. *South Carolina Fall*, 1961. Mixed media, 55 x 20 in. RR 10 MOCA
4. *Trophy III*, 1961. Mixed media, 96 x 65 $^3/_4$ in. RR 11 MOCA

JAMES ROSENQUIST (Grand Forks, North Dakota, 1933) pp. 39, 78, 194

5. *White Cigarette*, 1961. Acrylic on canvas, 60 $^1/_2$ x 35 $^3/_4$ in. JR 1 MOCA
1. *Push Button*, 1960-1961. Acrylic on canvas, 82 $^3/_4$ x 105 $^1/_2$ in. JR 2 MOCA
3. *Capillary Action*, 1962. Acrylic on canvas, 92 $^1/_2$ x 136 $^1/_4$ in. JR 3 MOCA
24. *Waves*, 1962. Acrylic on canvas, 56 x 77 in. JR 4 MOCA

2. *A Lot to Like*, 1962. Acrylic on canvas, 92 $^1/_2$ x 203 in. JR 5 MOCA
23. *Vestigial Appendage*, 1962. Acrylic on canvas, 72 x 93 $^1/_4$ in. JR 6 MOCA
6. *Noon*, 1962. Acrylic on canvas, 36 $^1/_4$ x 48 $^1/_2$ in. JR 7 MOCA
4. *Shave*, 1964. Acrylic on canvas, 58 $^1/_4$ x 50 $^1/_2$ in. JR 8 MOCA

MARK ROTHKO (Dvinsk, Russia, 1903 - New York City, 1970) pp. 34, 76, 192-193

3.5. *Brown, Blue, Brown on Blue*, 1953. Acrylic on canvas, 115 $^3/_4$ x 91 $^1/_4$ in. MR 1 MOCA
18.2. *Violet and Yellow in Rose*, 1954. Acrylic on canvas, 83 $^1/_2$ x 67 $^3/_4$ in. MR 2 MOCA
4. *Purple Brown*, 1957. Acrylic on canvas, 84 x 72 in. MR 3 MOCA
3.6. *Black, Ochre, Red over Red*, 1957. Acrylic on canvas, 99 $^1/_4$ x 81 $^1/_2$ in. MR 4 MOCA
7. *Red and Brown*, 1957. Acrylic on canvas, 68 x 43 in. MR 5 MOCA
1. *Red and Blue over Red*, 1959. Acrylic on canvas, 93 x 80 $^3/_4$ in. MR 6 MOCA
3.3. *Black and Dark Sienna on Purple*, 1960. Acrylic on canvas, 119 $^1/_4$ x 105 in. MR 7 MOCA

ROBERT RYMAN (Nashville, Tennessee, 1930) pp. 126-128, 236-142

1. *Allied*, 1966. Oil on cotton, 76 x 76 in. RRY 1, The Solomon R. Guggenheim Foundation
93.2.21. *Standard nos. 1-2-3-4-5-6-8-9-10-11-12-13*, 1967. Enamel on steel, 12 panels, each 48 x 48 in. RRY 2, The Solomon R. Guggenheim Foundation
3.11. *Aacon*, 1968. Oil on linen, 98 x 98 in. RRY 3, The Solomon R. Guggenheim Foundation
11.23. *Impex*, 1968. Oil on linen, 96 x 96 in. RRY 4, The Solomon R. Guggenheim Foundation
12. *Classico I*, 1968. Acrylic on paper, 93 x 90 in. RRY 5, The Solomon R. Guggenheim Foundation
6. *Classico II*, 1968. Acrylic on paper, 62 x 67 in. RRY 6, The Solomon R. Guggenheim Foundation
96. *Classico IV*, 1968. Acrylic on paper, 91 x 91 in. RRY 7, The Solomon R. Guggenheim Foundation
98.26. *Murillo*, 1968. Acrylic on paper, 80 x 84 in. RRY 8
98.27. *J. Green I*, 1968. Acrylic on paper, 84 x 86 in. RRY 9, The Solomon R. Guggenheim Foundation
7. *Classico 20*, 1968. Polymer on paper, 123 x 113 in. RRY 10, The Solomon R. Guggenheim Foundation
94. *Four Units*, 1969. Enamelac on corrugated paper, 121 x 120 in. RRY 11, The Solomon R. Guggenheim Foundation
97.5. *Three Units (nos. 1-2-3)*, 1969. Enamelac on corrugated paper, 3 panels, each 60 x 60 in. RRY 12, The Solomon R. Guggenheim Foundation
97.4. *Five Units (nos. 1-2-3-4-5)*, 1969. Enamelac on corrugated paper, 5 panels, each 60 x 60 in. RRY 13, The Solomon R. Guggenheim Foundation
16. *Untitled*, 1969. Enamelac on fiberglass, 18 $^1/_2$ x 18 $^1/_2$ in. RRY 14
15. *Untitled*, 1969. Enamelac on fiberglass, 20 x 20 in. RRY 15
17. *Mylar Pieces (nos. 1-2)*, Milano 1969. Acrylic on mylar, 2 panels, each 15 x 15 in. RRY 17
19. *Mylar Three Pieces (nos. 1 2-3)*, Milano 1969. Acrylic on mylar, 3 panels, each 15 x 15 in. RRY 18
13.30. *Surface Veil I*, 1970. Oil on linen, 144 x 144 in. RRY 19, The Solomon R. Guggenheim Foundation
18. *General Painting*, 1970. Enamel on cotton, 49 x 49 in. RRY 20, The Solomon R. Guggenheim Foundation
20. *General Painting*, 1971. Enamel on cotton, 53 x 53 in. RRY 22, The Solomon R. Guggenheim Foundation
13.25. *Surface Veil II*, 1971. Oil on linen, 144 x 144 in. RRY 23, The Solomon R. Guggenheim Foundation
9.13. *Surface Veil III*, 1971. Oil on cotton, 144 x 144 in. RRY 24, The Solomon R. Guggenheim Foundation
8. *Lenox*, 1971. Enamelac on linen, 59 x 59 in. RRY 25, The Solomon R. Guggenheim Foundation
29. *Central*, 1971. Enamelac on cotton, 69 x 69 in. RRY 26, The Solomon R. Guggenheim Foundation
28. *Arista*, 1972. Enamelac on cotton, 70 x 70 in. RRY 27, The Solomon R. Guggenheim Foundation
24. *Emprise*, 1973. Gripz on canvas, 70 x 70 in. RRY 28, The Solomon R. Guggenheim Foundation
10.11. *Capitol*, 1973. Oil on canvas, 96 x 96 in. RRY 29, The Solomon R. Guggenheim Foundation
95.11. *Empire*, 1973. Oil on linen, 96 x 96 in. RRY 30, The Solomon R. Guggenheim Foundation
22. *Two Stones*, 1971. Lithograph 14/50, 29 $^1/_2$ x 29 $^1/_2$ in. RRY 31
14. *Zenith*, 1974. Oil on wood, 96 x 144 in. RRY 32, The Solomon R. Guggenheim Foundation

GEORGE SEGAL (New York City, 1924) p. 195

1. *Man in the Armchair (Helmut von Erffa)*, 1969. Plaster and wood, 49 ¹/₂ x 30 x 31 ¹/₂ in. GS 1 MOCA
1. *Sunbathers on the Roof Top*, 1963-1967. Plaster and mixed media, 34 ¹/₄ x 143 ¹/₂ x 96 in. GS 2 MOCA

RICHARD SERRA (San Francisco, California, 1939) pp. 97-99, 207-208

55.56. *Belts*, 1966-1967. 9 vulcanized ruber units and blue neon tubing, 84 x 288 x 20 in. RS 1, The Solomon R. Guggenheim Foundation
55. 7. *Untitled*, 1967. Vulcanized rubber, 96 in. long approx. RS 2, The Solomon R. Guggenheim Foundation
55. 8. *Angle Slabs*, 1967. Fiberglass encased in rubber, 6 x 121 x 6 in. RS 3, The Solomon R. Guggenheim Foundation
55. 9. *Tearing Lead from 1:00 to 1:47*, 1968. Lead sheeting torn into pieces, 16 x 270 x 144 cm. (6 ¹/₄ x 107 x 57 in.) RS 4, The Solomon R. Guggenheim Foundation
61. *Shovel Plate Prop*, 1969. Steel, 80 x 84 x 32 in. RS 5, The Solomon R. Guggenheim Foundation
5. *Untitled*, 1969. Lead and steel, 98 x 121 x 20 cm. (38 ¹/₂ x 47 ¹/₂ x 8 in.) RS 6, The Solomon R. Guggenheim Foundation
4. *Sign Board Prop*, 1969. Lead antimony, 60 x 60 x 33 in. RS 7, The Solomon R. Guggenheim Foundation
59. *Clothes Pin Prop*, 1969. Lead antimony, 100 x 90 x 6 in. RS 8, The Solomon R. Guggenheim Foundation
60. *Strike (to Roberta and Rudy)*, 1969-1971. Hot rolled steel plate, on edge 96 x 288 x ⁵/₈ in. RS 9, The Solomon R. Guggenheim Foundation
1. *One Cut Bisected Corners*, 1973. 2 hot rolled steel triangles on edge, placed in opposite corners of rectangular room, each 104 x 504 x 1 ¹/₄ in. RS 10, The Solomon R. Guggenheim Foundation
57.2. *Shafrazi*, 1974. Oil on linen, 114 ¹/₁₆ x 213 ¹/₄ in. RS 11, The Solomon R. Guggenheim Foundation
3. *Zadikians*, 1974. Oil on linen, 2 units, each 129 x 102 in. RS 12, The Solomon R. Guggenheim Foundation
58. *Different and Different Again Unequal Elevations*, 1973. 4 hot rolled steel units, 2 units each 12 x 180 x12 in. and 2 units each 12 x 14 x 12 in., 12 x 615 x 500 in. approx overall. RS 13, The Solomon R. Guggenheim Foundation
6. *Unequal Elevations*, 1975. 2 hot rolled steel units, 1 unit:12 x 24 x 12 in. against wall,1 unit:10 x 24 x 12 in. placed 960 in. apart. RS 14, The Solomon R. Guggenheim Foundation

JOEL SHAPIRO (New York City, 1941) p. 211

7. *Untitled*, 1971. Texas limestone, 5 ¹/₂ x 4 ³/₄ x 4 ³/₄ in. JS 1
3. *Untitled (Coffin)*, 1971-1973. Cast iron, 2 ¹/₂ x 11 ¹/₂ x 5 in. JS 2
6. *Untitled (Maquette for coffin)*, 1971. Pine and italian poplar, 2 ⁵/₈ x 11 ³/₄ x 5 in. JS 2A
1. *Untitled (Chair)*, 1973-1974. Cast iron, 3 x 1 ¹/₄ x 1 ¹/₄ in. JS 4
2. *Untitled (Table)*, 1974. Cast iron, 5 ³/₈ x 6 x 4 ⁷/₈ in. JS 6
5. *Untitled (Maquette for table)*, 1974. Bass wood, 5 ³/₈ x 6 x 4 ⁷/₈ in. JS 6A
4. *Untitled*, 1974. Cast brass, 2 ³/₈ x 5 ⁷/₈ x 5 ¹/₄ in. JS 7

ANTONI TAPIES (Barcelona, Spain, 1923) pp. 74, 190-191

7. *All White*, 1955. Mixed media on canvas, 146 x 97 cm. (57 ¹/₂ x 38 ¹/₄ in.) AT 1 MOCA
6. *Grey Relief Perforated by a Black Sign*, 1955. Mixed media on canvas, 149 x 97 cm. (57 ¹/₂ x 38 ¹/₄ in.) AT 2 MOCA
4. *Grey and Black Cross*, 1955. Mixed media on canvas, 146 x 114 cm. (57 ¹/₂ x 45 in.) AT 3 MOCA
8. *Grey on White*, 1956. Mixed media on canvas, 130 x 162 cm. (51 ¹/₄ x 63 ³/₄ in.) AT 4 MOCA
2. *Collage on a Black Ground*, 1956. Mixed media on canvas, 130 x 162 cm. (51 ¹/₄ x 63 ³/₄ in.) AT 5 MOCA
11. *Grey-Brown Composition*, 1957. Mixed media on canvas, 80 x 130 cm. (35 x 51 in.) AT 6 MOCA
15. *Brown-Ochre with Black Crevice*, 1957. Mixed media on canvas, 130 x 97 cm. (51 ¹/₄ x 38 ¹/₄ in.) AT 7 MOCA
10. *Ochre and Brown (New York)*, 1957. Mixed media on canvas, 54 x 81 cm. (21 ¹/₄ x 32 in.) AT 8 MOCA
3. *Black-Ochre with Perforations*, 1957. Mixed media on canvas, 146 x 114 cm. (57 ¹/₂ x 45 in.) AT 9 MOCA
5. *Sable-Ochre*, 1957. Mixed media on canvas, 195 x 130 cm. (76 ³/₄ x 51 in.) AT 10 MOCA

14. *Red-Brown*, 1958. Mixed media on canvas, 114 x 146 cm. (45 x 57 ¹/₂ in.) AT 11 MOCA
1. *Grey with Red Sign*, 1958. Mixed media on canvas, 146 x 89 cm. (57 ¹/₂ x 35 in.) AT 12 MOCA
16. *Hammered Grey*, 1959. Mixed media on canvas, 116 x 89 cm. (45 ¹/₂ x 35 in.) AT 13 MOCA
9. *Grey with Six Marks*, 1959. Mixed media on canvas, 260 x 190 cm. (102 ¹/₄ x 74 ³/₄ in.) AT 14 MOCA

VITTORIO TAVERNARI (Milan, Italy, 1919 - Varese, Italy 1987) p. 196

2. *Grande torso (il fiume)*, 1954. Wood, 150 x 58 x 45 cm. (59 x 23 x 17 ³/₄ in.) VT 1, The Solomon R. Guggenheim Foundation (Panza Gift)
1. *Figura sdraiata*, 1971. Bronze, 56,5 x 39,5 cm. (22 ¹/₄ x 15 ¹/₂ in.) VT 2
Figura, 1965. Drawing on paper, 69 x 49 cm. (27 ¹/₈ x 19 ¹/₄ in.) VT 3

JEAN TINGUELY (Fribourg, Switzerland, 1925 - Basilea, Switzerland, 1991) p. 278

4. *La Vittoria*, Milano 1970. Drawing, 41,6 x 29,4 cm. (16 ³/₈ x 11 ⁵/₈ in.) JTI 1
2. *La Vittoria (Vive Panza)*, Milano 1970. Drawing, 40,8 x 32,7 cm. (16 x 12 ⁷/₈ in.) JTI 2
3. *La Vittoria (Per Panza)*, Milano 1970. Drawing, 41,5 x 33 cm. (16 ³/₈ x 13 in.) JTI 3
1. *La Vittoria (Mille grazia)*, Milano 1970. Drawing on both sides, 41 x 33 cm. (16 ¹/₈ x 13 in.) JTI 4

HAP TIVEY (Portland, Oregon, 1947)

Three Quarter Sphere, 1971. We approach a ³/₄ sphere from an ante chamber with two doors and two light disks. A stair lead us from the ante chamber to the floor of the sphere and this plane seems to hang suspended in space with physical contact only at the doorway. The only feature other than the door is a large confortable reclining chair placed near the edge of the platform. The color and the space begin to transform as soon as we start the program by pressing a button on the arm of the chair. HT 1, The Solomon R. Guggenheim Foundation (Panza Gift)
Santa Barbara Rooms, 1977. This gallery installation relies on a hallway flooded with natural light during the day and lit by exterior sources at night. Four rooms are constructed which use one light screen wall and three sheet rock or plaster walls. Doorways lead from the hallway into each successive room allowing light from each screen to interact with retinal changes incurrent by proceeding room. Each room:114 x 114 x 144 (minimum) in. HT 2, The Solomon R. Guggenheim Foundation (Panza Gift)
Sodium Exchange, 1977. One room divided in half by a two part screen. One side has a sodium source of light lasted side has a sodium source of light located behind a baffle. The other side has a white source which projects directly onto the screen. The halves of the room should be approximate squares with minimum ceiling height 114 in.. The screen runs floor to ceiling, wall to wall and it is framed by cardboard sheets. HT 3, The Solomon R. Guggenheim Foundation (Panza Gift)
Visual Corridor/Physical Corridor, 1977. This installation presents a dialogue between the eye's experiences in light as vicarious events with accompanying expectations and physically corroborated expectations. One space may be observed but not entered; another may be observed by entering. One must be examined remotely by projecting physical presence; another examined interiorly. Each share varying degrees of remoteless and immediacy. HT4,
Asian Masters, 1978. One room divided by scrim. The front room contains four circular cavities, the back is defined by a scrim in front and a scrim/screen at the rear. The front scrim is a neutral plane which diffuses the apposing details as the visual angles moves from perpendicular to oblique. HT 5, The Solomon R. Guggenheim Foundation (Panza Gift)

DAVID TREMLETT (St. Austell, England, 1945) pp. 295-296

1. *Cue*, 1974. 21 drawings in asymetical shape on wall, each 12,7 x 20 cm. (5 x 8 in.), 1 paper 25 x 25 cm. (10 x 10 in.) DT 1

2. *Watching the Way the Rabbits Run in Milwaukee*, 1975. 4 pencil
   drawings, photograph and lettering on paper, 76 x 128 cm.
   (30 x 50 ¹/₂ in.) DT 2
5. *Watching the Way the Rabbits Run in Kalgoorlie*, 1975. 4 pencil
   drawings, photograph and lettering on paper, 76 x 128 cm.
   (30 x 50 ¹/₂ in.) DT 3
6. *Watching the Way the Rabbits Run in Aberdeen*, 1975. 4 pencil
   drawings, photograph and lettering on paper, 76 x 128 cm.
   (30 x 50 ¹/₂ in.) DT 4
   Form one work of 6 parts:
7. *Scotland 1/1 (Lock Ness)*, 1975. 8 drawings and lettering on
   paper 33,5 x 91,5 cm. (13 ¹/₄ x 36 in.) DT 6
3. *Scotland 1/2 (Lock Ness)*, 1975. 8 drawings and lettering on
   paper 33,5 x 91,5 cm. (13 ¹/₄ x 36 in.) DT 7
4. *Scotland 1/3 (Lock Ness)*, 1975. 8 drawings and lettering on
   paper 33,5 x 91,5 cm. (13 ¹/₄ x 36 in.) DT 8
8. *Scotland 1/4 (Lock Ness)*, 1975. 8 drawings and lettering on
   paper 33,5 x 91,5 cm. (13 ¹/₄ x 36 in.) DT 9
10. *Scotland 1/5 (Lock Ness)*, 1975. 8 drawings and lettering on
    paper 33,5 x 91,5 cm. (13 ¹/₄ x 36 in.) DT 10
9. *Scotland 1/6 (Lock Ness)*, 1975. 8 drawings and lettering on
   paper 33,5 x 91,5 cm. (13 ¹/₄ x 36 in.) DT 11

JAMES TURRELL (Los Angeles, California, 1943) pp. 156-163, 283

3. *Argus*, 1976. Light projected on wall of an empty dark room.
   JT 1, The Solomon R. Guggenheim Foundation (Panza Gift)
1. *Afrum I*, 1967. Light projected into corner of an empty dark
   room. JT 2, The Solomon R. Guggenheim Foundation
   (Panza Gift)
139.140. *Virga*, Varese 1976. Ambient skylight and fluorescent light,
   room:147 x 176 x 369 in. JT 3, The Solomon R.
   Guggenheim Foundation (Panza Gift) on permanent loan to
   FAI
136.137.138. *Sky Space I*, Varese 1976. An overhead portal cut (100 x
   100 in.) to outside sky, interior fill light, room: 236 x 142 x
   142 in. JT 4, The Solomon R. Guggenheim Foundation
   (Panza Gift) on permanent loan to FAI
134.135. *Sky Window I*, Varese 1976. A vertical portal cut to outside sky,
   interior fill light, hallway: 98 x 584 in. JT 5, The Solomon R.
   Guggenheim Foundation (Panza Gift) on permanent loan to
   FAI
4. *Wallen*, 1976. Light projected on wall of an empty dark room.
   JT 10, The Solomon R. Guggenheim Foundation (Panza Gift)
2. *Iltar*, 1976. Wall (400 x 657 cm. = 158 x 259 in.) with cut (200 x
   327 cm. = 79 x 129 in.) placed at 300 cm. (118 in.) from
   endwall of room, artificial light. JT 11, The Solomon R.
   Guggenheim Foundation (Panza Gift)
   Shanta Blue, 1967. Pale blue light projected into corner of an
   empty room, ideal ceiling height 144 in. JT 16, The
   Solomon R. Guggenheim Foundation (Panza Gift)
   Inside Out, 1976. Rectangular cut (264 x 84 in.) in a room wall to
   outside sky, interior fill light, room: 192 x 576 x
   336 in. JT 17, The Solomon R. Guggenheim Foundation
   (Panza Gift)
   Arkar's Visit, 1985. Dark space with seating, red and blue light
   projection on end wall, room: 144 x 624 x 360 in. JT 18,
   FAI (Fondo per l'Ambiente Italiano) on permanent loan to
   Guggenheim
   Jadito's Night, 1985. Dark space, blue/green and red light
   projection on end wall, room: 144 x 480 x 432 in. JT 19,
   FAI (Fondo per l'Ambiente Italiano) on permanent loan to
   Guggenheim
141. *Night Passage*,1987. Rectangular cut (79 x 129 in.) in portition
   wall, light, room: 157 x 259 x 603 in. JT 20, The Solomon R.
   Guggenheim Foundation (Panza Gift)
   Arela, 1985.(Phaedo series) Rectangular cut (70 x 240 in.) in
   portition wall, room:144 x 672 x 432 in. JT 21, FAI (Fondo
   per l'Ambiente Italiano) on permanent loan to Guggenheim

CY TWONBLY (Lexington, Virginia, 1929) p.195

1. *Untitled*, 1957. Mixed media on canvas, 20 x 25 cm. (8 x 10 in.)
   CT 1

LAWRENCE WEINER (New York City, 1940) pp. 140-143, 170, 270

4. *Cat. No. 029. THE RESIDUE OF A FLARE IGNITED UPON A
   BOUNDARY*, 1969. LW 1, The Solomon R. Guggenheim
   Foundation (Panza Gift)

6. *Cat. No. 052. ONE KILOGRAM OF LACQUER POURED UPON A
   FLOOR*, 1969. LW 2
117.153. *Cat. No. 051. 1000 GERMAN MARKS WORTH MEDIUM BULK
   MATERIAL TRANSFERRED FROM ONE COUNTRY TO
   ANOTHER*, 1969. LW 3
5. *Cat. No. 085. A STAKE SET IN THE GROUND IN DIRECT LINE
   WITH A STAKE SET IN THE GROUND OF AN ADJACENT
   COUNTRY*, 1969. LW 4, The Solomon R. Guggenheim
   Foundation (Panza Gift)
   Cat. No. 089. A WALL STRIPPED OF PLASTER OR WALLBOARD,
   1969. LW 5
119. *Cat. No. 090. THE JOINING OF FRANCE GERMANY AND
   SWITZERLAND BY ROPE*, 1969. LW 6
   Cat. No. 091. A STAKE SET, 1969. LW 7, The Solomon R.
   Guggenheim Foundation (Panza Gift)
   Cat. No. 146. A RUBBER BALL THROWN ON THE SEA, 1969.
   LW 8
   Cat. No. 147. A STONE WALL BREACHED, 1969. LW 9
   *Cat. No. 148. AN AMOUNT OF MATERIAL PLACED UPON THE
   OCEAN NORTH OF THE COAXIAL CABLE AN AMOUNT OF
   MATERIAL PLACED UPON THE OCEAN SOUTH OF THE
   COAXIAL CABLE*, 1970. LW 10,
   The Solomon R. Guggenheim Foundation (Panza Gift)
1. *Cat. No. 150. A STONE LEFT UNTURNED*, 1970. LW 11
118. *Cat. No. 151. EARTH TO EARTH ASHES TO ASHES DUST TO
   DUST*, 1970. LW 12, The Solomon R. Guggenheim
   Foundation (Panza Gift)
   Cat. No. 157. TO THE SEA, 1970. LW 13, The Solomon R.
   Guggenheim Foundation (Panza Gift)
   Cat. No. 158. ON THE SEA, 1970. LW 14, The Solomon R.
   Guggenheim Foundation (Panza Gift)
   Cat. No. 159. FROM THE SEA, 1970. LW 14A, The Solomon R.
   Guggenheim Foundation (Panza Gift)
   Cat. No. 160. AT THE SEA, 1970. LW 15, The Solomon R.
   Guggenheim Foundation (Panza Gift)
   Cat. No. 161. BORDERING THE SEA, 1970. LW 16, The Solomon
   R. Guggenheim Foundation (Panza Gift)
3. *Cat. No. 099. SMUDGED*, 1970. LW 17
7. *Cat. No. 100. FLUSHED*, 1970. LW 18
   Cat. No. 101. MARRED, 1970. LW 19
116. *Cat. No. 102. REDUCED*, 1970. LW 20
   Cat. No. 218. WEAKENED FROM WITHIN, 1970. LW 21
   Cat. No. 229. BESIDE ITSELF, 1970. LW 22
2. *Cat. No. 238. OVER AND OVER OVER AND OVER AND OVER
   AND OVER AND OVER AND OVER*, 1971. LW 23,
   The Solomon R. Guggenheim Foundation (Panza Gift)
   Cat. No. 276. TO HAVE AND HAVE NOT, 1972. LW 24,
   The Solomon R. Guggenheim Foundation (Panza Gift)
   Cat. No. 277. TO HAVE AND TO HOLD, 1972. LW 25,
   The Solomon R. Guggenheim Foundation (Panza Gift)
   Cat. No. 278. TO SEE AND BE SEEN, 1972. LW 26,
   The Solomon R. Guggenheim Foundation (Panza Gift)
   Cat. No. 279. TO GIVE AND TO TAKE, 1972. LW 27,
   The Solomon R. Guggenheim Foundation (Panza Gift)
   Cat. No. 280. TO SHOW AND TO TELL, 1972. LW 28,
   The Solomon R. Guggenheim Foundation (Panza Gift)
   *Cat. No. 257. AFFECTED AS TO PRESSURE AND/OR PULL
   EFFECTED AS TO PRESSURE AND/OR PULL*, 1971. LW 29
   *Cat. No. 282. LOUDLY MADE NOISE (forte) AND/OR
   MODERATELY LOUDLY (mezzoforte)*, 1972. LW 30
   *Cat. No. 283. SOFTLY MADE NOISE (piano) AND/OR
   MODERATELY SOFTLY (mezzopiano)*, 1972. LW 38
   *Cat. No. 284. NOISE MADE VERY LOUDLY (fortissimo) AND/OR
   MODERATELY LOUDLY (mezzoforte)*, 1972. LW 39
   *Cat. No. 285. NOISE MADE VERY SOFTLY(pianissimo) AND/OR
   MODERATELY SOFTLY (mezzopiano)*, 1972. LW 40
   *Cat. No. 258. AFFECTED AS TO HEAT AND/OR COLD EFFECTED
   AS TO HEAT AND/OR COLD*, 1971. LW 45
   *Cat. No. 259. AFFECTED AS TO EXPLOSION AND/OR
   IMPLOSION EFFECTED AS TO EXPLOSION AND/OR
   IMPLOSION*, 1971. LW 46
   *Cat. No. 260. AFFECTED AS TO CORROSION AND/OR VACUUM
   EFFECTED AS TO CORROSION AND/OR VACUUM*, 1971.
   LW 47
   *Cat. No. 261. AFFECTED AS TO NOISE AND/OR SILENCE
   EFFECTED AS TO NOISE AND/OR SILENCE*,1971. LW 48
   First Quarter, 1972. 16 mm. black and white film, sound, 80
   min.. LW 52

DOUG WHEELER (Globe, Arizona, 1939) pp. 166, 291-293

1. *Ace Gallery Installation (Environmental light)*, January 1970.
   End projection wall 181 x 352 in. in square room, neon
   light inbedded in floor, walls and ceiling for uniform light

gradiation to umbra cavidity, ceiling bordered white transparent scrim. DW 1, The Solomon R. Guggenheim Foundation (Panza Gift)

5. *Eindhoven Stedelijk Van Abbemuseum Installation (Environmental light),* 1969-1970. 144 x 192 in. DW 2

2. *Amsterdam Stedelijk Museum Installation (Environmental light),* September 1969. 192 x 384 in., room:192 x 384 x 384 in. DW 3

13. *Tate Gallery Installation,* 1970-1975. Anamorphic compressed entrance to 222° hemispherical arc, neon light circumference, scrim, room:192 x 843 x 633 in. DW 4, The Solomon R. Guggenheim Foundation (Panza Gift)

9. *Suspended Volume in Reflected Spectrum,* 1975. The effective usable space is the 360 x 144 in. high walk around square room perimeter. The suspended volume should be white as the walls and floor and its sides opaque. The incident light reflection should be from a natural overhead source where the reflection off of the top of the volume would filter around its edges shrewding its presence and creating a torque of ambient spectral circumnavigation, 144 x 288 x 288 in. DW 5

3. *PSAD Synthetic Desert III,* 1971. Anechoic chamber, neon gradational floor illumination, plan:480 x 480 in. DW 6, The Solomon R. Guggenheim Foundation (Panza Gift)

12. *CC OSZ 75 Counter Orientation Space,* 1975. Bi-axis entrance - white low incident ambience 9 in. coving gradiating from entrance slits creating cavity of minimal geometric relationships - floor ceiling walls same featureless surface sheared 360° hemisphere into positive and negative orienting 180° hemisphere, 144 x 504 x 504 in. DW 7

4. *Luminefepous Space,* 1968-1975. An environment ideally kinestetic proportions. All planal areas (floor, ceiling, walls) joined by cove, base coat paint flat white and sprayed fluorescent phosphors in bluish white range on all surfaces, black UV fluorescents indirectly inside entrance frame, 144 x 288 x 288 in. DW 8, The Solomon R. Guggenheim Foundation (Panza Gift)

11. *RM LA DW 75 Invisible Reflecting Horizontal Plane,* 1975. Dissect space (given) into bisymetrical halves where eye level becomes implied plane between virtual ceiling below the disected plane, and actual ceiling above. Any space should be at least 144 in. high and where skylights can't be used due to logistic, then fluorescent would be installed top to bottom - covered so as to obscure source and allow an even projection, 144 x 312 x 240 in. DW 9

10. *WM NY DW 75 Sequential Planal Rotational Piece,* 1975. Light projection on 3 walls, ceiling and floor of a room,153 x 468 x 288 in. DW 10, The Solomon R. Guggenheim Foundation (Panza Gift)

145.146.14. *SA MI DW SM 2 75 Continum Atmospheric Environment,* 1975. The space is filled with quartz haligen and UV light that operates on a 6 minute cycle, ceiling height approx twice that of man, depth and width equal, and at least 5 times man's reach. DW 11, The Solomon R. Guggenheim Foundation (Panza Gift)

8. *Invisibly Defined Cube in Free Space,* 1971. Visually featureless white space - where penetration through quiet zone will give vague definition of voidal (sound dampened) presence or volume - scrim obscures pyramid accoustical absorbers - inlayed absorbers indistinguishable from surrounding relecting (sound) surface (floor), 144 x 432 x 432 in. DW 12

7. *LC OP 75 70 DW Space Corridor - Dissected 360° Hemisphere,* 1970-1975. Space corridor - dissected 360° hemisphere, constricted entrance - emiting natural daylight across domed red arizona clay floor - wall/ceiling white, 192 x 840 x 600 in. DW 13

6. *Diagonal Light Passage - Synthetic Shear DW 7 4 75,* 1975. All surfaces flat white - adjust entering light beam to cross diagonally to opposite entrance, except ceiling high - size propotional - up-down, 144 x 480 x 336 in. DW 14

IAN WILSON (New York, 1940) p.134

111. *Discussion: January 1972.* IW 1
Discussion: June 1972. IW 2
Discussion: April 8, 1973. IW 3
Discussion: May 5, 1974. IW 4
Discussion: May 9, 1974. IW 5
Discussion: November 3, 1974. IW 6
Discussion: October 30, 1974. IW 9
Discussion: May 12,1977. IW 13

Credits

Contents

Typesetted by
Oldoni Prestampa
Milan

Color separations by
Graphic Color
Milan

Printed by
Leva S.p.A. Arti Grafiche
Sesto S. Giovanni (Milan)

Bound by
Legatoria Torriani
Cologno Monzese (Milano)